Knowing Brother Joseph Again: Perceptions and Perspectives

Davis Bitton

Kofford Books
Salt Lake City, Utah

2011

2015   14   13   12   11   5   4   3   2   1

Greg Kofford Books, Inc.
P.O. Box 1362
Draper, UT 84020
www.koffordbooks.com

Library of Congress Cataloging-in-Publication Data

Bitton, Davis, 1930-2007.
  Knowing Brother Joseph again : perceptions and perspectives / Davis Bitton. — 2nd ed.
      p. cm.
  Rev. ed. of: Images of the prophet Joseph Smith / Davis Bitton. 1996.
  Includes bibliographical references and index.
  ISBN 978-1-58958-123-4
  1. Smith, Joseph, 1805-1844. 2. Church of Jesus Christ of Latter-day Saints—Presidents—Biography. 3. Mormons—United States—Biography. I. Bitton, Davis, 1930- Images of the prophet Joseph Smith. II. Title.
  BX8695.S6.B46 2010
  289.3092—dc22
  [B]
                                    2010038479

Knowing Brother Joseph Again

For JoAn, eternal friend and companion,

a convert, first to Jesus Christ,

then to his modern prophet.

Contents

Publisher's Preface

Greg Kofford

In 1996, Davis Bitton, one of Mormon history's preeminent and much-loved scholars, published a collection of essays on Joseph Smith under the title, *Images of the Prophet Joseph Smith.* When the book went out of print and the publisher went out of business, I approached Davis about doing an updated version that would also include some of his other work on the Mormon prophet. Davis was interested, especially as the bicentennial of Joseph Smith's birth approached in December 2005, and set energetically to work. He had the project partially finished when his health failed. He died on April 13, 2007, at age seventy-seven. With the cooperation and approval of JoAn Bitton, to whom he dedicated this work and who selected the title, we have completed the preparation. On her behalf, we thank Ardis E. Parshall and Courtney J. Lassetter, both of whom offered encouragement and support.

Introduction

This is not a conventional biography of Joseph Smith, but its intended purpose should not be hard to grasp. That purpose is to trace how Joseph Smith has appeared from different points of view. It is the image of Joseph Smith rather than the man himself that I seek to delineate. Those unfamiliar with Joseph Smith may gain some general orientation from the brief chronology I provide. The most thoughtful full biography is now Richard Lyman Bushman's *Joseph Smith: Rough Stone Rolling* (New York: Alfred A. Knopf, 2005).

Even when we have cut through the rumor and misinformation that surround all public figures and agree on many details, differences of interpretation remain. St. Augustine may have been the first, but was certainly not the last, to discover that understanding even oneself is deficient, inconsistent, shifting, and ultimately imperfect. How flawed, then, must be any effort to write the life of another person! But we humans keep trying. Perhaps I can clarify the thrust of this book by imagining a brief conversation after a reader has finished reading Chapter 1 on Joseph Smith as a hero.

"This is nothing but a sappy pro-Mormon description. How ridiculous! Why, you are trying to say that Joseph Smith, of all people, is a hero right up there with some of the greatest."

"No," I answer. "You have missed the point. I do not say that Joseph Smith *was* a hero."

"Well, you make him sound like one. How can that be good history?"

"You read carelessly or hurriedly. We start with the fact that some people saw him as a hero. That's a simple fact."

"Well, I suppose if you include his pitiful followers."

"And if some people saw him in those terms, we might like to understand why. To get at the answer we must first understand how the term *hero* was used at the time."

"But most people didn't see him in this positive light," the critic sputters. "I don't like him and in no way consider him a hero."

"The fact remains that some people saw him under this heading. He was a hero to them. Rather than ignore that fact, we should try to understand. Isn't that the historian's goal?"

"Just don't make it sound like Joseph Smith was worthy of a statue in Arlington National Cemetery."

"Be patient, my friend. This book is a series of probes, examinations of Joseph Smith from different angles. The hostile point of view gets a chapter to itself. We will recognize the harsh characterizations and try to understand what was being said."

"I think I get it. This is not a book about Joseph Smith. It is a book about different images of Joseph Smith."

"Exactly."

Joseph Smith knew that some would believe him, while others—the great majority—would not. He did hope to persuade as many as possible into trying an "experiment" upon his words. Many of those who did ended up with their own strong image—they called it a witness or testimony—of the reality of Smith's prophetic calling.

We live in an age of relativism. What is beautiful for one is not for another, what is good and moral for one is not for another, and what is true for one is not for another. Such an attitude, widespread in the world, condemns those who testify of truth. Pope Benedict XVI is one who wrestles with what relativism means for Christians. How can they claim any superiority for their religion? How can they preach the gospel to all the world? Isn't it evidence of a simple mind, a mind lacking in tolerance, to proclaim the good news of Christ?

I shudder at the thought that my presentation here will lead to such soft relativism. I do not think that everything is up for grabs, with each person's opinion being equally valid. Just as Jesus was either the Savior and Redeemer of the world or he was not, so Joseph Smith was either a true, authorized prophet of God or he was not. In recounting his visions, either he spoke the truth or he did not.

Yet the fact remains that different people saw him in different ways. Even his followers emphasized different facets at different times. All human beings are complex and resist the reductionism that would dismiss them with a single adjective or noun. People like Joseph Smith are rich and complex. As Leonard J. Arrington and I wrote in 1979, Joseph Smith "was, in the words used by Carl Van Doren to describe Benjamin Franklin, a 'harmonious human multitude'–a complex mix of half a dozen different elements, each of which in a simpler man might have constituted an entire personality."[1] From their own perspectives, different people saw him differently or focused on a different facet of his personality at different times. Inescapably, what they observed or found out about him was refracted through the lens of their own experience. Some of the different, flickering, not always compatible views are the subject of this book.

The torrent of published writings on the Joseph Smith shows no sign of diminishing. Rather than offering a list of titles, I refer the reader to two indispensable guides: (1) David J. Whittaker, ed., *Mormon Americana: A Guide to Sources and Collections in the United States* (Provo, Utah: BYU Studies, 1995), which includes Dean C. Jessee, "Sources for the Study of Joseph Smith," and David J. Whittaker, "Joseph Smith in Recent Research"; and (2) The Joseph Smith entries in James B. Allen, Ronald W. Walker, and David J. Whittaker, eds., *Studies in Mormon History, 1830–1997: An Indexed Bibliography* (Urbana: University of Illinois Press, 2000).

Note

1. Leonard J. Arrington and Davis Bitton, *The Mormon Experience: A History of the Latter-day Saints* (New York: Alfred A. Knopf, 1979), 19.

Chronology

For readers new to the subject, this minimal chronology, which is no substitute for a biography, allows one to situate Joseph in space and time.

Dec. 23, 1805	Joseph Smith Jr. born in Sharon, Windsor County, Vermont.
Winter 1812–13	Painful leg operation removes pieces of bone.
Summer 1816	Family moves to Palmyra, New York.
Spring 1820	The First Vision.
Jan. 18, 1827	Marriage of Joseph Smith Jr. and Emma Hale.
April 1829	Oliver Cowdery begins to act as scribe as Joseph Smith dictates translation from metal plates.
March 1830	Book of Mormon published by E. B. Grandin in Palmyra, New York.
Apr. 6, 1830	Organization of the Church of Jesus Christ with six members.
Oct. 1830	Four missionaries preach the gospel in Ohio. Sidney Rigdon is baptized.
Feb. 1, 1831	Having left New York, Joseph and Emma Smith arrive in Kirtland, Ohio.
March 24, 1832	Joseph tarred and feathered by mob at Hiram, Ohio.
Feb. 14, 1835	Quorum of Twelve Apostles organized.
March 27, 1836	Dedicates Kirtland Temple.
Jan. 12, 1838	Leaves Kirtland, Ohio, to escape violence.
March 14, 1838	Arrives with family at Far West, Missouri.
Oct. 27, 1838	Governor Lilburn W. Boggs of Missouri orders Mormons to leave the state or suffer extermination.

Oct. 31, 1838	Surrenders to Missouri militia.
Dec. 1, 1838	Imprisoned at Liberty, Missouri.
March 15, 1839	Allowed by guards to escape.
May 10, 1839	Moves to Commerce, Illinois, later renamed Nauvoo.
March 17, 1842	Organizes Female Relief Society.
March 18, 1844	Gives "last charge" to the Twelve Apostles.
June 10, 1844	Orders destruction of *Nauvoo Expositor* press.
June 12, 1844	Arrested on charge of riot for destroying press.
June 25, 1844	Surrenders at Carthage, Illinois
June 27, 1844	Shot to death by mob at Carthage Jail.

Chapter 1

Joseph Smith as Hero

Joseph Smith a hero? For many, the idea is ridiculous. On the other hand, for faithful Latter-day Saints the term is, if anything, inadequate to define his significance. But in recognizing different angles of vision from which he could be viewed and the resulting different perspectives on his life—which is the essential thrust of this book—perhaps it is a good place to start. For as odious as Joseph Smith appeared to many, those who looked at him with different eyes could see him as a hero.

To properly appreciate this aspect of his persona we must see him against the backdrop of nineteenth-century heroism. What, then, had Joseph Smith's generation inherited from previous centuries and their view of the heroic? How did he measure up against the heroic yardstick of his day? These are the questions we will explore in the present chapter.

To start with, the label *hero* makes no sense without certain minimum attributes. Different lists have been compiled. For literary scholar Roy Porter, the hero is:

- an extraordinary individual, with the ability "to perform extraordinary feats or miracles or to give inspired teaching," who demonstrates his powers in warfare or some other kind of dangerous or violent situation, but heroism also "may be expressed in any number of ways that are viewed as extending the range of achievement for a particular society or group."
- a human being—not divine, in other words, and consequently showing some human failings.
- the object of heightened admiration.

Porter seems to restrict the term to someone who is dead but whose "venerated memory" is kept alive by telling "his biography in circles for whom is memory had social significance. The traditions of the hero, for Porter, are "essentially folklore material."[1]

Bill Butler, a historian of ideas, lists thirty different attributes of the hero.[2] Some apply most obviously to the founders of major religions: e.g., preceded by legends, of unknown parentage, conceived miraculously, etc. Some of Butler's other points, derived from specific heroic figures, are by no means considered necessary for all heroes: "rescued or taught by wild or supernatural beings"; "consecrated by acquiring weapons"; or "initiated by being given a name."

Selecting from Butler's larger list, however, we find several features with possible applicability to our present subject: a life "more difficult than that of most people"; "a constant wanderer"; "larger-than-life actions, size, beauty, courage, intelligence"; wielding "supernatural weapons"; living a dangerous life that "can bring death to his friends as often as to his enemies"; "a supernatural or sacrificial death."

Joseph Campbell, well-known authority on myth, sees in heroes a three-phase sequence of "a separation from the world, a penetration to some source of power, and a life-enhancing return."[3] "If we could dredge up something forgotten not only by ourselves but by our whole generation or our entire civilization, we should become indeed the boon-bringer, the culture hero of the day—a personage of not only local but world historical moment."[4] For his followers, the Mormon prophet did exactly that, "rendering the modern world spiritually significant."[5] But by ranging back and forth across the centuries and geographically from culture to culture, which some would see as his great strength, Campbell is fundamentally unhelpful in setting a framework for heroism in the nineteenth century.[6]

Looming largest as historical hero in European and American consciousness at the beginning of the nineteenth century was Napoleon. He was not the culture-hero who defends society, according to one authority, but the outlaw adventurer with "boundless ambition," willing "to break with law and convention." To achieve the lofty status of hero, in his own understanding of the term, Napoleon needed to exhibit "the rebellious aura of the adventurer." His could not be a life of ease or convention. He wished to be seen as the "Man of Destiny."[7] When Joseph Smith was growing up as a boy, Napoleon was winning some of his great battles, escaping from Elba to return to France in the Hundred Days, losing the battle of Waterloo, and then living out his life on St. Helena.

Dixon Wecter, a historian of popular culture, has studied a sequence of Americans from Captain John Smith to Franklin Delano Roosevelt. In the late eighteenth century, Benjamin Franklin, George Washington, and Thomas Jefferson were all seen as heroes, to be followed in the nineteenth century by Daniel Boone, Davy Crockett, Abraham Lincoln, Robert E.

Lee, and others.[8] Of these it will be most helpful for our present purposes to consider Old Hickory—Andrew Jackson.

Historian John William Ward has supplied the standard study of Jackson's image.[9] In 1815, when Joseph Smith was just nine years old, Jackson became a national hero as a result of the American victory in the battle of New Orleans. In the actual battle, British troops were not noticeably cowardly, although their leadership put them in an impossible situation. Nor did the American troops display any particular skill in marksmanship. The fact remains, however, that when the shooting subsided, the British casualties were 2,000, while the Americans lost only eight killed and thirteen wounded.

The battle was one thing, its image another. Soon one heard that the victory was due to American marksmanship. This version of the events received a fresh infusion of popularity in the 1820s through the song "The Hunters of Kentucky." Here is one stanza:

> But Jackson he was wide awake,
> and wasn't scared with trifles,
> For well he knew what aim we take
> with our Kentucky rifles;
> So he marched us down to "Cyprus Swamp";
> The ground was low and mucky;
> There stood "John Bull," in martial pomp,
> *But here was old Kentucky.*

In essence, the claim was being made that uncorrupted nature, in the form of soldiers fresh from the forests and the fields, triumphed over the pomp of old Europe. Not the beneficiary of a pampered childhood or an aristocratic education, Jackson had grown from infancy to maturity "as the forest trees grow." This very lack of training was significantly one of the important aspects of Jackson as hero. Lacking academic degrees and formal study, he nevertheless possessed (or was presented as possessing) strength of mind, even genius, an ability to cut through to the essential, to rise above petty detail to the broad generalization. As a newspaper correspondent put it, "His mind seems to be clogged by no forms."[10] No dandy, no intellectual, Jackson faced as his opponent in the 1828 election John Quincy Adams, a Harvard professor. One criticism that Jackson's opponents made was that he would embarrass the United States. "What will the English malignants . . . the Edinburgh and Quarterly reviewers . . . say of a people who want a man to govern them who cannot spell more than about one word in four?" As it turned out, Ward comments, the people, "didn't give much of a damn what the English malignants thought."[11] To be an American hero for his generation required some connection with the divine. Soon after the battle of New Orleans, a great Te Deum was celebrated. The Catholic *abbé* extolled Jackson as God's representative: "To *Him*, therefore, our most fervent thanks are due for our late unexpected rescue, and it is Him we chiefly intend to praise, when considering you, general, as *the man of his right hand*, whom he has taken pains to fit out for the important commission of our defence."[12] Although Jackson may not have been particularly religious, an important part of his image as hero for his age was the assumption that God watched over him, assisted him, and even intervened in his behalf.

What of Joseph Smith? Could he be seen as a hero by the definitions presented above? Against the backdrop of the Jacksonian era, consider the following:

1. Joseph Smith came from lower-class origins. More so than Jackson, certainly more so than William Henry Harrison, he could claim to have been born in a log cabin. He didn't stay in the simple structure in Sharon, Vermont. Heroes never do.

2. He exhibited physical courage. When only seven years of age, he became afflicted with a bone infection that ultimately required surgery. The first incision was eight inches long on his lower leg. The second time the surgeon reopened the wound, he went as deep as the bone. The third operation was even more excruciating. The surgeon bored into the bone of his leg, first from one side, then from the other, and broke off a piece of bone with a pair of pincers. This process was repeated three times in order to remove the necessary amount of infected bone. The boy refused to be tied down, saying he could "tough it out" if his father would hold him in his arms. And he refused to take any wine to mitigate the pain.[13]

About twenty years later, after the Church had been organized and while he was living on the Johnson farm near Kirtland, Ohio, Joseph Smith was awakened in the night by a mob of armed men who burst into the house, choked him into unconsciousness, dragged him outside, tore off his clothes, beat him, scratched him, smeared his naked body with hot tar, and rolled him in feathers. He staggered back home. His wife Emma was so frightened when she saw him that she swooned, thinking he was covered with blood. A blanket was thrown around him. All night his friends worked, using lard to loosen the tar and then scrape it off, often removing pieces of skin with the tar. The next morning he appeared on schedule at a worship service, much to the surprise of two mob leaders who were in the congregation. Joseph preached a sermon, making no reference to his experience of the night before, and afterwards baptized three new members into the Church.[14] Many such incidents could be adduced. To his followers they showed a courageous leader who drew upon unseen sources of strength.

3. He challenged the establishment. This is too obvious to require evidence, but it may be worth reminding ourselves of how steadily he pursued his course, taking on, as it were, the entire world. "Courage means many things besides physical bravery: taking an unpopular position, standing up for principle, persevering, forging accomplishment out of adversity." This description by historian Peter Gibbon is readily seen in Joseph Smith.[15]

4. Against incredible opposition, he kept bouncing back. His entire life can be seen as a series of experiences taking this form. At one of the lowest points, his people having been expelled from Missouri, Joseph languished with a few associates in Liberty Jail. One might think he was down for the count. But during the crucial months of late 1838 and early 1839, he was binding his fellow prisoners to him even more closely, putting forth teachings that inspired (and still do), regrouping his own and his people's resources. In the immediate aftermath of his escape, he established a new center on the banks of the Mississippi River and then sent out apostle-missionaries, themselves in the depths of poverty, to far-away England.

5. Audaciously, he played for high stakes. This was inherent in his initial claim to religious authority, but also in such dramatic actions as leading a so-called army, Zion's Camp, to rescue the beleaguered Saints in Missouri. However humble he was before God in a spiritual sense, there was nothing modest about Joseph Smith's undertakings and style. But then modesty is not a trait we readily associate with Alexander the Great, Napoleon, or Old Hickory.

6. He was a builder. It may have been enough for the heroes of history and legend to defeat the dragon, to save their family or people, but the greatest of them had constructive achievements to their credit, as witness the biblical King David, Napoleon, and Andrew Jackson. Not satisfied simply to denounce the political, economic, and religious institutions of his day, Joseph Smith launched his own (or as he would say, God's) counter-systems—political, economic, social, and especially ecclesiastical. Even if all did not succeed, he gave sufficient impetus to the new Church—and the ancillary utopian aspects—that they were able to survive his death.

If George Washington was *pater patriae,* the father of his country, Joseph Smith was *pater ecclesiae,* father of his church. Both Washington and Smith would insist on adding the words "under God."

7. Finally, let us consider Joseph Smith's personal style. Although some have extended the concept of hero to include intellectual and artistic

geniuses, it is hard to think of a recluse or a balding, bespectacled milque-toast as a true hero.[16] In the public arena, the hero is able to be noticed—indeed, to command attention—and to attract and keep followers. This flair, however we define it, Joseph Smith had. It was impossible to ignore him. He was striking in appearance. Certainly he had his moments of private relaxation and casual conversation, even humor; but when he spoke, people listened, whether in the question-answer format that became common near the end of his life or in sermons and orations. He was a natural leader of men. Joseph Smith had charisma.

Listen to Wilford Woodruff, as early as 1836, writing in his journal after listening to thirty-year-old Joseph Smith preach in the newly dedicated Kirtland Temple: "There is not a greater man than Joseph standing in this generation. The gentiles look upon him & he is to them like bed of gold conce[a]led from human view: they know not his principle, his spirit, his wisdom, virtue, phylanthropy, nor his calling. His mind like Enochs swells wide as eternity. Nothing short of a God can comprehend his soul."[17]

Or here is the testimony of George Q. Cannon: "Whether engaging in manly sport, during hours of relaxation, or proclaiming words of wisdom in pulpit or grove, he was ever the leader. His magnetism was masterful, and his heroic qualities won universal admiration. Where he moved all classes were forced to recognize in him the man of power. Strangers journeying to see him from a distance, knew him the moment their eyes beheld his person." If this last claim seems extravagant, we should be aware that George Q. Cannon is recalling his own experience when landing at the pier in Nauvoo. Crowds of people were milling about, but when Cannon spotted the Prophet he "knew him instantly."[18]

But, it may be said, this is loading the dice. Of course, his followers saw him in glowing terms. That is what made them followers. Non-Mormons, at least anti-Mormons, saw him differently, as we shall see in a later chapter. The answer, of course, is that all heroes could be seen in negative terms. We don't know what the Trojans were saying about Agamemnon, or the Philistines about Saul and David, but we do know of the hostile caricatures of George Washington, Napoleon Bonaparte, and Andrew Jackson. Heroism is very largely in the eye of the beholder. But without certain characteristics, an individual is simply not convincingly labeled a hero. Of humble origins, lacking formal education, not hampered by traditional forms, extraordinarily intelligent, ready with the repartee that showed his acuity, resolute of purpose, of penetrating eye, a natural leader, protective of women and children, somehow connected with or approved by God—such was the litany of attributes of Andrew Jackson, at least in the image held by his followers. Without exception, such also were the attributes of Joseph Smith.

Even some outside observers recognized that Joseph was far from ordinary and might very well have a significance beyond their present estimate. As early as 1840 a visitor to Nauvoo remarked on the way in which leading people gathered to hear Joseph's pronouncements: "His bearing towards them was like one who had authority, and the deference which they paid him convinced us that his dominion was deeply seated in the empire of their consciences."[19]

In 1842, the *New York Herald* editorialized: "This Joe Smith is undoubtedly one of the greatest characters of the age. He indicates as much talent, originality, and moral courage as Mahomet, Odin, or any of the great spirits that have hitherto produced the revolutions of past ages."[20]

Later, Josiah Quincy, mayor of Boston (after describing Andrew Jackson in terms far from adulatory), wrote of Joseph Smith:

> It is by no means improbable that some future textbook, for the use of generations yet unborn, will contain a question something like this: What historical American of the nineteenth century has exerted the most powerful influence upon the destinies of his countrymen? And it is by no means impossible that the answer to that interrogatory may be thus written: *Joseph Smith, the Mormon prophet.* And the reply, absurd as it doubtless seems to most men now living, may be an obvious commonplace to their descendants.[21]

Quincy goes on to say that "such a rare human being is not to be disposed of by pelting his memory with unsavory epithets." Joseph Smith, he wrote, was a "sturdy self-asserter," a "fine-looking man" of "commanding appearance." But he was more. Comparing Joseph to Elijah Potter of Rhode Island, Quincy wrote: "Of all men I have met, these two seemed best endowed with that kingly faculty which directs, as by intrinsic right, the feeble or confused souls who are looking for guidance."

Quincy's words are often quoted by Latter-day Saints. Positive remarks from an intelligent, well-known Bostonian were a welcome contrast to the denunciations we shall consider later. But too much must not be read into the words. Quincy was not entirely complimentary and was much too sophisticated to take the Mormon religion seriously. But he could not deny that the Mormons had an extraordinary leader. "Born in the lowest ranks of poverty, without book-learning and with the homeliest of all human names," Quincy concluded, Joseph Smith "had made himself at the age of thirty-nine a power upon the earth."[22]

Smith's willingness to think in grandiose terms was evidenced in 1843 when he proposed to the U.S. government that he be given the contract for enforcing the law on the Overland Trail to Oregon. Had this offer been accepted—and we know not whether it was even taken seriously—there might well have been a generation who thought of the entire country west of the Mississippi as Smith country. He would have been the godfather over thousands of miles in the West. That he could even think in such terms tells something of the man.

Within the long tradition of heroism it is worth remembering the importance of being seen on horseback. "Perhaps we have not really been able to believe in heroes since the triumph of the internal combustion engine," a Renaissance historian remarks as he notes the popularity of equestrian monuments in Renaissance Italy.[23] After establishing a new city of Nauvoo, Illinois, Joseph Smith became its mayor and a commander of the Nauvoo Legion. He could wear his officer's uniform on public occasions, could lead the troops in parade, and could commission (or at least encourage) an artistic rendition of himself that is squarely in the tradition of the equestrian statue.

In 1844, Joseph Smith threw his hat into the ring for the presidency of the United States. How serious was he? Did he think he stood a chance? He told Josiah Quincy that in a close election he might be the balance of power.[24] *Views of the Presidency*, his campaign pamphlet, sets forth his dissatisfaction with much of the present social-political order.[25] What would be the message, the pitch, of those out on the stump promoting his candidacy? Speaking to non-Mormons, they could not well emphasize that Joseph Smith was a prophet. That would be a turn-off. But they could, in addition to expounding his specific policy proposals, convey their own conviction that he was a towering personality capable of providing strong leadership—in short, a hero.

Already in Joseph Smith's lifetime the notion of hero was complex. Later it would fragment further. Thomas Carlyle's famous *On Heroes, Hero-Worship and the Heroic in History* (1841) discusses the hero as divinity, the hero as prophet, the hero as poet, the hero as priest, the hero as man of letters, and the hero as king.[26] In these terms, Joseph Smith stands forth not only as prophet-hero but as a political, economic, and military hero. In his single person, he managed to refract several of the main components of heroic possibility.

"Hero" was a title Smith never claimed for himself. Primary for him was his role as "prophet, seer, and revelator." Serving as spokesman for God on earth far transcended being a hero as the term was usually understood.

But one could be both, and the distinction could be useful. Thus, it might have been possible to see Smith as a genuine hero—thinking, for example, of the putative voters in the 1844 presidential election—without accepting his prophetic claims. Even among his followers, one imagines, there were those still struggling with the religious aspect who were mesmerized by the hero.

As they looked upon Joseph Smith, especially as they remembered him, Latter-day Saints saw someone who in a short lifetime had accomplished great things. He had been a crucial player in the cosmic plan of God. With a flair for the dramatic, he had asserted his claims in a way that could not be ignored. Like a Titan, he strode across the historical stage. For his followers of the Jacksonian era, he was a true hero. The term "hero" has experienced a metamorphosis. When used today, it often carries very different meaning from its meaning in the past. For many, military heroes were rendered obsolete by the anti-war movement in the 1970s. When asked to identify their heroes, young people often mention sports stars or performers of rock music. But these individuals' patent deficiency as role models, which some of them remind us they never claim to be, renders the term "hero" meaningless when applied to them. Cynicism—suspicion about the motives and private life of all public figures—is the prevailing attitude.[27] Heroism melts before modern investigative reporting and the glare of television cameras.

Political philosopher Sidney Hook sees the hero as fundamentally incompatible with modern democracy.[28] A more profound explanation comes from George Roche, a college president, who wrote that heroes cannot exist in an age of moral relativism, confirming Hawthorne's earlier pronouncement that "a hero cannot be a hero unless in an heroic world."[29] At the very least, the hero himself cannot be a relativist.[30] The term is devaluated almost beyond recognition when people, asked to name their heroes, simply point to sports and entertainment stars.[31]

Sociologist Robert Nisbet sees six attributes as essential to the hero.[32] First, says Nisbet, there must be an "unshakable belief in one's own charismatic nature—that is, belief that one is on a mission not merely to instruct the world but to liberate it, from dogma and superstition, from torment and tyranny." Second, there is the "heroic deed," which can be a book. Third is "the hero's obsessive sense of coming, as it were, upon a midnight clear, all the world hushed in unconscious anticipation." Fourth is "the all-important exile or ostracism as the direct and immediate consequence of the great deed." Fifth, there must be enemies. "Without hostile opposition, above all treachery, one cannot possibly become a hero." Finally, says Nisbet, talent or genius is not enough; the hero must be "larger than life."

There is little difficulty in demonstrating that Joseph Smith fulfilled each of these requirements for heroism. In fact, in commenting on one of the attributes, Nisbet writes: "Jesus, Buddha, Caesar, Cromwell, Washington, and Joseph Smith all knew, as true heroes must, their respective wildernesses, exiles, castigations by contemporaries, even their Elbas and Golgothas."[33] For present-day Mormons, Joseph Smith's religious titles—especially prophet, seer, and revelator—have become central while his heroic attributes are clouded over. Many who staunchly accept him as a prophet know little of his biography. But those in tune who have sufficient interest in history can still see him in the heroic mold. Consider the following summary by Mormon biographer John Henry Evans:

> Here is a man who was born in the stark hills of Vermont; who was reared in the backwoods of New York; who never looked inside a college or high school; who lived in six States, no one of which would own him during his lifetime; who spent months in the vile prisons of the period; who, even when he had his freedom, was hounded like a fugitive; who was covered once with a coat of tar and feathers, and left for dead; who, with his following, was driven by irate neighbors from New York to Ohio, from Ohio to Missouri, and from Missouri to Illinois; and who, at the unripe age of thirty-eight, was shot to death by a mob with painted faces.
>
> Yet this man became mayor of the biggest town in Illinois and the state's most prominent citizen, the commander of the largest body of trained soldiers in the nation outside the Federal army, the founder of cities and of a university, and aspired to become President of the United States.[34]

Such is the stuff of hero-worship.

Eight years after Joseph's death, William Willes expressed his admiration in the following verse:

> Say, Who beheld the pious rage
> 'Mong sects in this *enlightened* age,
> And saw them differ, foam, and rage?
> The Prophet, Joseph Smith.
> Who made the resolution rare
> To ask the Lord in secret prayer,
> "Which sect did all the truth declare?"
> The Prophet, Joseph Smith.
> Who was encompassed and assailed
> By powers of darkness, yet ne'er quailed
> And wrestled until he prevailed?

> The Prophet, Joseph Smith.
> Who saw the Lord descend and say,-
> "Hear thou my son, he'll show the way,
> "If you will now his laws obey?"
> The Prophet, Joseph Smith.
> Who took the Plates the angel shewed,
> And brought them from their dark abode,
> And made them plain by power of God?
> The Prophet Joseph Smith.
> Who did receive the power to raise
> The Church of Christ in Latter-days,
> And call on men to mend their ways?
> The Prophet Joseph Smith.
> Who bore the scorn, the rage, the ire,
> Of those who preach for filthy hire,
> Was called by them "Imposter, Liar?"
> The Prophet, Joseph Smith.
> Who brought the truth of God to view,
> And led God's faithful people through,
> And built the city of Nauvoo?
> The Prophet, Joseph Smith.
> Who fell by ruthless mobbers' hands?
> Whose heart's-blood stained Columbia's land?
> Who died fulfilling Christ's command?
> The Prophet, Joseph Smith.[35]

Whatever one may think of the author's literary skills, it is clear that for him Joseph Smith was a hero.

In the immediate aftermath of Joseph Smith's death, with no sense of incongruity, W. W. Phelps could write the words familiar to all Mormons:

> Hail to the Prophet, ascended to heaven!
> Traitors and tyrants now fight him in vain.
> Mingling with Gods, he can plan for his brethren;
> Death cannot conquer the hero again.[36]

Notes

1. Roy Porter, "Heroes in the Old Testament," in T*he Hero in Tradition and Folklore*, edited by H. R. E. Davidson (London: Folklore Society, 1984), 90-111.

2. Bill Butler, *The Myth of the Hero* (London: Rider and Company, 1979).

3. Joseph Campbell, *The Hero with a Thousand Faces* (1949; rpt., Cleveland, Ohio: World Publishing Company, 1956), 35.

4. Ibid., 17.

5. Ibid., 388.

6. For a critique of Campbell's approach, see Owen Jones, "Joseph Campbell and the Power of Myth," *Intercollegiate Review* 25 (Fall 1989): 13–24. The first Latter-day Saint to apply an archetypal approach to Joseph Smith of whom I am aware was Clifton Holt Jolley, "The Martyrdom of Joseph Smith: An Archetypal Study," *Utah Historical Quarterlky* 44 (Fall 1976): 329–50.

7. Shoshana Knapp, "Napoleon as Hero," in *Perspectives on Nineteenth-Century Heroism*, edited by Sara M. Putzell and David C. Leonard (Potomac, Md.: Studia Humanitatis, 1982).

8. Dixon Wecter, *The Hero in America: A Chronicle of Hero-Worship* (1941; rpt., Ann Arbor: University of Michigan Press, 1963). See also Marshall W. Fishwick, *American Heroes: Myth and Reality* (Washington, D.C.: Public Affairs Press, 1954), with chapters on Smith, Washington, Boone, and others. See especially Paul K. Longmore, *The Invention of George Washington* (Berkeley: University of California Press, 1988).

9. John William Ward, *Andrew Jackson: Symbol for an Age* (1953; rpt., New York: Oxford University Press, 1962).

10. Quoted in ibid., 53.

11. Ibid., 65.

12. Quoted in ibid., 104.

13. Lucy Mack Smith, *History of Joseph Smith* (1853; rpt., Salt Lake City: Bookcraft, 1958), chap. 15; Donna Hill, *Joseph Smith: The First Mormon* (Garden City, N.Y.: Doubleday, 1977), 35–36.

14. Hill, *Joseph Smith*, 145–46.

15. Peter H. Gibbon, *A Call to Heroism: Renewing America's Vision of Greatness* (New York: Atlantic Monthly Press, 2002), 5.

16. Thomas Carlyle, in *On Heroes, Hero-Worship, and the Heroic in History* (1841) included not only Muhammad and Oliver Cromwell as heroes but also Shakespeare, Dante, Samuel Johnson, and Martin Luther. Gibbon, *A Call to Heroism*, 25.

17. Scott G. Kenney, ed., *Wilford Woodruff's Journal*, 9 vols. (Midvale, Utah: Signature Books, 1983–84), April 9, 1837, 1:138–39.

18. George Q. Cannon, *Life of Joseph Smith, the Prophet* (1888; Salt Lake City: Deseret Book, 1964 printing), 20.

19. Ibid.

20. *New York Herald*, November 7, 1842.

21. Josiah Quincy, *Figures of the Past* (Boston: Little Brown, 1883), 376–400.

22. Ibid.

23. Randolph Starn, "Reinventing Heroes in Renaissance Italy," *Journal of Interdisciplinary History* 17 (Summer 1986): 77.

24. Quincy, *Figures of the Past*, 399.

25. "Joseph Smith's Presidential Platform," *Dialogue: A Journal of Mormon Thought* 3 (Autumn 1968): 17–36, including Richard D. Poll, "Joseph Smith and the Presidency, 1844"; Martin B. Hickman, "The Political Legacy of Joseph Smith"; a photographic reprint of *General Smith's Views*; and editorial footnotes.

26. Carlyle, *On Heroes, Hero-Worship and the Heroic in History* (1841). See also D. Sonstroem, "Double Vortex in Carlyle's *On Heroes and Hero Worship*," *Philological Quarterly* 59 (Fall 1980): 531–40.

27. For a searching discussion see Gibbon, *A Call to Heroism.*

28. Sidney Hook, *The Hero in History* (1943; rpt., Boston: Beacon, 1955), chap. 11.

29. George Roche, *A World without Heroes: The Modern Tragedy* (Hillsdale, Mich.: Hillsdale College Press, 1987), 7 and *passim*. Russell Kirk, who wrote the introduction to this volume, quotes Hawthorne (v).

30. "When the primordial sentiments of a people weaken, there invariably follows a decline of belief in the hero. To see the significance of this, we must realize that the hero can never be a relativist." Richard M. Weaver, *Ideas Have Consequences* (Chicago: University of Chicago Press, 1948), 31.

31. See symposium "Where Have All the Heroes Gone?" in *Critic* 335 (Fall 1976): 28–35; F. R. Lloyd, "Home Run King," *Journal of Popular Culture* 9 (Spring 1976): 983–95; P. A. Hutton, "From Little Bighorn to Little Big Man: The Changing Image of a Western Hero," *Western Historical Quarterly* 7 (January 1976): 19–45; W. M. Clements, "Savage, Pastoral, Civilized: An Ecology Typology of American Frontier Heroes," *Journal of Popular Culture* 8 (Fall 1974): 254–66.

32. Robert Nisbet, *Prejudices* (Cambridge, Mass.: Harvard University Press, 1982), 152–58.

33. Ibid., 154.

34. John Henry Evans, *Joseph Smith, an American Prophet* (New York: Macmillan, 1933), v.

35. William Willis [Willes], "The Prophet, Joseph Smith," *Millennial Star* 14 (1852): 303–4.

36. W. W. Phelps, "Praise to the Man," *Hymns of the Church of Jesus Christ of Latter-day Saints* (Salt Lake City: Church of Jesus Christ of Latter-day Saints, 1985), no. 27.

Chapter 2

A Prophet—In the Book of Mormon

"His own visions and visitations are not more marvelous than those reported throughout the Book of Mormon, which, in fact, they closely resemble." —Hugh Nibley

Arriving at Kirtland, Ohio, he entered the Whitney store, extended his hand to the proprietor, and said, "N. K. Whitney! Thou art the man."

"You have the advantage of me," said Whitney. "I could not call you by your name as you have me."

"I am Joseph the Prophet," Smith answered, smiling.[1]

That was the way he identified himself. That is what his mother called him. That was the most common designation used by his people. "The Prophet Joseph Smith"—this continues to be the standard language used by Latter-day Saints when referring to him.

But what does it mean to be a prophet? The term can be slippery. With its home base in the Bible, the term is assigned to "major" and "minor" writers from Isaiah to Malachi. But its application has been extended. Girolamo Savonarola, for example, was called a prophet at the end of the fifteenth century.

What did the term *prophet* mean to Joseph Smith? One promising way of discovering the answer, it seems to me, is through the Book of Mormon. Some critics of the Book of Mormon consider it simply a product of Joseph Smith's mind, a pious fraud produced entirely within the context of early national America. Mormons have traditionally accepted Joseph's own account of the book's miraculous discovery and translation from ancient plates. Some have attempted to come up with a compromise, ranging from the natural, ingenuous insertion of King James language when it seemed appropriate to a more complex meld of ancient and modern into a targum-like sacred text. What all of these theories—the hostile one of fraud, the traditional one of believers, and the efforts at compromise—have in common is the recognition that somehow the words of the Book of Mormon passed through the brain of Joseph Smith.

Using that simple fact as a point of departure, I would like to explore some passages that must have seemed especially relevant to Joseph Smith. I am referring not to moral teachings but to descriptions that touched very close to the reality of his own life experience. No one can prove that he produced these passages (or thought, pronounced, or read them) with his own life in mind, but I think we can assume that he would have responded with special sensitivity to words that seemed close to his own experiences.

Perhaps before even considering the examples, I should make it clear that this reading does not imply a fabrication, with Joseph incorporating his own experiences into a text ostensibly dealing with ancient people.[2] In fact, some of his own peak experiences and tribulations that closely resonate with the Book of Mormon came after its publication. All I wish to suggest here is that, far more than those of us who are average readers, he would have been especially tuned in to many of the passages in the book.[3]

Of obvious relevance are passages that specifically refer to a future prophet. When Lehi, blessing his son Joseph, tells of a future seer who will also be named Joseph after his father (2 Ne. 3:15), we understand this to be a strikingly specific ancient prophecy from the sixth century B.C. referring to the nineteenth-century prophet. But here I have in mind not such an obvious, explicit reference but rather various descriptions made in the course of the Book of Mormon account that, on their face, do not apply to Joseph Smith.[4]

Let us start with the description of visions. Lehi's vision at the very beginning ("he thought he saw God") led to praise, "for his soul did rejoice, and his whole heart was filled" (1 Ne. 1:15). By the time he was dictating these words of the Book of Mormon to a scribe, Joseph had also experienced visions. Did his soul rejoice? Was his heart filled? Would he have reflected on the comparison, saying, in effect, "Yes, that is the way one feels after such a marvelous experience"? It is instructive to consider all the visions in the Book of Mormon in the same light: Would they have rung true to Joseph Smith? Would he have seen in them parallels to his own supernatural communications? I make mention of these revelatory experiences with humility and an advance awareness that our usual categories of thought may not suffice to explain them.

The Book of Mormon describes a future time—from the context, obviously referring to the generation of Joseph Smith—when there would be different churches, "when the one shall say unto the other: Behold, I, I am the Lord's; and the others shall say: I, I am the Lord's; and thus shall every one say that hath built up churches, and not unto the Lord" (2 Ne. 28:3). Is this description unrelated to the circumstance of different competing religions in upstate New York, "some crying 'Lo, here!' and others 'Lo, there!' Some were contending for the Methodist faith, some for the Presbyterian, and some for the Baptist" (JS—H 1:5). Is the frequent alignment of "contention" with unrighteousness and departure from the ways of God in the Book of Mormon unrelated to the sectarian strife of the early nineteenth century? As the words of the scriptural text passed through his mind and came from his lips, or afterwards as he read them, would Joseph Smith have been oblivious to the contemporary scene? It was the resurrected Savior who is quoted in the Book of Mormon as saying: "For verily, verily I say unto you, he that hath the spirit of contention is not of me, but is of the devil, who is the father of contention, and he stirreth up the hearts of men to contend with anger, one with another" (3 Ne. 11:29).

In addition to a general context of contending, incompatible claims, some of the elements of Joseph Smith's First Vision as he later described it were a strong desire, a recognition that God would communicate (prompted by the epistle of James), the request in prayer, and a gratifying sense of being forgiven for his sins. In the Book of Mormon, we read of Nephi's great desire, his recognition that God granted revelations (1 Ne. 10:17–19), his request (19:3), followed, of course, by a sublime revelation. Later, Enos pled with the Lord, crying unto him "in mighty prayer and supplication." Finally came the voice of the Lord: "Enos, thy sins are forgiven thee, and thou shalt be blessed" (Enos 2–5). Are we to think that such passages struck no chord of response in Joseph Smith, who, recalling his First Vision in 1832, wrote, "I saw the Lord and he spake unto me saying Joseph my son thy sins are forgiven thee"?[5] In a sense, then, we have in the Book of Mormon, published in 1830, not a report of the 1820 First Vision, but descriptions of other visions that include several of its constituent elements.

Then there is the reaction of the unbelievers. In Lehi's case "the Jews did mock him" (1 Ne. 1:19). Indeed, mockery was the standard response. When Lehi had a dream-vision of the tree of life, the faithful disciples were far fewer in number than the inhabitants of "a great and spacious building" who were "in the attitude of mocking and pointing their fingers" in scorn (1 Ne. 8:27). Later Nephi foresaw a generation when the record (the Book of Mormon) would come forth, when, as noted above, there would be different competing churches. Their message would be, "Hearken unto us, and hear ye our precept; for behold there is no God today, for the Lord and the Redeemer hath done his work, and he hath given his power unto men. Behold, hearken ye unto my precept; if they shall say there is a miracle wrought by the hand of the Lord, believe it not; for this day he is not a God of miracles; he hath done his work" (2 Ne. 28:5–6).

It is hard to believe that Joseph Smith could have dictated these words or later read them without thinking of his own visions and, for example, the Methodist minister who "treated my communication not only lightly, but with great contempt" (JS–H 1:21).

How do believers react to ridicule? So desperate are we for approval, so responsive to peer pressure, that many, even after conversion ("after they had tasted of the fruit"), will become ashamed and fall away (1 Ne. 8:28). But Nephi, after his own vision, came to recognize the large and spacious building as "vain imaginations and pride of the children of men" (1 Ne. 12:18). He reaffirmed his own sincerity—that he was not faking or trying to win notoriety: "For the fulness of mine intent is that I may persuade men to come unto the God of Abraham, and the God of Isaac, and the God of Jacob, and be saved" (1 Ne. 6:4). And rather than being swayed by the amused and condescending ridicule of cultured despisers, he "heeded them not" (1 Ne. 8:33).

Would Joseph Smith have gone over such descriptions without thinking of the superciliously negative reaction to his own stubborn insistence that he had seen a vision? "Why does the world think to make me deny what I have actually seen? For I had seen a vision; I knew it, and I knew that God knew it, and I could not deny it, neither dared I do it; at least I knew that by so doing I would offend God, and come under condemnation" (JS—H 1:25).

One of the most basic premises of Joseph Smith from the First Vision onward was that God was still a God of miracles and that He did speak to His children according to their need and their faith, in contrast to the common attitude that such divine interventions occurred only in Bible times. In the Book of Mormon, after Nephi had heard of his father's momentous dream and desired to see and know for himself, he wrote, almost as if insisting over and over again:

> I, Nephi, was desirous also that I might see, and hear, and know of these things, by the power of the Holy Ghost, which is the gift of God unto all those who diligently seek him, as well in times of old as in the time that he should manifest himself unto the children of men.

> For he is the same yesterday, to-day, and forever; and the way is pre-pared for all men from the foundation of the world, if it so be that they repent and come unto him.
>
> For he that diligently seeketh shall find; and the mysteries of God shall be unfolded unto them, by the power of the Holy Ghost, as well in these times as in times of old, and as well in times of old as in times to come; wherefore, the course of the Lord is one eternal round. (1 Ne. 10:17–19)

Joseph Smith was ridiculed by ministers and critics who told him that "there were no such things as visions or revelations in these days; that all such things had ceased with the apostles, and that there would never be any more of them" (JS—H 1:21). Would not Nephi's fervent declaration have had direct application?

The Book of Mormon contains other passages describing the way prophets are received. For example, another Nephi was denounced by the Establishment, the judges, for wanting to "raise himself to be a great man, chosen of God, and a prophet" (Hel. 9:16). Ridicule and suspicion—these were the response of respectable people to the words of prophets. And anger. Samuel the Lamanite uttered these telling words:

> And now when ye talk, ye say: If our days had been in the days of our fathers of old, we would not have slain the prophets; we would not have stoned them, and cast them out.
>
> Behold ye are worse than they; for as the Lord liveth, if a prophet come among you and declareth unto you the word of the Lord, which testifieth of your sins and iniquities, ye are angry with him, and cast him out and seek all manner of ways to destroy him; yea, you will say that he is a false prophet, and that he is a sinner, and of the devil, because he testifieth that your deeds are evil. (Hel. 13:25–26)

It might be held that this is simply a restatement of how prophets are always received—a type established by such ancient prophets as Jeremiah. But beyond that, I am here suggesting that Joseph Smith must have recog-nized significant points of close similarity to his own life experience.

In the course of his memorable dream, Lehi, after tasting the fruit that "filled my soul with exceedingly great joy" began to be "desirous that my family should partake of it also" (1 Ne. 8:12). Likewise Joseph Smith was anxious to share his great divine encounters with his family members. In the Book of Mormon narrative it is Father Lehi, Nephi, Sam, and even-tually Jacob and Joseph (younger children born in the wilderness) who are the steadfast believers, while Laman and Lemuel personify doubt and murmuring. In a characteristic burst of sibling jealousy, they complain that their brother "has taken it upon him to be our ruler and our teacher" (1 Ne. 16:37). When he began to build a ship, they said, "Our brother is a fool" (1 Ne. 17:17).

The alignment was not always so stark. At one point even Lehi faltered (1 Ne. 16:20), and the elder brothers were able at times to submit sufficiently that Nephi "had great hopes of them, that they would walk in the paths of righteousness" (1 Ne. 15:5). But in the final analysis, friction in the family led to schism.

What has all of this to do with Joseph Smith? How would he have recognized any of his own life in the scriptural account? The desire to share his convictions with other members of the Smith family was certainly present. We have no evidence of sibling rivalry, and the two older brothers, Alvin and Hyrum, did not reject their younger brother's claims. But perhaps for a time there was a concern in Joseph's mind about this possibility. Was Joseph ever called a fool? Did any family members protest that he, like Nephi, was following in the footsteps of a visionary father? Did the Smith family members, or some of them, complain of the "hard things" (1 Ne. 16:1) Joseph was telling them?

We are too lacking in detailed information about the Smith family dynamics during the decade of the 1820s to answer with certainty, and what we do know shows a rather incredible degree of family unity. Nevertheless, it seems highly unlikely that Joseph looked upon these Book of Mormon passages just cited as being totally unrelated to his own family existence, as apprehension of possible reactions if not allusions to actual happenings. One can well imagine that, in his family, Joseph, like Nephi, spoke "in the energy of my soul" (1 Ne. 16:24).

The family of Joseph Smith Sr. and Lucy Mack Smith was not always at the bottom of the social scale. There was some education, some degree of literacy, and, for a while, even the possibility of at least moderate wealth. But the expectations were disappointed, and most of the time—I am thinking of the move from Vermont to New York and the hard-scrabble existence of clearing fields and trying to pay off a mortgage during the fifteen years leading up to 1830—it must have seemed like bare survival. In Lucy Mack Smith's history, we gain a picture of a family looked down upon, not quite acceptable in polite society, yet sincere, hardworking, religious, and conscious of a special destiny.

Would the depths of Joseph Smith's soul have been provoked by references in the Book of Mormon to "the pride of the world" (1 Ne. 11:36), "the vain imaginations and the pride of the children of men" (1 Ne. 12:18)?

Lehi recalled that his son Joseph was born "in the wilderness of mine afflictions" (2 Ne. 3:1). Many times, especially after 1830, Joseph Smith must have felt that he was in the wilderness of his own afflictions.

Against this background, Joseph was faced with awesome challenges. Had he been able to look ahead from the spring of 1830, when the Book of Mormon was published and the Church was organized, how would he have reacted? It was not going to be a quick or an easy triumph. Accompanying the slings and arrows of persecution would come sickness, drivings from place to place, prison, and finally death.

Would he, then, have recognized some consolation in Lehi's great blessing on Jacob about the necessity of "opposition in all things" (2 Ne. 2:11)? Would he, too, have prayed that the Lord would consecrate his afflictions to his gain (2 Ne. 2:2)? And would he have been able to proclaim with Nephi, "I will go and do the things which the Lord hath commanded, for I know that the Lord giveth no commandments unto the children of men, save he shall prepare a way for them that they may accomplish the thing which he commandeth them" (1 Ne. 3:7)?

One of the recurring commonplaces in the Book of Mormon has to do with the inadequacy of words to express certain things. We should, it appears, recognize different levels to this problem. First is the distinction between speaking and writing, oral utterance as opposed to written accounts. It was quite possible to be "powerful" in the former while weak in the latter. Writing, as any teacher of composition knows, requires one to know about such practical matters as spelling, paragraphing, and punctuation. As found in the scriptures, too, mastery of some literary forms was included. Not just anybody who has the gift of gab is a skilled writer. And the words on a page are not presented by a human voice, with its pauses and emotional overtones. Here is Moroni's statement: "Thou hast also made our words powerful and great, even that we cannot write them; wherefore, when we write we behold our weakness, and stumble because of the placing of our words; and I fear lest the Gentiles shall mock at our words" (Ether 12:25).

Then, beyond this distinction, human language, oral or written, is inadequate to express the things of the Spirit. Specifically, as prophets and mystics seem to agree, our human language systems, functional enough in workaday situations, are incapable of expressing that which lies outside their cultural context.

Again, what has all of this to do with Joseph Smith? In the late 1820s, this young man was somehow producing a book of over 500 pages. He might have been quite articulate when talking to friends and family, but putting down something in writing was different. He was also experiencing additional encounters with God and angels—the revelations now found at the beginning of the Doctrine and Covenants. Can he possibly have been oblivious to his own frustrations when going over passages dealing with the specific problems of language, the difficulty of expressing the things of eternity, an awareness of weakness in writing, and an apprehension that future readers would "mock"? Again, in the same sense as before, we have "autobiographical" elements, unidentified as such, in the Book of Mormon itself.

The Book of Mormon tells of a series of prophets, great leaders chosen by God. Did Joseph Smith see himself as a modern equivalent of these men? It is hard to believe that he made no comparisons.

Consider Mormon and the skeletal account of his life we are given. When he was "about ten" Mormon received a kind of calling from Ammaron, who said, "I perceive that thou art a sober child, and art quick to observe" (Morm. 1:2). When Joseph Smith was the same age, he was still recovering from the traumatic leg operation that had occurred when he was seven. He traveled to Salem and spent time with his paternal Uncle Jesse. His mother remembered him as "remarkably well disposed." At age eleven, Mormon was "carried by my father into the land southward" (Morm. 1:6). At the same age, in 1816, Joseph Smith accompanied his family in a move from Vermont to New York. When Mormon was fifteen, "being somewhat of a sober mind, therefore I was visited of the Lord, and tasted and knew of the goodness of Jesus" (Morm. 1:15). It was in his fifteenth year, as Joseph Smith later wrote, that he experienced the First Vision, seeing the Father and the Son (JS—H 1:7ff). When he was "about twenty-four" Mormon was to take the sacred plates from their hiding place in the hill Shim. Joseph Smith, who had turned twenty-four on December 23, 1829, was completing the translation of the Book of Mormon prior to its publication in the spring of 1830.

When Moroni took over the guardianship of the plates from his father, we find him addressing the future generation in which the record would come forth. It would come forth at a time when many disbelieved, did not believe in Christ, "imagined up" a god unto themselves, and despised those who believed in miracles. The similarity to Joseph Smith's time, at least as he experienced it, is obvious. But there are even interesting specifics. Consider some parallels:

Mormon 9
27. Doubt not, but be believing, and begin as in times of old, and come unto the Lord with all your heart . . .

Mormon 8
26 . . . and it shall come in a day when it shall be said that miracles are done away . . .

14 . . . for he truly saith that no one shall have them to get gain; but the record thereof is of no worth; and whoso shall bring it to light, him will the Lord bless.
15. For none can have power to bring it to light save it be given him of God; for God wills that it shall be done with an eye single to his glory; for the welfare of the ancient and long dispersed covenant people of the Lord.

Joseph Smith—History 1
11. I was one day reading the Epistle of James, first chapter and fifth verse, which reads: If any of you lack wisdom, let him ask of God, that giveth to all men liberally, and upbraideth not, and it shall be given him. [The passage of course continues: *But let him ask in faith, nothing wavering* (emphasis mine).]

21. Some few days after I had this vision, I happened to be in company with one of the Methodist preachers, who was very active in the before mentioned religious excitement; and, conversing with him on that subject of religion, I took occasion to give him an account of the vision which I had had. I was greatly surprised at his behavior; he treated my communication not only lightly, but with great contempt, saying it was all of the devil, that there were no such things as visions or revelations in these days, that all such things had ceased with the apostles, and that there would never be any more of them.

46. Moroni . . . added a caution to me, telling me that Satan would try to tempt me (in consequence of the indigent circumstances of my father's family), to get the plates for the purpose of getting rich. This he forbade me, saying that I must have no other object in view in getting the plates but to glorify God, and must not be influenced by any other motive than that of building his kingdom; otherwise I could not get them.

By now, it seems unnecessary to ask the question: Could or did Joseph Smith see himself and his own experiences in the Book of Mormon? In addition, of course, prophecies in the Book of Mormon refer to the future individual who will "bring forth" this sacred record: Ether 5:1–3 even seems to forget the writer's point of view. In his position as a prophet standing alone, Moroni had been commanded to "seal up" both the record and the interpreters for a distant future generation. He quotes moving words from the Lord, including His direct admonition to both Gentiles and the house of Israel: "Come unto me." But at this point, abruptly, Moroni interjects a passage of counsel to the future prophet:

> I have told you the things which I have sealed up; therefore touch them not in order that ye may translate; for that thing is forbidden you, except by and by it shall be wisdom in God.
>
> And behold, ye may be privileged that ye may show the plates unto those who shall assist to bring forth this work;
>
> And unto three shall they be shown by the power of God; wherefore they shall know of a surety that these things are true.

These words put us squarely into the experience of Joseph Smith, who, on the occasion of Moroni's first appearance to him, had heard similar cautions about his motives and intimations that he would be able to show the plates to some individuals (JS—H 1:42, 46). Does Moroni not seem to be addressing Joseph Smith specifically? In any case, how can the words have been dictated by Joseph Smith in the late 1820s (or later read by him) without an acute awareness of their personal relevance? After all, Joseph was impecunious and, like all human beings, thought about financial security. And under some combination of circumstances only months before the publication of the Book of Mormon in 1830, witnesses had testified of seeing the plates.

At the end of Joseph Smith's life, in Carthage Jail with death staring him in the face, he turned to the Book of Mormon. One has to wonder how this action fits with the claim that the whole thing was a fraud. If he would not then be prompted to admit that the jig was up and confess his gigantic confidence scheme, at the very least, one would suppose, he should have turned to the Bible looking for a passage about forgiveness. Instead he found his solace in the Book of Mormon, in Ether 12, where he read the following moving words:

> And it came to pass that I prayed unto the Lord that he would give unto the Gentiles grace, that they might have charity.

And it came to pass that the Lord said unto me: If they have not charity it mattereth not unto thee, thou hast been faithful; wherefore, thy garments shall be made clean. And because thou hast seen thy weakness, thou shalt be made strong, even unto the sitting down in the place which I have prepared in the mansions of my Father.

And now I, Moroni, bid farewell unto the Gentiles, yea, and also unto my brethren whom I love, until we shall meet before the judgment-seat of Christ, where all men shall know that my garments are not spotted with your blood. (Ether 12:36–38)

As quoted by John Taylor in Doctrine and Covenants 135:5 the word "Moroni" is replaced with the three dots of an ellipsis so that the reader would realize, in case it were not sufficiently obvious, that Joseph Smith in 1844 could utter the same words in his own right. If in Carthage Jail he read the entire Book of Mormon chapter, he might well have recognized more than a little from his own life: the necessity for faith before receiving a "witness," rejection by people who would not believe because they saw not, the reaction of those who would mock ("Fools mock, but they shall mourn"), and the simple statement that, at the judgment, all would know that he (Moroni/Joseph?) had "seen Jesus, and that he hath talked with me face to face" (Ether 12:39).

Much in the Book of Mormon moves beyond such connections: the panoramic visions of the future, the history of wars and migrations, and the religious teachings in memorable passages about such subjects as the resurrection of the dead. I have no desire to suggest that the book is only a reflection of Joseph Smith's life.[6] Smith with Book of Mormon similarities that occurred after the book's publication, and forces comparisons that do not hold up under scrutiny. Moreover, the bulk of the Book of Mormon text is untouched by such an interpretation. My interpretation here emphatically leaves room for the authenticity of the Book of Mormon. I can attest that other readers will find passages which reflect some of their feelings and life situation. Yet we have seen enough, I suggest, to be convinced that, to a remarkable degree, the Book of Mormon contains many passages that could easily be seen as describing not only the external circumstances but also some of the most sacred and intimate aspects of the nineteenth-century Prophet.

One explanation would be that, in fabricating the book, Joseph inserted some feelings based on his own experiences (although this does suggest, awkwardly for some, that he had genuine religious experiences). Another is that the process of translation was sufficiently flexible that he used words and feelings of his own precisely at the points where they were appropriate in describing other prophets who, human beings after all, had anticipated some of his experiences and emotions. I find it sufficient to say that, whether in the process of dictating it to his scribe or in later correcting, reading, or pondering it, Joseph Smith would encounter in the Book of Mormon more than a few passages that resonated powerfully in his soul.

Notes

1. Elizabeth Ann Whitney, "A Leaf from an Autobiography," *Woman's Exponent* 7, no. 7 (September 1, 1878): 51.

2. I do not therefore accept the assumptions and conclusions of the following, although I note some of the same passages: William D. Morain, "The Sword of Laban: Joseph Smith, Jr. and the Unconscious," paper presented at Mormon History Association, Ogden, Utah, May 1993, and his subsequent book, *The Sword of Laban: Joseph Smith, Jr., and the Dissociated Mind* (Washington, D.C.: American Psychiatric Press, 1998); Robert D. Anderson, "The Sword of Laban: The Book of Mormon as Autobiography," paper presented at Sunstone Symposium, Salt Lake City, August 1993; his "The Autobiography of Joseph Smith in Third Nephi," paper presented at Sunstone Symposium, Salt Lake City, August 1994; and his *Inside the Mind of Joseph Smith: Psychobiography and the Book of Mormon* (Salt Lake City: Signature Books, 1999); nor Dan Vogel's *Joseph Smith: The Making of a Prophet* (Salt Lake City: Signature Books, 2004).

3. Unlike John L. Brooke, *The Refiner's Fire: The Making of Mormon Cosmology, 1644–1844* (New York: Cambridge University Press, 1994), who sees the Book of Mormon as an "autobiography" of the Prophet, I leave room for a genuine ancient history, an honestly lived life, and a shock of recognition.

4. For a listing of nine prophecies, which are not my subject matter in this chapter, see Richard Wadsworth, "Does the Book of Mormon Prophesy of the Prophet Joseph Smith?" *Ensign* 19 (April 1989): 52–53.

5. Dean C. Jessee, ed., *The Personal Writings of Joseph Smith* (Salt Lake City: Deseret Book, 1984), 6.

6. For parallels between the Book of Mormon and Joseph Smith's life, Robert D. Anderson, "Toward an Introduction to a Psychobiography of Joseph Smith," *Dialogue: A Journal of Mormon Thought* 23 (Fall 1994): 249–72, has a simple explanation: The book was a disguised, perhaps unintentional, autobiography. This interpretation, as stated, is unconvincing. It does not recognize possibilities of recognition rather than a simple one-directional influence and does not account for life experiences of Joseph.

Chapter 3

"Like Unto": Ancient Prototypes of a Modern Prophet

"You could not discover the limits of the self even by traveling along every path: so deep a logos does it have." —Heraclitus

Like everyone, Joseph Smith had his own uniqueness. But looking back, he could find commonalities with earlier prophets that made it possible to see them as anticipators. To a greater or lesser degree, sometimes with remarkable details, he replayed the broad themes and patterns of their life in the modern age. To employ a scriptural phrase, he was "like unto" them.[1] Biographers satisfied with secular interpretations show no interest in such things; but in this tone deafness, they miss overtones that had significant resonance with the Prophet and his followers.

Joseph seldom introduced himself as "Joseph, the prophet," as he did to Newel K. Whitney in Kirtland, Ohio; and he frequently used his title of "General" in Nauvoo, but there is no question that he saw himself and his life's mission as a prophet. Of course, that term could be cynically applied to him, as it was to Robert Matthews ("Matthias the Prophet"), meaning a self-proclaimed prophet obviously suffering from delusions of grandeur or some form of mental illness.[2] Others meant to put Joseph Smith in the company of Muhammad, a prophet to his people but, in the view of middle-class Americans of the past century, one with a false message.

In common parlance, a prophet is one who foretells future events. Deuteronomy 18:21–22 offers this well-known test of the prophet's legitimacy: Does or does not the thing foretold by the prophet come to pass? To the extent that insight into the future was part of Joseph Smith's role, he satisfied the expectation. He came across to his followers as a latter-day John the Revelator, telling in detail of the judgments to come.[3]

More basic is the fact that a prophet proclaims the word of God to his generation, itemizing its sins and calling it to repentance, with the wrath to come either implied or explicitly described.[4] An hour's reading in the revelations of the Doctrine and Covenants should demonstrate clearly enough that Joseph Smith supplied copious evidence of both kinds of message: he foretold coming events, and he delivered "a voice of warning" to the modern world.

Joseph Smith also brought forth additional scriptures, thus enlarging the usual prophetic role. Besides the revelations of the Doctrine and Covenants, he translated the Book of Mormon and the book of Abraham from ancient documents. "Translation" cannot be understood in the usual sense, for he did not claim to know the original language of these texts and could accomplish the task only "by the gift and power of God" as John Taylor asserted in his eulogy (D&C 135:3). An enormous scholarly literature exists on these scriptures that the Mormons accept along with the Bible. The simple point here is that written scriptures were among the most important productions of this prophet.

But beyond simply itemizing different aspects of his prophetic role, there is a more satisfying way, I believe, to get at what the term "prophet" meant to Joseph Smith. Looking back across the centuries, he was aware of other prophets. Which, if any, of these did he identify with? Of course, he had his own personality, his own setting; but looking back, he could find shared experiences that made it possible to see earlier prophets as role models, as anticipators. To some degree he was "like unto" them. Chapter 2 noted a few such connections between Joseph Smith and Book of Mormon characters. To further grasp this dimension of his prophetic role, it is rewarding to turn our attention to some of the ancient biblical patriarchs and prophets.

Enoch. We do not know much about Enoch from the Bible. Seven generations removed from Adam, he "walked with God" and "God took him" (Gen. 5:24). At age twenty-five, Joseph Smith added more details, including a great panoramic vision from Enoch's vantage point of the future course of world events (Moses 5–6). Without attempting a comprehensive analysis, let me simply observe that the city of Zion, far in the future from the point of view of ancient Enoch, would be built up in the last days and would join Enoch's righteous city: "And the Lord said unto Enoch: Then shall thou and all thy city meet them there, and we will receive them into our bosom, and they shall see us; and we will fall upon their necks, and they shall fall upon our necks, and we will kiss each other" (Moses 7:63).

Since the New Jerusalem, the latter-day Zion, was to be built up in Jackson County, Missouri, under the leadership of Joseph Smith, it is clear that he envisioned some kind of parallel. One characteristic of Enoch's righteous society was that there were no poor among them; Joseph Smith, anxious to establish justice in his day, strove mightily to get his followers to follow a system of communalism (*not* communism), which he, significantly, called the Order of Enoch.[5]

The first Zion, having been lifted up to heaven, would somehow rejoin the latter-day Zion. Enoch would meet his counterpart, the great prophet-seer-revelator-translator (D&C 107:92) of the last dispensation. There may even be a subtle suggestion that Enoch had appeared to his latter-day successor: "He is a ministering Angel to minister to those who shall be heirs of Salvation and appered [sic] unto Jude as Abel did unto Paul."[6]

Clearly Joseph Smith admired the ancient great-souled patriarch, telling a Nauvoo audience: "The reason why I feel so good is because I have a big soul. There are men with small bodies who have got souls like Enoch. We have gathered our big souls from the ends of the earth."[7] But deeper than admiration is the sense of identity, of performing parallel roles. We are not at all surprised to discover that one of the code names used to designate Joseph Smith in the early revelations was that of Enoch.[8]

Abraham. Also highly significant for the latter-day prophet was the ancient patriarch Abraham. The book of Abraham, now part of the Pearl of Great Price, adds many details not found in the Bible and reinforces the central importance of Abraham. That Joseph Smith breezily made up the additional biographical incidents seems unlikely in view of the striking confirmation in other extrabiblical sources published only in the late twentieth century.[9]

Parallels between the lives of Abraham and Joseph Smith are also noticeable. Joseph Smith's prayer, leading to the First Vision at age fourteen, "echoes young Abraham's prayer at the same age. . . . Both men had been foreordained; both received the priesthood, preached the gospel, and encountered formidable opposition; both spoke face to face with divine messengers and God himself; both possessed a Urim and Thummim, translated ancient records, and wrote scripture; and both founded an influential community of believers."[10]

Other connections include an appearance by Abraham to Joseph Smith. "A central purpose of the restoration is to make Abraham's promises effective for his descendants, who through temple ordinances may receive the blessings of Abraham." Despite his special mission, Joseph Smith claimed no monopoly on these blessings; instead, all Saints "are commanded to come to Christ by 'doing the works of Abraham,'" whose life constitutes a pattern.[11]

Joseph. The naming of Joseph Smith after the biblical Joseph, who was sold into Egypt, is alluded to in the Book of Mormon. Lehi, blessing his son Joseph (another individual with this same name), quoted the ancient Joseph's prophecy of a future seer: "And his name shall be called after me; and it shall be after the name of his father. And he shall be like unto me" (2 Ne. 3:15). The Book of Mormon was published in 1830; here was a passage referring to Joseph Smith, then twenty-four years old. To claim that he would in any significant way be like the ancient Joseph of Egypt seems rather audacious.

That the ancient Joseph was a type of Christ is one of the longstanding truisms of Christian biblical exegesis. BYU religion professor Joseph Fielding McConkie has listed fifteen similarities between Joseph and Jesus.[12] But remarkably, the ancient Joseph also typified and foreshadowed his nineteenth-century namesake. Apostle Neal A. Maxwell has noted some of the similarities between the ancient Joseph and nineteenth-century Joseph Smith. Both had "inauspicious beginnings"; both had visions when young; both were hated; both "knew sibling jealousy or other ill feelings; both were "falsely accused; both were "generous to those who betrayed them"; both were "jailed and knew what it was to be in a 'pit'"; both prophesied; both knew separation from family and friends; and both were "amazingly resilient in the midst of adversity."[13] Others have also listed and commented upon the many parallels between the two Josephs.[14]

It would be claiming too much to say that Joseph Smith consciously saw to it that his life replayed much of the ancient Joseph's experience, but at times he was conscious of similarities. Writing from Liberty Jail, he said, "I feel like Joseph in Egypt.[15]

Moses. There is no greater Old Testament figure than Moses, who led the children of Israel out of Egypt. Teaching the Israelites anciently, Moses declared, according to the account preserved in Deuteronomy 18:15: "The Lord thy God will raise up unto thee a Prophet from the midst of thee, of thy brethren, like unto me; unto him shall ye hearken." This passage has an interesting exegesis in Jewish and Christian traditions. Christians have typically seen it as referring to Jesus Christ (Acts 3:22–23). Interestingly, in one of the Angel Moroni's early visits to Joseph Smith, he quoted passages of scripture, including Acts 3:22–23. "He said that that prophet was Christ; but the day had not yet come when 'they who would not hear his voice should be cut off from among the people,' but it soon would come" (JS—H 1:40).

The Book of Mormon, too, states very clearly that Jesus fulfilled the prediction of being one "like unto Moses." Speaking to the Nephites in the western hemisphere, the resurrected Lord proclaimed: "Behold, I am he of whom Moses spake, saying: A prophet shall the Lord your God raise up unto you of your brethren, like unto me; him shall ye hear in all things whatsoever he shall say unto you" (3 Ne. 20:23).

But this is not quite the end of it. Others, too, could emulate Moses or look to his life as a foreshadowing of their later experience. Thus, Nephi, demonstrating to his murmuring brothers that God's powers could do marvelous things, listed a series of remarkable parallels between the family of Lehi and the ancient followers of Moses: The exodus began with God's call; a miracle had occurred at the Red Sea; manna had been supplied in the wilderness; water had gushed forth from a rock; although led by God, the ancient Israelites had also murmured; nevertheless, God had both chastised and led them; finally they reached the promised land. The Lehites were like unto the children of Israel; and by strong suggestion, both Lehi and Nephi were like unto Moses (1 Ne. 17:23–32).[16]

It is not entirely surprising to read that the future prophet whose name would be Joseph after his father's would be "great like unto Moses" (2 Ne. 3:9). After ancient Joseph prophesied that Moses, or "a Moses," would have judgment in writing but would not be "mighty in speaking" and that God would raise up a "spokesman—referring, of course, to Aaron— he went on to make a similar prophecy about the future prophet Joseph, son of a Joseph (2 Ne. 3:17–18). Sidney Rigdon was in 1833 declared a "spokesman" unto the people and unto Joseph Smith (D&C 100:9). In 1844, almost in passing, Joseph remarked, "Moses was a stammering sort of a boy like me.[17]

As early as September 1830, the comparison was made: "But, behold, verily, verily, I say unto thee, no one shall be appointed to receive commandments and revelations in this church excepting my servant Joseph Smith, Jun., for he receiveth them even as Moses" (D&C 28:2).

The book of Moses, part of the Joseph Smith Translation of the Bible, first published in *Evening and Morning Star*, now included in the Pearl of Great Price, has the Lord explaining to Moses that "in a day when the children of men shall esteem my words as naught and take many of them from the book which thou shalt write, behold, I will raise up another like unto thee, and they shall be had again among the children of men— among as many as shall believe" (Moses 1:41). This is a specific reference to Joseph Smith, who is again likened to Moses.

In 1834, as the Missouri Saints were being driven from their homes, a revelation spoke of Zion's future redemption: "Behold, I say unto you, the redemption of Zion must needs come by power; Therefore, I will raise up unto my people a man, who shall lead them like as Moses led the children of Israel" (D&C 103:15–16). That this individual was the president of the Church should have been made clear early in 1835 by these words: "And again, the duty of the President of the office of the High Priesthood is to preside over the whole church, and to be like unto Moses" (D&C 107:91). But it is not going too far, I think, to say that it was Joseph Smith, the founding prophet of the last dispensation, who was preeminently likened unto Moses.[18]

In describing an 1836 blessing in Kirtland, Joseph Smith wrote: "I then took the seat, and father [Joseph Smith Sr.] annoint[ed] my head and sealed upon me the blessings, of Moses, to lead Israel in the latter days, even as Moses led them in days of old."[19] The following year, at a meeting in the Kirtland Temple, according to Wilford Woodruff's diary, "Elder Brigham Young one of the twelve gave us an interesting exhortation & warned us not to murmur against Moses (or) Joseph or the heads of the church."[20] In important ways, like Brigham Young after him, Joseph Smith could be seen as a Moses to his people.

John the Baptist. John the Baptist, as portrayed in the New Testament, is a rather enigmatic figure. He does not loom large in terms of the amount of attention given to him. Yet he was clearly too imposing to ignore, and Jesus granted him more than a little importance. Scholars have suggested that the rivalry between his followers and those of Jesus continued for many years. Religion professor Robert J. Matthews has given the most thorough Latter-day Saint appreciation of this "bright and burning light."[21]

As he thought of John the Baptist, Joseph Smith might well have identified with his roughness. Lacking the outward sophistication of the world, the Baptist spoke from the wilderness. His message to his generation was direct: Repent! All his life, Joseph was acutely aware of his own disadvantages and his lack of education. He well knew that he would not cut an imposing figure in the drawing rooms of New York and Philadelphia. Yet he had something to say and fearlessly raised his voice of warning to the world.

John the Baptist also, of course, died a martyr. To the extent that he had premonitions about his own violent death, Joseph might well have thought of this comparison along with other biblical apostles and prophets.

Most importantly, John the Baptist was a forerunner. He prepared the way of the Lord and testified of Him. As we all remember, a connection was drawn between him and Elias. One of the important meanings of "Elias" in LDS understanding is "preparer" (*Bible Dictionary*). Was he the Elias whose return had been predicted? Yes and no. Reading the New Testament passages, we recognize ambiguity on this matter, no doubt reflecting disagreement in the first century. John both denied and admitted that he was Elias. Traditional exegesis has fastened on the fact that he was a forerunner, a herald of the Messiah.

That Joseph Smith was drawn into this same pattern of thinking is obvious on the surface. For him, the second coming of the Lord was nigh. As a kind of parallel or latter-day version of the Baptist, Joseph was also the forerunner and herald. The similarity was made quite explicit in the revision and expansion of the Bible now known as the Joseph Smith Translation. Joseph's translation of Matthew 17:11–14 contains Jesus's response to the question of whether he himself was Elias:

> And again I say unto you that Elias has come already, concerning whom it is written, Behold, I will send my messenger, and he shall prepare the way before me; and they knew him not, and have done unto him, whatsoever they listed.
>
> Likewise shall also the Son of Man suffer of them. But I say unto you, Who is Elias?
>
> Behold, this is Elias, whom I send to prepare the way before me.
>
> Then the disciples understood that he spake unto them of John the Baptist, and also of another who should come and restore all things, as it is written by the prophets.

"And also of another" refers, of course, to Joseph Smith himself. As BYU religion professor Robert L. Millet has written, "Joseph Smith was the final great Elias before the Messiah, an Elias of the Restoration.[22]

Paul. The Apostle Paul, seen by some as the real founder of Christianity, may not be an obvious model for Joseph Smith. Yet after describing the ridicule and rejection heaped on him by those to whom he related his First Vision, Joseph later wrote:

> I have thought since, that I felt much like Paul, when he made his defense before King Agrippa and related the account of the vision he had when he saw a light, and heard a voice; but still there were but few who believed him; some said he was dishonest, others said he was mad; and he was ridiculed and reviled.
>
> But all this did not destroy the reality of his vision. . . . So it was with me. (JS—H 1:24–25)

As problems accumulated in his life, Joseph wrote: "Deep water is what I am wont to swim in. It has all become a second nature to me; and I feel, like Paul, to glory in tribulation" (D&C 127:2). Later, only a month before his death, Joseph Smith, who had been reading from 2 Corinthians 11, wrote: "I, like Paul, have been in perils, and oftener than anyone in this generation. As Paul boasted, I have suffered more than Paul did. I should be like a fish out of water, if I were out of persecutions."[23]

Richard L. Anderson, a longtime student of Paul, has been struck by the number of similarities between that New Testament apostle-prophet and Joseph Smith. Both had a "first vision." Both delayed giving a description of the event. Both had revelations of the resurrected Lord. Both put forth insightful doctrinal instruction but did not claim to know all the answers. Testifying courageously on the basis of their firsthand experiences, both were "considered blasphemers by their contemporaries." Both had visions of the degrees of glory. Both prayed for their contemporary believers and worked to help them understand how to live Christian lives. Both sacrificed beyond measure for the work. Both bore powerful testimonies. Both anticipated martyrdom. Widely separated in time, culture, and incidental trappings, the lives of Paul and Joseph Smith nevertheless possessed "dramatic common denominators."[24]

To find significant parallels and even points of identity with other prophets would no doubt be possible. Daniel, Peter, John the Beloved, and Nephi are just a few of the possibilities that suggest themselves. Striking parallels with the prophet Mormon have already been pointed out. (See chap. 2.) But most important by far are the points of resemblance between Joseph Smith and Jesus Christ.

Jesus Christ. Joseph Smith, of course, did not consider himself superior to or even equal to Jesus Christ. Jesus was divine, the only begotten Son of God. Joseph was human. Joseph accepted the divine Sonship of Jesus Christ, His divine role as Creator, and His unique atonement, never claiming any such significance for himself.

Nevertheless, there are more than a few points at which Joseph Smith made comparisons between himself and Jesus, and other Mormons were not ashamed to do the same. Before declaring any such comparison blasphemous, let us see what specifically they meant.

First, both Joseph Smith and Jesus endured great difficulty and persecution. This is a general observation true of all the prophets and, of course, was predicted by Jesus to be the lot of his followers: "Blessed are ye, when men shall revile you, and persecute you" (Matt. 5:11). At one of Joseph's moments of greatest trial, in Liberty Jail in 1839, he pondered the deeply introspective question: "The Son of Man hath descended below them all. Art thou greater than he?" (D&C 122:8). The implied answer, of course, is that Christ had suffered and sacrificed far more, but it is significant that the comparison came to mind.

The end of Joseph Smith's life provoked further comparison with Jesus. In each case, there were traitors. In each case, there was a voluntary submission. And in each case, there was a claim of innocence.

Neither Joseph nor his followers ever claimed that he was atoning for the sins of the world. What they were saying, in effect, is that, on a lesser level, Joseph Smith was experiencing something akin to what Christ experienced.[25]

But unmistakable similarities are there. Both Jesus and Joseph were born in lowly surroundings. Both had rather short lives. Both were prophets (John 6:14). Both founded churches—Jesus his church in "the meridian of time," Joseph the same church restored in "the fulness of time." In the thought categories of Latter-day Saint dispensationalism, these were the two greatest outpourings of God's revelations and authority. Joseph Fielding McConkie lists ten points of identity.[26] Francis M. Gibbons, General Authority and biographer of modern prophets, has pointed out differences but also similarities.[27] In important ways, then, Joseph Smith was "like unto" Christ.

In conclusion, what are we to make of such remarkable parallels across time? It seems to me that two different frames of reference are useful here. The first is typology. The word has different meanings but here refers to a conception of human time that saw a relationship between an earlier person or event and a later one. More specifically, as developed by Christians in the patristic period, following leads laid down in the New Testament itself, Old Testament persons, events, or even objects were seen as foreshadowing the New Testament. Most commonly it was Christ Himself who was typified by such personages as David or Joshua, but even Noah's ark could be seen as a type pointing to Christ's atoning sacrifice on the cross or the church He established.[28]

The typological understanding of human experience was pervasive in the Middle Ages, but it continued for many generations longer. Far more than we had earlier thought, typological thinking was still widely accepted in colonial and early national America.[29] And the idea is explicitly spelled out in the Book of Mormon.[30] I argue that the typological mindset, far from being confined to the Bible and the Book of Mormon, extended into Joseph Smith's self-concept and self-presentation. Like John Bunyan, who in *Grace Abounding* had seen himself as an antitype of Moses,[31] Joseph

Smith saw himself as having been prefigured by prophets from the distant past. For his generation he was an Enoch, a Moses, a Joseph, a Paul, and, to a lesser degree, even a Jesus.

The second frame of reference I wish to invoke is that of identity as projected or created in autobiography. To determine who or what one is, is far from a simple matter.[32] Part of the problem is determining which categories, labels, or roles one will select as most determinative of one's essence, or, more likely, experience as inevitable—as imposed from outside. As several studies have conclusively pointed out, autobiography as a literary form has had for its characteristic task self-fashioning, invention of the self, and at times a conscious modeling on the lives of earlier prototypes.[33]

Did Joseph Smith set out consciously to imitate the earlier heroic figures? Was his life a deliberate playing out of a role he had selected for himself? If such questions are simply another way of charging him with charlatanry, perhaps we should be cautious, remembering the honorable tradition of *imitatio* as a way of elevating our individual lives.[34] And it is worth stating something rather obvious: It is far easier to select a noble individual of the present or the past as one's ideal than it is to replicate that life to any significant degree. However motivated, Joseph was living a life—acting out a role or roles—of immense, archetypal scope.

I have not here attempted to make a case that Joseph Smith was a prophet. Instead, I have probed some aspects of his self-concept, which were then conveyed to his followers. Clearly he identified strongly with certain figures from the deep past—Enoch, Abraham, Joseph, Moses, John the Baptist, Paul, and Jesus—with whom he was connected by invisible threads. He thought of himself as, like them, a prophet, and for his followers that was what he was.[35]

Notes

1. See Deut. 18:15, 18: "The Lord thy God will raise up unto thee a prophet from the midst of thee, of thy brethren, like unto me; unto him ye shall hearken"; "I will raise them up a prophet from among their brethren, like unto thee." This is the one place in the Bible that I can find where the phrase is used to compare one man to another. In other places it is used in the negative to emphasize the superiority of God ("none like unto") or to

compare things or situations ("The Kingdom of God is like unto . . ."). In the Book of Mormon the phrase is more commonly used to compare men.

2. Paul E. Johnson and Sean Wilentz, *The Kingdom of Matthias* (New York: Oxford University Press, 1994).

3. Two of the most specific works on this subject are Nephi L. Morris, *Prophecies of Joseph Smith and Their Fulfillment* (2d ed.; Salt Lake City: Deseret Book, 1926); and Duane S. Crowther, *The Prophecies of Joseph Smith* (Salt Lake City: Bookcraft, 1963).

4. Abraham J. Heschel, *The Prophets* (New York: Jewish Publication Society of America, 1962).

5. Commenting on deed-forms found in the papers of Edward Partridge, B. H. Roberts said: "The first of the following deed-forms was used in consecrating property to the Church; the second, in securing the stewardship to those entering into the law of consecration and stewardship, sometimes called the order of Enoch, because it was the law under which the Patriarch Enoch and his people lived." Joseph Smith et al., *History of the Church of Jesus Christ of Latter-day Saints,* edited by B. H. Roberts, 7 vols. (Salt Lake City: Church of Jesus Christ of Latter-day Saints, 1932–51), 1:365 note 25. See also Leonard J. Arrington, Feramorz Y. Fox, and Dean L. May, *Building the City of God: Community and Cooperation among the Mormons* (Salt Lake City: Deseret Book, 1976), chap. 2; and Leonard J. Arrington, "Early Mormon Communitarianism: The Law of Consecration and Stewardship," *Western Humanities Review* 7 (Autumn 1973): 341–69.

6. Joseph Smith, Sermon, October 5, 1840, in Andrew F. Ehat and Lyndon W. Cook, eds., *The Words of Joseph Smith* (Provo, Utah: BYU Religious Studies Center, 1980), 41.

7. *History of the Church*, 6:300.

8. This code name appears in pre-1981 editions of the Doctrine and Covenants (see, for example, sections 92, 96, and 104, and revelations published in *History of the Church*, 1:352, 2:54). On the general topic, including scholarly fascination with the apocryphal Book of Enoch, see Hugh Nibley, *Enoch the Prophet* (Salt Lake City: Deseret Book/Provo, Utah: Foundation for Ancient Research and Mormon Studies [FARMS], 1986). For comparisons with the Enoch of the kabbalah, see Harold Bloom, "The Religion-Making Imagination of Joseph Smith," *Yale Review* 80 (April 1992): 29–30, 32.

9. Hugh Nibley, *Abraham in Egypt* (Salt Lake City: Deseret Book, 1981); and his serialized manuscript, "A New Look at the Pearl of Great Price," *Improvement Era* 71–73 (January 1968–May 1970).

10. E. Douglas Clark, "Abraham," *Encyclopedia of Mormonism,* 4 vols. (New York: Macmillan, 1992), 1:8.

11. Ibid.

12. Joseph Fielding McConkie, *His Name Shall Be Joseph* (Salt Lake City: Hawkes Publishing, 1980), 78–79.

13. Neal A. Maxwell, "A Choice Seer," *Ensign* 16 (August 1986): 6–15.

14. McConkie, *His Name Shall Be Joseph*, 80–83; Ann N. Madsen and Susan Easton Black, "Joseph and Joseph: 'He Shall Be Like unto Me' (2 Nephi 3:15)," in *The Old Testament and the Latter-day Saints* (Salt Lake City: Randall Books, 1986), 25–40.

15. Quoted in Neal A. Maxwell, *But for a Small Moment* (Salt Lake City: Bookcraft, 1986), 106–7.

16. George S. Tate, "The Typology of the Exodus Pattern in the Book of Mormon," in *Literature of Belief: Sacred Scripture and Religious Experience,* edited by Neal A. Lambert (Provo, Utah: BYU Religious Studies Center, 1981), 245–62.

17. *History of the Church,* 6:478.

18. John A. Widtsoe, *Evidences and Reconciliations*, 3 vols., 2d ed. (Salt Lake City: Bookcraft, 1951), 1:197.

19. Dean C. Jessee, ed., *The Personal Writings of Joseph Smith* (Salt Lake City: Deseret Book, 1984), 145.

20. Entry for January 10, 1837, in Dean C. Jessee, ed., "The Kirtland Diary of Wilford Woodruff," *BYU Studies* 12 (Summer 1972): 382.

21. Robert J. Matthews, *A Burning Light: The Life and Ministry of John the Baptist* (Provo, Utah: Brigham Young University Press, 1972).

22. Robert L. Millet, "Joseph Smith among the Prophets," in *Joseph Smith: The Prophet, the Man,* edited by Susan Easton Black and Charles D. Tate Jr. (Provo, Utah: BYU Religious Studies Center, 1993), 19.

23. *History of the Church,* 6:408.

24. Richard L. Anderson, "Parallel Prophets: Paul and Joseph Smith," *Ensign* 15 (March 1985): 12–17.

25. "All prophets to one degree or another are in the similitude of the Savior. Prophets stand as living types or models of the Christ." McConkie, *His Name Shall Be Joseph*, 216.

26. Ibid., 218–19.

27. Francis M. Gibbons, "The Savior and Joseph Smith: Alike Yet Unlike," *Ensign* 21 (May 1991): 32–33.

28. The most important single study is Henri de Lubac, *Exégèse médiévale: Les quatre sens de l'écriture,* 4 vols. (Paris: Aubier, 1959). But see

also Paul J. Korshin, *Typologies in England, 1650–1820* (Princeton, N.J.: Princeton University Press, 1982).

29. Sacvan Bercovitch, *Typology and Early American Literature* (Amherst: University of Massachusetts Press, 1972); Sacvan Bercovitch, *The Puritan Origins of the American Self* (New Haven, Conn.: Yale University Press, 1975); Ursula Brumm, *Die religiöse typologie im amerikanischen Denken* (Leiden, Netherlands: Brill, 1963).

30. In addition to George S. Tate's article cited above, see Bruce W. Jorgensen, "The Dark Way to the Tree: Typological Unity in the Book of Mormon"; and Richard Dilworth Rust, "'All Things Which Have Been Given of God . . . Are the Typifying of Him': Typology in the Book of Mormon," all three in *Literature of Belief: Sacred Scripture and Religious Experience,* edited by M. Gerald Bradford (Provo, Utah: BYU Religious Studies Center, 1981).

31. Linda H. Peterson, *Victorian Autobiography: The Tradition of Self-Interpretation* (New Haven, Conn.: Yale University Press, 1986), esp. 6–7, 10, 21.

32. See P. Gleason, "Identifying Identity: A Semantic History," *Journal of American History* 15 (Winter 1984): 365–85; G. F. Macdonald, ed., *Perception and Identity* (Ithaca, N.Y.: Cornell University Press, 1979); and R. K. Fenn, "Religion, Identity and Authority in the Secular Society," in *Identity and Authority: Explorations in the Theory of Society,* edited by Roland Robertson and Burkart Holzner (New York: St. Martin's, 1979), 119–44.

33. See esp. Stephen J. Greenblatt, *Renaissance Self-Fashioning: From More to Shakespeare* (Chicago: University of Chicago Press, 1980); Paul J. Eakin, *Fictions in Autobiography: Studies in the Art of Self-Invention* (Princeton, N.J.: Princeton University Press, 1985); and Peterson, *Victorian Autobiography.* On modeling see especially Karl F. Morrison, *The Mimetic Tradition of Reform in the West* (Princeton, N.J.: Princeton University Press, 1982); also Glenn W. Olsen, "St. Augustine and the Problem of the Medieval Discovery of the Individual," *Word and Spirit* 9 (1987): 129–56, esp. its bibliography. An important article is Georges Gusdorf, "Conditions and Limits of Autobiography," reproduced in translation in James Olney, ed., *Autobiography: Essays Theoretical and Critical* (Princeton, N.J.: Princeton University Press, 1980), 28–48.

34. From a lengthy scholarly literature on the imitation of Christ, I cite one example: John D. Laurance, *Priest as Type of Christ: The Leader of the Eucharist in the Salvation History according to Cyprian of Carthage* (New York: Peter Lang, 1984).

35. See Kenelm Burridge, *New Heaven, New Earth* (1960), quoted in Marvin S. Hill, "The 'Prophet Puzzle' Assembled: or, How to Treat Our Historical Diplopia toward Joseph Smith," *Journal of Mormon History* 3 (1976): 104–5.: "If we are confronted with evidence of a divine revelation, we cannot think it irrelevant or irrational or fantasy or wishful thinking. We must take it seriously and try to account for what actually occurs. Even if our private assumptions do not admit of such a thing as divine revelation, we must admit that for others it does exist."

Chapter 4

In the Mormon Folk Memory

At his death in 1844, Joseph Smith's life had spanned less than thirty-nine years, his leadership of the church he had organized only fourteen. Yet his impact on his followers continued. Their grief-stricken numbness in mid-1844 was soon followed by recollections, as those who had known him leaned on the back fence or sat around the fireplace and exchanged stories. In the East, in the Midwest, and later especially in Utah, those who had known Joseph Smith told and retold the stories of their experiences with him.

As years passed, oldtimers who remembered the Prophet were called upon to give their recollections in meetings and celebrations or write a piece for the newspaper or one of the Church magazines. The stories were told and retold, sometimes improved upon, sometimes published. In turn, as published versions were picked up and transmitted orally, there was some repetition. Those who remembered were soon outnumbered by those who knew Joseph only by reputation. But the telling of stories continued.

This was the posthumous Joseph Smith as he lived in the collective memory of his people. Unable to listen to the actual voices of those who, in the late nineteenth century, told these stories, we are a step away from the ideal terrain for folklore research. However, by drawing upon sermons—which in Mormon usage were conducive to spontaneous recollections—as well as diaries and letters, we get close to the real-life situations in which these stories were told. Also, since the published stories were almost always an extension of previously told stories in the oral tradition, and since, once published, they had a feedback effect in being picked up and told again and again, there is no reason to exclude published anecdotes from present consideration.[1] Several collections of stories about Joseph Smith have been published.[2] My purpose here is not to compile another collection but rather to propose a usable taxonomy with examples for each category. Also, I assess the value of this material for both the biographer and the historian.

Human Qualities

In many stories, Joseph Smith's warm and endearing qualities as a human being were mentioned. Contrary to the negative image of "ol' Joe Smith" promulgated during his lifetime, these storytellers seemed to say, "No, he was a good person. Here is what I remember about him."

In the Mormon collective memory, Joseph emerges as a loving husband and father, someone who was kind to children. Margaret Burgess, daughter of William McIntyre, told of a touching incident when Joseph came to the McIntyre home, took her starving infant sister from their sick mother "to his own home where his wife gave it nourishment from her own breast, she having buried her own babe." When the McIntyre infant died, Joseph "grieved as if he had lost one of his own," embraced "the little cold form," and said, "Mary, oh my dear little Mary." Margaret also remembered when, as a toddler she wandered into a side lane and became stuck in the mud. Joseph saw her there, came over, lifted her out, cleaned the mud from her shoes with tufts of grass, wiped the tears from her face with his handkerchief, and carried her home to her mother.[3]

Story after story attests to the Prophet's generous and affectionate attitude toward children, demonstrating that he was open to the impulses of the heart and identifying him with the simple virtues of childhood.[4]

Contrary to his detractors' efforts to portray him as a lazy ne'er-do-well, Joseph Smith's people remembered him as a hard worker.[5] Jesse W. Crosby recalled details that showed Joseph as a neat and responsible householder who "always left his fence clear of everything that might gather fire, such as underbrush, loose limbs, and tall strong weeds." In his wood yard "logs were neatly piled and all trash cleared away. If he did not finish the log on which he was chopping the remnant was laid back on the pile and not left on the ground for a stumbling block. The chips he made he picked up himself into a basket and put them in a wooden box which stood in the woodyard, or carried them into the house to be burned." His fields "were always in good condition and yielded well." When visitors came, "their teams were fed the best of hay and his barn was full." Crosby's reminiscence continues, "No other orchard had as fine fruit as did his." And "if an inferior cow was by any means shoved onto him it would be but a short time before she became a first class milker."[6]

In pioneer Utah, where there was apparently a certain amount of littering and poor upkeep—as witness Brigham Young's repeated scold-

ings—it was valuable to recall such a Joseph Smith, the master householder and manager, at the center of a charming domestic scene reminiscent of
the Dutch masters.

Physical Strength

Closely related to the human qualities were stories of Joseph's great
physical strength. He was not quite Paul Bunyan in these stories, perhaps,
but some of his friends would have put him in the same league with Daniel
Boone and Davy Crockett. This was the Joseph of exuberant spirits, who
could wield an ax with the best of men.[7] He would bat a ball into the next
county,[8] win any stick-pulling contest,[9] and straighten out an iron axle-tree
that had been bent so severely that it resisted the efforts of several other
men.[10]

His prowess at fighting and defeating tough braggarts started when
he was a boy and continued into manhood. In wrestling, he could defeat all
comers.[11] In one interesting variant of the champion wrestler, Joseph threw
Howard Coray, a friend who was smaller and lighter, and broke his leg.
Full of remorse, Joseph then carried the injured man into his own house,
set his leg, and tenderly nursed and blessed him.[12] In another variant, it
was not Joseph who won the wrestling match but Joseph who, standing on
the side, inspired young Mormon Philemon Merrill with faith sufficient
to throw a bully.[13] Nauvoo, the city of Joseph, was no place for rivermen—
half-hoss and half-alligator though they might be—to intimidate God-
fearing people.

There are other examples of Joseph's astounding physical strength.
According to one story, he carried an exhausted friend (probably Oliver
Cowdery) by night through a swamp away from a pursuing mob to safety—an all-night ordeal that conjures up images of Aeneas carrying the
aged Anchises from burning Troy.[14]

On another occasion Joseph found himself in a stagecoach. When
the driver went into an inn for a drink, he came out much the worse for
it. When the horses took fright and started to gallop at an increasing
speed, the Prophet calmed the excited passengers. Then, in the manner of a
Western movie hero, he went through the window, pulled himself up into
the driver's seat, gathered the reins, and brought the horses under control.[15]

The nineteenth-century American hero was a man of physical
strength. George Washington could throw a dollar across the Potomac,
and Abraham Lincoln was a champion rail-splitter. These were the qualities that Americans admired in their heroes. Frail asceticism was not in

their catalogue of heroic virtues.[16] For Mormons, Joseph Smith measured up to the expectation.

Supernatural Glow

In addition to strength, affection, and cheerfulness, what some Latter-day Saints remembered about their prophet was a hard-to-define quality, a presence that commanded attention and for them signaled his special connection to God. His eyes looked right through them.[17] When he spoke, his words were so powerful that they shook the very souls of his listeners.[18] When he touched them or shook their hand, they were electrified. Emerging from a revelatory experience, he looked strangely different, his face glowing in an unforgettable manner.[19] These were clues of the divine power possessed by God's prophet. At least, this was the way the Saints remembered him.

Miracles

Even when they might not remember any actual words that Joseph uttered, his faithful followers in later years could recall certain incidents when he had performed miracles. I have in mind here not prophecies (verbal pronouncements about the future), but rather acts with no obvious natural explanation. Joseph once said he had a task that must be performed that very night. He turned to a young man and asked if he would do it. The young man said he would before morning. The young man "testified that he did do the job although he had to travel five hundred miles to do it—500 there and 500 back." The teller of this story explained:

> I do not doubt but that if Joseph Smith required such a thing to be done, said it must be done, and delegated a man to do it who was willing, it would be done, and that by the person being wafted through the air by the power of God, equal to translation; whether the person went in body or in spirit, whether the distance was 500 or 5000 miles, it would be all the same. If he required such a thing it would be because God required it and all things are possible with God. That is my faith in the Prophet Joseph Smith.[20]

The Zion's Camp expedition of 1834 provided the setting for other recollected miracles.[21] In 1884 Zera Cole recounted that one night the company was camped on a prairie far from water. The weather was warm, and the men and animals were thirsty. "Joseph called for a shovel and as if surveying for the most convenient place for all started in to digging a hole like a well with his own hands, about the size of a wash tub, and but little deeper when water came up and filled the hole, so that all the men and horses had plenty to drink. The ground seemed as dry, when they camped, as prairies generally are."[22] If Moses could bring forth a gushing well by striking the rock of Horeb with his staff, it seemed fitting to the Mormon faithful that their prophet would have similar powers.

Healings were the most frequent miracles. Especially memorable were those occurring at Nauvoo in the widespread cases of malaria and cholera in July 1839.[23] Charles R. Dana recalled an occasion in 1841 when his wife was sick "nigh unto death." He went in search of Joseph and, eyes full of tears, asked him to come administer to her. At first Joseph, who was preoccupied with another matter, said he could not but, on second thought, said he would come presently. Here is Dana's account of what happened:

> My heart leaped for joy. I hurried home. I had not much more than got there before Bro. Joseph came bounding over the bottom like a chased roe. He asked me, "How long has she been so sick?" He then walked the house for some minutes. I began to fear that he considered her past recovery, but he finally went to the fire, warmed his hands, throwed his cloak off, went to the bed, laid his hands on her, and while in the midst of his administering to her he seemed to be baffled. The disease or evil spirit rested upon him, but he overpowered it and pronounced great blessings upon her. After he took off his hands he turned to me and said, "That sister will get well, take good care of her." . . . She began to amend from that hour. I firmly believe that if he had not been called in that she would have died.[24]

Joseph Smith did not heal every person of every ailment, but such examples of miraculous healing continued to inspire his followers as they recounted them in later years. It is perhaps necessary to say that he saw himself as an instrument of God. It was the Almighty who actually accomplished the healing.

Doctrinal Sayings

If the remembered deeds and miracles were inspiring to the Saints, more substantive in content were the Prophet's words, his sayings. Many of them were expressed not in writing or even in sermons but in individual conversations. As the Saints remembered him, Joseph gave answers to all kinds of doctrinal questions, some important, others seemingly trivial. Toward the end of the century, Oliver B. Huntington attributed to Joseph Smith the sayings that Noah's ark had been built in or near South Carolina; that houses previously inhabited by wicked people should be thoroughly cleaned, fumigated, and dedicated by prayer, lest the wicked spirits afflict the new inhabitants; and that "every living thing that knows enough to run when you point your finger at it, will be resurrected."[25] Such utterances were essentially oracular. One of the most curious of such statements, again from Huntington, is the following: "The inhabitants of the moon are more of a uniform size than the inhabitants of the earth, being about 6 feet in height. They dress very much like the quaker style and are quite general in style, or the one fashion of dress. They live to be very old, coming generally near a thousand years."[26] Oliver Huntington wrote that he heard this description from Philo Dibble, who was accustomed to going up and down through Utah communities giving lectures on Church history.

One question with important doctrinal implications has to do with the Mormon belief in a Mother in Heaven, most commonly known from one verse in Eliza R. Snow's hymn, "O My Father." As late as 1916, Susa Young Gates recalled what she had earlier heard from Zina D. Huntington Smith Young (Oliver B. Huntington's sister). Zina had lost her mother under trying circumstances and, filled with intense grief, asked the Prophet whether she would know her mother on the other side.

> "Certainly you will," was the instant reply of the Prophet. "More than that, you will meet and become acquainted with your eternal Mother, the wife of your Father in Heaven."
> "And have I then a Mother in Heaven?" exclaimed the astonished girl.
> "You assuredly have. How could a Father claim His title unless there were also a Mother to share that parenthood?"[27]

These Huntingtons got around. A fascinating family with close ties with both Joseph Smith and Brigham Young, they enjoyed talking about such things and seem to have seen it as their personal mission to preserve the choice experiences and sayings of Joseph Smith.

One question of special interest to many Mormons was the location of the lost ten tribes of Israel who, as part of the winding-up scene were expected to return. What had Joseph to say on this subject? In 1884 Abraham H. Cannon noted in his diary that he had called upon Eliza R. Snow, who said she had heard Joseph Smith say, "When the ten tribes were taken away, the earth was divided, so that they occupy a separate planet from this."[28] Martha Cragun Cox heard the same story from her father, who told her that the Prophet had said to him "that at the north pole the earth is convex or cup shaped with the deepest sea resting there. The planet that belonged to that part of the world would in time return to its place, strike the earth at that part, completing the sphere."[29] These reports led Eliza R. Snow to compose a hymn, three stanzas of which follow:

Thou, earth, was once a glorious sphere
    Of noble magnitude,
And didst with majesty appear,
    Among the worlds of God.

But thy dimensions have been torn
    Asunder piece by piece,
And each dismember'd fragment borne
    Abroad to distance space. . . .

And when the Lord saw fit to hide
    The "Ten Lost Tribes" away,
Thou wast divided to provide
    The orb on which they stay.[30]

The whole "doctrine," besides resting on the recollection of Eliza Snow and Martha Cox, was found in the family tradition of Patriarch Homer M. Brown, who in 1924 told in lavish detail of a conversation between his grandfather, Benjamin Brown, and the Prophet.[31]

The trouble was that others remembered differently. In 1886, when asked what the Prophet had said regarding the ten tribes, Anson Call wrote: "I have heard Joseph say that the ten tribes were in the northern interior of the earth, and that they retain their tribe relations and their strength and manhood, that they have not dwindled, as we have, for they have been favored of the Lord, and have retained their organizations and understood well the redemption and have ever had in their midst the true prophets of the Lord."[32] Did Joseph Smith make both statements? Or only one? Or neither? Or did he use a crucial word like "perhaps" or "possibly" that was forgotten in the later traditions?[33] In any case, one of the problems of oral tradition as a source of doctrinal truth is well illustrated.

The pithiness of many of these sayings, especially those that were passed on in successive generations, probably reveals something of Joseph Smith's preaching style. The aphorism—the oracular, single-sentence utterance containing a truth, a principle, or an alleged fact—is familiar in some of the sections of the Doctrine and Covenants. (See, e.g., D&C 130-131.) After his arrival in Nauvoo, starting in January 1840, the Prophet participated occasionally in a kind of study group, minutes of which were kept by William Patterson McIntyre. Although various people participated in the discussions and gave reports on special topics, it is interesting to note that on almost every question, Joseph had the last word and gave his views in a series of short pronouncements.[34] The constant questions coming from the Saints, who assumed that he had answers to all questions, must have reinforced whatever natural tendencies he had in this direction. To say that his typical style was conducive to aphoristic declarative statements is not to claim that all the remembered sayings are genuine, for it is precisely such short sentences that could be easily distorted or misremembered. More important, perhaps, is the fact that later recollections often failed to include the context, the question or situations that evoked the Prophet's answer. And one has to suspect that an occasional tongue-in-cheek mood was lost, if not on his hearers, at least by those in later generations who passed on the Smith apocrypha with utter seriousness.

Practice and Policy

Recalling what Joseph Smith had said or done became more crucial in matters of practice and policy. In 1883, when the Kirtland School of the Prophets was reorganized in Salt Lake City, the only survivor of the original School of the Prophets from the 1830s was Zebedee Coltrin. Coltrin was called in and asked to explain the procedures. Did they have the ceremony of washing of feet? Did they kneel when praying or did they raise their hands? And what was the manner of administering the sacrament in Joseph's day? On this last question, Coltrin answered: "The Sacrament was also administered at times when Joseph appointed after the ancient order; that is, warm bread to break easy was provided, and broken into pieces as large as my fist, and each person had a glass of wine and sat and ate the bread and drank the wine; and Joseph said that was the way that Jesus and his disciples partook of the bread and wine; and this was the order of the church anciently, and until the church went into darkness."[35]

Similar questions were raised regarding procedures in the Kirtland Temple. It is significant that Church leaders, nearly forty years after the Martyrdom, still felt obligated to find out Joseph Smith's way of doing something. Yet after finding out the facts as best they could, the brethren did not feel obligated to follow Joseph on every jot and tittle, for they recognized that often he had acted in haste due to the exigencies of the time.

The importance of remembered conversations is illustrated by the policy prior to 1978 of not ordaining black men to the priesthood, a practice which went back to the early years of the Church, but with at least some inconsistencies.[36] Some Church members, troubled by the apparent discrimination, cited the great vision of Peter that extended the gospel to the Gentiles as evidence of God's desire to treat all races alike. In 1879, a small group met in Provo, Utah, to attempt to establish what Joseph Smith had taught. Present were Abraham O. Smoot (a Kentuckian), President John Taylor, Brigham Young Jr., Secretary L. John Nuttall, and Zebedee

Coltrin. The whole discussion was based on Coltrin's recollection. All the way back in 1834, Coltrin and John P. Greene (Brigham Young's brother-in-law) had argued over the question and finally took the matter to Joseph, who, according to Coltrin, said, "Brother Zebedee is right, for the Spirit of the Lord saith the Negro has no right nor cannot hold the Priesthood."[37] Although this recollection did not determine policy in this case, it did much to reinforce it. The exclusionary policy came to an end, of course, in 1978 with a revelation "extending priesthood and temple blessings to all worthy male members of the Church" (D&C, Official Declaration—2).

Prophecies

Many of Joseph Smith's remembered sayings were predictions about the future. Some of these predictions were canonical, written down as revelations in the 1820s or 1830s. Some were fulfilled in his lifetime; some, such as the prophecy of a war between the states to begin in South Carolina, were fulfilled later. Some, such as the prophecy that the Mormons would return to claim their "inheritances" in Jackson County, Missouri, are yet to be fulfilled.[38] The study of the Prophet's prophetic utterances is a specialty in itself and has been the subject of at least three books.[39] The prophetic recollections passed on by word of mouth were usually not the great cosmic utterances but rather short statements, often one-liners, easily remembered. All were fulfilled to the narrator's satisfaction; in fact, this was usually the point of the story.

In one of these mini-prophecies, as it was later remembered, Joseph once told W. W. Phelps and his wife that they never should taste death. Well, they died. Was this, then, an unfulfilled prophecy? Not in the mind of true believers. Here is the explanation later given:

> The manner of the fulfillment of that promise is rather singular. They supposed, and so did all that knew of the promise, that they were to never die; but the Lord does business in his own way and his way is not as the way of a man.
>
> Before Brother Phelps died he lost all his judgment, lost all his mind[,] reason, consciousness and all sense. He knew nothing, not even his name, nor how to eat, thus being unable to taste of anything; not even death. His mind gradually dwindled, withered and dried up. His wife was killed instantly, so quickly that she had not time to taste of death. She was killed as she was dipping up a bucket of water from the ditch, a gust of wind hurled a board from a house and it struck her on the neck breaking it instantly. She never tasted of death nor even felt the blow.[40]

Another sepulchral prediction was the Prophet's prediction to Zina Baker Huntington, mother of Oliver and Zina, that "her flesh should never see corruption." This was first taken to be a promise that she would never die, but of course she did. When the "old burying ground" in Nauvoo was moved outside the city, however, it was necessary to disinter her body, which was found to be "full, plump and looked natural in feature without a 'smell of corruption or decay.'"[41] Again, according to this report, the Prophet was vindicated.

One of the favorite, noncanonical Joseph Smith prophecies was that the day would come when the Constitution of the United States would hang, as it were, by a thread and that it would be saved by the elders of the Church. Usually the first reference to this prophecy is cited as Brigham Young's sermon on the Fourth of July 1854.[42] In 1855 Jedediah Grant remembered something similar although the imagery was slightly different: "What did the Prophet Joseph say? When the Constitution shall be tottering, we shall be the people to save it from the hand of the foe."[43] Three years later in 1858, Orson Hyde made a slight but important correction: "I believe he said something like this—that the time would come when the Constitution and the country would be in danger of an overthrow, and said he, 'If the Constitution be saved at all, it will be by the elders of this Church.'"[44] In 1870, Eliza R. Snow, citing her own memory, repeated the basic prophecy without Hyde's qualification: the Constitution would hang by a thread and the Mormons would "rise up" and save it and "bear it off triumphantly."[45]

It will be illuminating to consider the probable basis for these later recollections. It is easy to demonstrate that Joseph Smith had great respect for the U.S. Constitution, especially venerating its provision for freedom of religion; that he was disappointed and disillusioned with the failure of the state and national governments to protect the Saints in Missouri and Illinois; that he was contemptuous of many office holders and politicians of his day; that he had grim forebodings about the future, in which he saw, among other things, increased mob violence and the outbreak of a war between the states; that, being unable to endorse any of the major candidates in 1844 and seeing no other alternative, he put himself forth as a candidate for the presidency; and that, in long-range terms, he saw some kind of political kingdom which would, in effect, be controlled by the Mormon leaders but would include non-Mormons and would protect all people in their rights. This whole congeries of ideas reflecting Joseph Smith's point of view in the Nauvoo period (roughly 1840–44), would seem to provide a plausible basis for expecting him to say something of the kind—the Constitution was in danger, would totter or hang by a thread, and would be saved by the Church—although it seems likely, from a naturalistic perspective, that he was thinking either in terms of his possible election in 1844 or, more likely, the establishment of a Mormon theocracy in Nauvoo or elsewhere that would become stronger and stronger, a bastion of security while the rest of the country was collapsing in violence and warfare.[46]

Interestingly enough, primary documents in the LDS Church History Library reveal that the basic assertions about the failure of the Constitution did not have to await the disappointments and disillusionment of 1842 and 1843 or the organization of the political kingdom and Joseph's decision to be a candidate in 1844. The following was written by Orson Pratt on January 21, 1841:

> He [Joseph Smith] says . . . the government is fallen and needs redeeming. It is guilty of Blood and cannot stand as it now is but will come so near desolation as to hang as it were by a single hair!!! Then the servants goes to the nations of the earth, & gethers [sic] the strength of the Lord's house, a mighty army!!! And this is the redemption of Zion, when the Saints shall [have] redeemed that government & reinstated it in all its purity and glory!!! That America may be an asylum for the remnant of all nations.[47]

This curious statement is third hand. Orson Pratt was recounting to George A. Smith what Parley P. Pratt had written in a letter. The original germ is probably found in a sermon delivered by Joseph Smith on July 18, 1840. Unfortunately there are no verbatim transcriptions of most of his sermons, but the following notes, apparently taken at the time by Martha Jane Knowlton, suffice to make the point:

> We shall build the Zion of the Lord in peace until the servants of that Lord shall begin to lay the foundation of a great and high watch Tower. . . . Then the Enemy shall come as a thief in the night and scatter the servants abroad. When the seed of these 12 Olive trees are scattered abroad they will wake up the Nations of the whole Earth. Even this Nation will be on the very verge of crumbling to pieces and tumbling to the ground and when the constitution is upon the brink of ruin this people will be the Staff up[on] which the Nation shall lean and they shall bear the constitution away from the very verge of destruction.

The same sermon contains fulsome prophecies about the future glory of Nauvoo. "It is evident that the prophecies about Nauvoo, like Jackson County before it," Dean C. Jesse has wisely remarked, "were contingent upon human conditions and failings."[48]

The Constitution-by-a-thread prophecy therefore rests on an actual statement made by Joseph Smith in 1840, not long after the failure of his effort to obtain help from the U.S. government. What may be more interesting is the fact that it was not until after 1850 that this prophecy began to be a favorite among members of the Church. From that time forward, I believe, the prophecy was cited whenever the nation seemed on the verge of calamity or the Saints felt threatened by national policies. Thus, the Utah War seemed a possible fulfillment, as did the Civil War. When the anti-polygamy campaign got underway during the 1860s, 1870s, and especially in the 1880s, the Saints saw themselves as beleaguered defenders of the Constitutional principle of freedom of religion. What was more natural than to recall over and over again something like this: "The Prophet told us this would happen. The Constitution would hang by a thread, but if we just stand for our rights, eventually we will save it."

In the twentieth century and into the twenty-first, the uses of the Constitution-by-a-thread prophecy have been what might be expected: Those who decry the political trends of the times—the New Freedom, the New Deal, and the welfare state—have seen everything from the progressive income tax to the U.S. Supreme Court decision on prayer in the schools as fulfillment of the first part of the prophecy. Psychologically, it served the triple purpose of providing confirmation of the Prophet's calling (he had told them all this would happen), reassurance for the future (the Constitution would be saved), and enhancement of their self-importance (they would be the ones to save it). A prophecy with possibilities of such frequent application is understandably one of the favorites in the lexicon of remembered sayings of Joseph Smith.[49]

Occasion for Stories

To tell anecdotes about the Prophet Joseph Smith needed no special motivation, for Latter-day Saints found them inherently interesting. Yet certain events provided a special stimulus. In the 1860s, for example, when the Reorganized Church of Jesus Christ of Latter Day Saints (now Community of Christ) sent missionaries (including the sons of Joseph Smith Jr.) to Utah, it was natural that certain recollections would come to the fore. Later, the litigation over ownership of the Temple Lot in Independence, Missouri, resulted in many statements about the early Church. Every year on the anniversaries of Joseph Smith's birth (December 23) and death (June 27), the thoughts of some turned to the Prophet, often in sacrament meeting talks or testimonies. The April 6 anniversary of the Church's organization was another such occasion. And in 1880 began a series of jubilee (fifty-year) commemorations—of the organization of the Church, Zion's Camp, the founding of the Relief Society, the Prophet's death, and the pioneers' arrival in the Salt Lake Valley—in connection with which recollections were very naturally part of the celebrations.

The number of those who remembered Joseph Smith and who had had direct encounters with him steadily decreased over time. In 1873, Brigham Young, speaking in Logan, said: "I believe I will do myself the favor, and gratify myself so far as to ask those of my brethren and sisters now present, who were personally acquainted with Joseph Smith, to raise their right hands. (A very few hands up.) There is a few, but very few, not above one to twenty, and perhaps not more than one to fifty in this congregation who ever saw Joseph Smith." By the 1890s those who had been in their twenties at the Prophet's death were roughly in their seventies; those who had been children were now their fifties and sixties. Life expectancy being shorter than at present, these survivors were not numerous. It was natural to pay some deference to them. These factors help explain the character of many of the stories—the plethora of childhood recollections of the kindly Prophet, for example. Thinking in these terms, we can readily perceive that the lifespan in which the firsthand experiences were told stretched from 1844 to about 1914, with some tendency to cluster in the generation following the death of Brigham Young in 1877.

T. Edgar Lyon tells of attending a fast and testimony meeting with his father in the Salt Lake City Twentieth Ward:

> What I experienced there was my first meaningful acquaintance, even though vicariously, with Joseph Smith and the story of the restoration of the gospel and the Church of Jesus Christ on earth. This was the most exciting meeting I had ever attended. The people who bore their testimonies had known Joseph and Hyrum Smith personally, and related their recollections of them, their love of Joseph Smith as a decidedly human being, and their appreciation of the religious and spiritual understanding he had given them. I think I missed but few fast and testimony meetings after that introductory one. Gradually I became aware that there were two distinct groups in the fast meeting. One numbered about twenty or twenty-five people who seemed very old to me, and the other group was made up of those of younger age, such as my parents. In the older group were women in black dresses trimmed with white collars and cuffs. They wore small black bonnets tied under their chins with black silk ribbons. The men were dressed in black suit and ties, and practically all had full beards and gray or white hair. When the meeting was opened for testimony these were the ones who rose and bore their testimonies,

and were still at it when the bishop closed the meeting. Gradually I became aware that they were known as "The Old Nauvooers."[50]

Lyon recalls some of the stories he heard from these people. Coming from eyewitnesses, the stories stuck with him and helped form his own affectionate regard for Joseph Smith.

Value of Material

What is the value of these remembered stories? In a certain genre of faith-promoting discourse (sermons, magazine articles, and even books), they continue to be cited as evidence of the Prophet's awesome qualities without any hint that their reliability might be suspect. But even among Mormons some of the stories were too strong for ready belief. In 1898 the *Improvement Era* carried the following editorial, probably written by Joseph F. Smith, then a counselor in the First Presidency and son of the martyred Hyrum Smith:

> We fear that many things that are reported as coming from the Prophet Joseph, and other early elders in the church, by not being carefully recorded or told with strict regard for accuracy, have lost something of their value as historical data, and unwarranted additions have sometimes been made to the original facts, until it is difficult to determine just how far some of the traditions which have come to us may be accepted as reliable representations of what was said or what was done.[51]

Even though presented in a faith-promoting way, in other words, the stories about Joseph Smith cannot always be uncritically accepted at face value.

The most recent and most comprehensive collection has a provocative discussion of reliability. "That soul who has filled his mind with truth will instinctively resonate to the voice of truth," writes compiler Mark L. McConkie. "Those familiar with gospel patterns and doctrines will have feelings about what is written by the early Saints and others that more accurately describe what is involved than academic scholarship can generally yield."[52] In isolation, this statement might be subject to ridicule, but when all of McConkie's comments are taken together, they do not add up to rejecting careful scholarship, for he is fully cognizant of the hazards of memory and imagination.

Anecdotes about Joseph Smith told in later generations are not, in and of themselves, a reliable source of Latter-day Saint doctrine. The four standard works (Bible, Book of Mormon, Doctrine and Covenants, and Pearl of Great Price), official declarations or proclamations, general handbooks of instructions, and the current teachings of living apostles or prophets—these are the authoritative statements of present-day Mormonism.

Too often critics or novices try to hang around the necks of Latter-day Saints beliefs that these believers have never heard of. But rejecting all later testimony out of hand, perhaps on the grounds that the testifier is not available for cross-examination, is going too far. Many of the anecdotes ring true. If they can be pinned down close to the actual time and place they were supposed to have occurred, if they are consistent with the rest of what is known about the Prophet, and especially if there is confirmation from other evidence, they have credibility.

Mormons have rightly protested when unfriendly biographers have uncritically accepted the affidavits taken from Joseph Smith's neighbors in 1833 and later; they were collected without adequate controls. It would be ironic to turn around and accept at face value the sayings and stories passed on by word of mouth fifty or a hundred years later. The stories and sayings of Joseph Smith as told after his death are indeed valuable source material, if not always for the life of the Prophet, then for his popular image among his people.

Joseph himself stated: "I told them that a prophet was a prophet only when he was acting as such."[53] Despite this protestation, the words of a prophet often assumed a sacrosanct quality. Inevitably his followers clung to his words. Recollections become more than simple reminiscence or idle conversation; they carried the potential, if accepted, of being authoritative. "Whatever he told us came from the Lord we accepted," recalled Mercy Thompson in 1893, "and when he said the word of the Lord was thus and so, we knew it was so, and believed it without witnessing it ourselves, for we knew he would not tell us anything came from the Lord that did not come from the Lord."[54]

Mormonism in its first hundred years offers an illuminating case study of the transmission of testimony and some of the problems that can emerge as those who were acquainted with the founding prophet gradually die off and finally—as someone has said about the post-apostolic period of early Christianity—none remains who can say, "I saw."

Notes

1. A modern folklorist who has drawn heavily on printed material is Richard M. Dorson, in his *Jonathan Draws the Longbow* (Cambridge, Mass.: Harvard

University Press, 1946). Stories about historical figures are considered fair game for the modern folklorist who takes an enlarged view of his discipline. For further discussion of this question, see Richard M. Dorson, *American Folklore and the Historian* (Chicago: University of Chicago Press, 1971) and his *Folklore: Selected Essays* (Bloomington: Indiana University Press, 1971).

2. In 2003 Mark L. McConkie published *Remembering Joseph: Personal Recollections of Those Who Knew the Prophet Joseph Smith* (Salt Lake City: Deseret Book, 2003). Utilizing earlier compilations and adding many additional examples, McConkie's work is takes two formats. The printed book, organized topically in five broad categories, presents only a sampling. An accompanying compact disk contains all of the printed material plus additional sources arranged alphabetically by author. An earlier collection of stories about Joseph Smith include Hyrum L. Andrus and Helen Mae Andrus, comps., *They Knew The Prophet* (Salt Lake City: Bookcraft, 1974); and Edwin F. Parry, comp., *Stories about Joseph Smith the Prophet* (Salt Lake City: Deseret News Press, 1934). A primary source full of similar material is Oliver Boardman Huntington, Journal, typescript, Brigham Young University and LDS Church History Library. Other stories that appeared in sermons were published in the *Journal of Discourses*, 26 vols. (Liverpool and London: Latter-day Saints' Book Depot, 1854–86). See citations in the index under Joseph Smith's name. A useful collection of Mormon folklore, although inadequate for the present topic, is Austin Fife and Alta Fife, *Saints of Sage and Saddle* (Bloomington: University of Indiana Press, 1956).

3. "Stories from the Notebook of Martha Cox," in Parry, *Stories about Joseph Smith the Prophet*, 23–27.

4. Among many references to Joseph Smith's fondness for children are Parry, *Stories about Joseph Smith the Prophet*, 31; Andrus and Andrus, *They Knew the Prophet*, 46, 99, 101, 102, 120, 127, 151, 154, 166. See also Leonard J. Arrington, "The Human Qualities of Joseph Smith, the Prophet," *Ensign* 1 (January 1971): 35–38.

5. Andrus and Andrus, *They Knew the Prophet*, 1, 5.

6. Andrus and Andrus, *They Knew the Prophet*, 143.

7. Parry, *Stories about Joseph Smith the Prophet*, 43.

8. Andrus and Andrus, *They Knew the Prophet*, 103, 140; Parry, *Stories about Joseph Smith the Prophet*, 97.

9. Andrus and Andrus, *They Knew the Prophet*, 89.

10. Leland Homer Gentry and Todd M. Compton, *Fire and Sword: A History of the Latter-day saints in Northern Missouri, 1836–39* (Salt Lake City: Greg Kofford Books, 2010), 124.

11. Ibid., 80, 89, 112, 117; Parry, *Stories about Joseph Smith the Prophet*, 27–29.

12. Andrus and Andrus, *They Knew the Prophet*, 135.

13. "Philemon's Faith," *Friend*, August 1974, 47; Parry, *Stories about Joseph Smith the Prophet*, 87.

14. Andrus and Andrus, *They Knew the Prophet*, 14, 15; Huntington, Journal, 161; see Addison Everett's version in John W. Welch with Erick B. Carlson, eds.

Opening the Heavens: Accounts of Divine Manifestations, 1820-1844 (Provo, Utah: Brigham Young University Press/Salt Lake City: Deseret Book, 2005), 228-30.

15. Parry, *Stories about Joseph Smith the Prophet*, 88.

16. Dorson, *American Folklore*, 201; see also Dixon Wecter, *The Hero in America* (New York: Charles Scribner's Sons, 1941).

17. Andrus and Andrus, *They Knew the Prophet*, 34, 42, 43, 59, 68, 107; see also Gary L. Bunker and Davis Bitton, "Mesmerism and Mormonism," *BYU Studies* 15 (Winter 1975): 146-70.

18. Andrus and Andrus, *They Knew the Prophet*, 44, 59, 111, 120, 164, 172.

19. Andrus and Andrus, *They Knew the Prophet*, 23, 34, 42, 43, 59, 68, 107; *Journal of Discourses*, 9:89.

20. Huntington, Journal, 8-9.

21. *Journal of Discourses*, 19:38.

22. Huntington, Journal, 23, 34; Parry, *Stories about Joseph Smith the Prophet*, 29.

23. Wilford Woodruff, *Leaves from My Journal* (Salt Lake City: Juvenile Instructor Office, 1881), chap. 19.

24. Charles R. Dana, Autobiography, 1841, holograph, LDS Church History Library.

25. Huntington, Journal.

26. Ibid., 166, 168.

27. Susa Young Gates, *History of the Young Ladies' Mutual Improvement Association* (Salt Lake City: Deseret News, 1911), 16.

28. Abraham H. Cannon, Diary, photocopy of holograph, 4, LDS Church History Library, 4. On the ten tribes, see Walt Whipple, "A Discussion of Many Theories Concerning the Whereabouts of the Lost Ten Tribes," typescript, LDS Church History Library.

29. Biographical Sketch of Martha Cox, 104, holograph, LDS Church History Library.

30. Eliza R. Snow, "Thou, earth, was once a glorious sphere," in Jill Mulvay Derr and Karen Lynn Davidson, comps. and eds., *Eliza R. Snow: The Complete Poetry* (Provo, Utah: BYU Press, 2009), 408; Apostle Parley P. Pratt expressed the same idea in *Millennial Star* 1 (February 1841): 258.

31. Patriarch Homer M. Brown of Forest Dale in Salt Lake City, Narration given to Theodore Tobiason, October 1924, LDS Church History Library.

32. Anson Call, Letter to John M. Whitaker, January 30, 1886, LDS Church History Library. A generation later Israel Call, Anson's son, wrote that he heard his father say "on a number of occasions that the Prophet told him in company with others that the ten tribes were on a portion of this earth that had been taken away." Quoted in Robert W. Smith, *The Last Days* (Salt Lake City: Pyramid Press, 1947), 215.

33. "I heard him say, 'Peradventure, the Ten Tribes were not on this globe, but a portion of the earth had cleaved off with them and went flying into space," according to Bathsheba W. Smith, in Andrus and Andrus, *They Knew the Prophet*, 123.

34. William Patterson McIntyre, Minute Book, LDS Church History Library.

35. Zebedee Coltrin, quoted in Salt Lake Stake, School of the Prophets, Minutes, October 3, 1883, LDS Church History Library.

36. Lester E. Bush Jr., "Mormonism's Negro Doctrine: An Historical Overview," *Dialogue: A Journal of Mormon Thought* 8 (Spring 1973): 11-68.

37. Ibid., 31.

38. The Civil War prophecy (now D&C 87) was received in 1832, first published in 1851, and included in the Doctrine and Covenants in 1876. Although it was and is widely viewed as having its fulfillment in the American Civil War, the nullification ordinance passed by the South Carolina legislature in 1832 could be seen as a "rebellion," and the statement that "war shall be poured out upon all nations" must extend beyond the Civil War itself.

39. Nephi L. Morris, *Prophecies of Joseph Smith and Their Fulfillment* (Salt Lake City: Deseret Book, 1920); W. Cleon Skousen, *Prophecy and Modern Times* (Salt Lake City: Griffen Patterson Co., 1948); and Duane S. Crowther, *The Prophecies of Joseph Smith* (Salt Lake City: Bookcraft, 1963).

40. Huntington, Journal, 165.

41. Ibid., 165-66.

42. Brigham Young, quoted in Journal History of the Church of Jesus Christ of Latter-day Saints, chronological scrapbook of typed entries and newspaper clippings, 1830-present, July 4, 1854, LDS Church History Library.

43. Daniel Tyler, *The Mormon Battalion,* 350, as quoted in Preston Nibley, "What of Joseph Smith's Prophecy That the Constitution Would Hang by a Thread?" *Church News,* December 15, 1948.

44. *Journal of Discourses,* 6:152.

45. Eliza R. Snow, quoted in *Deseret News Weekly,* January 19, 1870, as quoted in Nibley, "What of Joseph Smith's Prophecy."

46. Klaus J. Hansen, *Quest for Empire: The Political Kingdom of God and the Council of Fifty in Mormon History* (East Lansing: Michigan State University Press, 1967); Marvin S. Hill, *Quest for Refuge: The Mormon Flight from American Pluralism* (Salt Lake City: Signature Books, 1989).

47. Orson Pratt, Letter to George A. Smith, January 21, 1841, LDS Church History Library.

48. Dean C. Jessee, ed., "Joseph Smith's 19 July 1840 Discourse," *BYU Studies* 19 (Spring 1979): 390-93.

49. Richard R. Vetterli, *The Constitution by a Thread* (Salt Lake City: Paramount Publishers, 1967). This prophecy even surfaced during Mitt Romney's presidential campaign. Thomas Burr, "Giuliani: Campaign Sent Article Tying Mitt to a Mormon Legend," *Salt Lake Tribune,* June 5, 2007, A-1. See the following references from the *Journal of Discourses* (7:15; 12:204; 21:8, 31-32; 10:318, 357; 22:143; 23:226, 239; 26:39, 142); *Juvenile Instructor* 31:524, 544; and *Conference Reports* (October 1938, 196; October 1942, 58; April 1950, 154; October 1952, 18. The most thorough discussion of this prophecy, its attribution to Joseph Smith, and its conflation with the "White Horse" prophecy, appear in Craig L. Foster, *A*

Different God? Mitt Romney's Presidential Campaign, the Religious Right, and the Mormon Question (Salt Lake City: Greg Kofford Books, 2008), chap. 3.

50. T. Edgar Lyon, "Recollections of 'Old Nauvooers': Memories from Oral History," *BYU Studies* 18 (Winter 1978): 143-50.

51. "Editor's Table," *Improvement Era* 1 (March 1898): 372.

52. McConkie, *Remembering Joseph*, 56.

53. Joseph Smith, *History of The Church of Jesus Christ of Latter-day Saints*, edited by B. H. Roberts, 7 vols., 2d ed. rev. (Salt Lake City: Church of Jesus Christ of Latter-day Saints, 1932-51), 5:265.

54. *Abstract of Evidence, Temple Lot Case*, 2:346.

Chapter 5

Through the Eyes of His Enemies

"[Joseph Smith is] one of the blackest and basest scoundrels that has appeared upon the stage of human existence since the days of Nero and Caligula."—Francis Higbee

"Such a rare human being is not to be disposed of by pelting his memory with unsavory epithets."—Josiah Quincy

"Deep water is what I am wont to swim in," wrote Joseph Smith in 1842 (D&C 127:2). The deep water included not only the outward trials of privation and pain and grief but also a verbal barrage of denunciation. Parents attempting to instill in their children a positive self-image would shudder at the prospect of such a negative onslaught during formative years. Yet this is what Joseph Smith experienced. What degree of psychological resilience is required to survive being relentlessly portrayed in demeaning terms?

To identify the different components of the hostile image, let us pay particular attention to the adjectives and nouns most commonly employed in the popular press whenever Joseph Smith was mentioned.

It was the First Vision experience of 1820, according to Joseph Smith's later account, that caused the initial furor.[1] When he told this experience to a Methodist preacher, "he treated my communication not only lightly, but with great contempt, saying it was all of the devil, that there were no such things as visions or revelations in these days; that all such things had ceased with the apostles, and that there would never be any more of them." Smith went on to describe a more general reaction of "prejudice against me among professors of religion. . . . While they were persecuting me, reviling me, and speaking all manner of evil against me falsely for so saying," Joseph continued, "I was led to say in my heart: Why persecute me for telling the truth?" We recognize the words of Jesus: "Blessed are ye, when men shall revile you, and persecute you, and shall say all manner of evil against you falsely, for my sake. Rejoice, and be exceedingly glad: for great is your reward in heaven: for so persecuted they the prophets which were before you" (Matt. 5:11–12).

It is not clear just how much Joseph Smith told. The experience of the First Vision was not trumpeted abroad; rather, after the initial scornful rejection by his minister and perhaps others, he treasured it up in his heart, leaving even some family members with vague, confused memories. But the tongues were wagging.

Between 1823 and 1827, he told some people, even outside his family, about the prospect of obtaining golden plates. Lacking the autobiographical statement of 1838, in which he made the sequence clear enough for most purposes, earlier contemporaries could be pardoned for a tendency to confuse that precious treasure with the buried treasure Smith was digging for in the employ of Josiah Stowell. In any case, in his early adulthood Joseph Smith acquired the label of "money digger," with a freight of associated meanings that was entirely pejorative. If he believed in the treasure-seeking activity himself, he was, in the eyes of his detractors, "superstitious," a dabbler in magic.[2] If he did not believe in such things but took advantage of others who were easily persuaded, he was a "charlatan," a "confidence man."

Which brings us to the Bainbridge hearing of 1826. Some later writers claimed that Joseph there charged with being an "impostor." But there is no such crime. Attorney and legal historian Gordon A. Madsen, who has studied the 1826 hearing thoroughly, concludes that instead Smith was charged and tried for being a "disorderly person." When the supposed victim, Josiah Stowell, testified in his behalf, Joseph was released.[3]

One important fact remains. Even before age twenty-one—and well before the organization of the Church in 1830—Joseph had critics and enemies. However, it was the publication of the Book of Mormon and the organization of the Church in the spring of 1830 that really brought Joseph Smith onto the public stage. On June 30, 1830, the *Palmyra Reflector* sarcastically wrote:

> The age of miracles has again arrived . . . and if the least reliance can be placed upon the assertions, daily made by the "Gold Bible" apostles, (which is somewhat doubtful), no prophet, since the destruction of Jerusalem by Titus, has performed half so many wonders as have been attributed to that spindle shanked ignoramus JOE SMITH. This fellow appears to possess the quintessence of impudence, while his fellow laborers are not far behind . . . denouncing dire damnation on such as may

withhold their approbation from one of the most ridiculous impostures ever promulgated.[4]

Ignorance, impudence, imposture. Nouns were readily turned into adjectives, and vice versa. Joseph was perceived as ignorant, brash, and fraudulent.

Using the pseudonym Obadiah Dogberry, Abner Cole, editor of the *Palmyra Reflector*, wrote a series on the new religion. He described Joseph Smith as "tall and slender—thin favored—having but little expression of countenance, other than that of dullness; his mental powers appear to be extremely limited, and from the small opportunity he has had at school, he made little or no proficiency." The defamation was extended to the entire Smith family: "We have never been able to learn that any of the family were ever noted for much else than ignorance and stupidity, to which might be added, so far as it may respect the elder branch, a propensity to superstition and a fondness for everything marvelous." Joseph made no "pretensions" to religion, Cole claimed, "until his late pretended revelation." He continued, "It is well known that Joe Smith never pretended to have any communion with angels, until a long period after the pretended finding of his book."[5]

Here is the germ of the theory that the Book of Mormon was first a romance or adventure story intended to make a profit. According to this view, the religious content was an afterthought, awkwardly pasted into the earlier version. Although Cole uses the word "prophet," it is always with the specific qualification that Smith was a "false" prophet. He was called "the pseudo prophet Joe Smith Junior" and compared him to such "imposters" as Walters the Magician, Joanna Southcote, and Jemima Wilkinson. We recognize the strategy of guilt by association.

Smith was also compared to Muhammad—not that Joseph had the military leadership or the natural abilities of Muhammad, mind you. "It is only in their ignorance and impudence," said Cole, "that a parallel can be found."[6] This comparison, not intended as a compliment, would be repeated in the future.

Even before the move of the New York Latter-day Saints to Ohio in January 1831, Joseph Smith was described by his detractors as ignorant, superstitious, impudent, and fraudulent. His followers, easily taken advantage of, were also ignorant and superstitious, In short, they were "dupes." Some of those closest to him were not dupes but "pious reprobates," suggesting knowing collusion.

In March 1831, the Book of Mormon, which had been lampooned even before its publication, was labeled a "hoax": "Many may persevere in sustaining the Hoax, after they are convinced of the imposition, rather than acknowledge they were duped by so barefaced and contemptible an artifice,"[7] The perpetrator of a hoax is of course a deceiver, a charlatan.

This same year, 1831, Thomas Campbell, a former associate of Sidney Rigdon, denounced the Mormons for their "blasphemous pretensions." Comparing them to the French prophets, the Quakers, and the Shakers, he concluded: "If the Mormonite prophets and teachers can show no better authority for their pretended mission and revelations than those impostors have done, we have no better authority to believe them than we have to believe their predecessors in imposition."[8] *Blasphemy, imposture, pretense.*

About the same time, Alexander Campbell, Thomas's son, published an extensive review of the Book of Mormon in his *Millennial Harbinger.*[9] Campbell called Joseph Smith a "liar" and a "knave," with recurring adjectives such as "impudent" and "ignorant." Again he cast Joseph in the company of discredited predecessors: "Every age of the world has produced impostors and delusions."[10] *Delusion, fanaticism, pretension, imposture*—the words by which mainstream Christianity had dismissed Anabaptists, Quakers, and a series of idiosyncratic religious leaders—were now hurled at the Mormons.

In 1831 skeptical observer David I. Burnett wrote of "a feigned revelation purporting to be literally new." The Mormons—a few hundred in number at this time—were "rabble." Joseph Smith was "a perfect ignoramous [sic]." His close associates were "accomplices."[11]

A landmark in anti-Mormon literature burst on the scene in 1834 in the form of Eber D. Howe's *Mormonism Unvailed.* Its subtitle disparages its subject: *A Faithful Account of That Singular Imposition and Delusion.* Howe put forth the "Spaulding theory," claiming that Joseph Smith purloined an unpublished romance written by Solomon Spaulding, a Presbyterian minister, adapted it, and published it as the Book of Mormon.[12] The book and the religion were thus an "artful imposition" on "credulous" believers. Smith was "our imposter." "No one but the vilest wretch on earth, disregarding all that is sacred, intrepid and fearless of eternity, would ever dared to have profaned the sacred oracles of truth to such base purposes."[13]

In reprinted letters by former Mormon Ezra Booth, one more negative label was added: *despot.* "Never was there a despot more jealous of his prerogative than Smith," he wrote, "and never was a fortress guarded with more vigilance and ardor against every invading foe."[14]

Mormonism Unvailed published affidavits from Palmyra neighbors condemning the entire Smith family as "ignorant," "lazy," "indolent," "intemperate," "superstitious," "visionary," and "dishonest." "Their word was not to be depended upon." Joseph Smith and his father were both "entirely destitute of moral character and addicted to vicious habits." Joseph was "saucy and insolent to his father" and "not very well educated." All the Smith men were "lazy, intemperate and worthless men, very much addicted to lying."[15]

Since these uncomplimentary affidavits betray a common authorship and are contradicted by other affidavits, they have been considered unreliable by Mormons. Some later biographers have used them, and one recent book attempted, unsuccessfully in my view, to rehabilitate them.[16] For present purposes, what matters is that they were among the early statements establishing the negative image of Joseph Smith.

A later example is John C. Bennett. After his baptism in 1839, Bennett had enjoyed a meteoric rise. Quickly he became chancellor of the University of Nauvoo, mayor of the city, and a counselor in the First Presidency. Then he clashed with Joseph Smith, fled from the city, and traveled throughout the United States giving lectures and interviews.[17] Bennett's voice would have had credibility—if one could overcome suspicions about his own honesty for having been a high-ranking Mormon himself.

Bennett's *The History of the Saints* (1842) carried a subtitle: *An Exposé of Joe Smith and the Mormons*. Claiming to have joined the Church as a subterfuge in the same way that Napoleon became a Muslim in Egypt, Bennett denounced Mormonism as "a frightfully corrupt system, that would enable them [the Mormons] to give free course to their lust, ambition, and cruelty—a system than which, one more abominable the arch-enemy of mankind himself could not have invented."[18] This was not a dispassionate book.

But what does Bennett say about Joseph Smith? Smith was "one of the grossest and most infamous impostors that ever appeared upon the face of the earth." Bennett itemizes Mormon profanity, drunkenness, swindling, robberies, and the attempted assassination of Missouri's ex-governor Lilburn Boggs. By now, polygamy had been introduced on a limited basis, proof for Bennett of his subject's depravity. For Bennett, Smith was a "polluted monster," a "holy debauchee."[19] Thus, in the negative image circulating among the public at large Joseph Smith now became also a rake, an adulterer, a seducer. Those who knew of Bennett's own sexual adventurism sensed a huge character flaw that gave him no standing to launch such charges.

Bennett's Joseph Smith was, again, a despot, the accusation made by Ezra Booth as early as 1833. Bennett charged that Smith's objective was to erect "a despotic military and religious empire the head of which [was] emperor and pope."[20] Smith had a nefarious plan to take over Illinois, Missouri, Iowa, and other states by force of arms, exterminating those who would not convert to Mormonism. Why, Bennett asks, should this be surprising? For Bennett, Mormons were like the extreme Anabaptists of the Reformation era, described by citing the 1534 Muenster debacle. They were all fanatics.[21]

Bennett could not have been more up to date. The term "fanaticism" was then often employed to describe "an overheating of the emotions that led otherwise normal people to entertain strange and enthusiastic doctrines."[22] The intemperance of Bennett's language can be conveyed only by direct quotation. Joseph Smith was "a most consummate blackguard, and dastardly coward . . . the most foul imposter that ever graced the earth. . . . a foul and polluted murderer. . . . Joe's licentiousness is unparalleled in the annals of time."[23] Bennett described the Mormon "hierarchy"—with Joseph Smith at the head—as guilty of "infidelity, deism, atheism; lying, deception, blasphemy; debauchery, lasciviousness, bestiality; madness, fraud, plunder, larceny;, burglary, robbery, perjury; fornication, adultery, rape, incest; arson, treason, and murder; and they have out-heroded Herod, and out-deviled the devil, slandered God Almighty, Jesus Christ and holy angels."[24] One can almost see Bennett flipping through the pages of a thesaurus.

In the pattern of anti-Smith rhetoric, Joseph Smith was not merely socially distasteful. He was a law breaker. We recall the abortive legal attacks of 1826 and 1830. The nature of the alleged crimes and misdemeanors changed from case to case as "vexatious lawsuits" hounded him. In 1838, when taken prisoner in Missouri, Joseph Smith was charged with murder, arson, burglary, larceny, theft, and stealing—multiple charges leveled by Judge Austin A. King against sixty-four defendants. A charge is not the same as a conviction, to be sure, but in the eyes of his enemies Joseph was a criminal of the blackest dye.[25]

One of the crimes charged against him was treason. Joseph Smith was thus a "traitor." In English usage, few crimes are more heinous. Treason includes the idea of turning against friends and loved ones, against one's own country, and stabbing it in the back. A traitor's loyalty is to the enemy. The charge of treason, made in the court of Judge Austin King in 1838, had no substance. It was used for one reason: to hold Joseph and his friends in prison.[26] Thus Liberty Jail and thus Carthage Jail. Hurling epithets and throwing him into a dungeon, his enemies could rejoice in his suffering and ultimately murder him. By now we are well conditioned to the reality that the truth of the allegation has little to do with its popularity and usefulness to those who wished to demonize the Mormon leader.

Bennett also did much to popularize the comparison of Joseph Smith to Muhammad.[27] First advanced in Palmyra in 1831, the comparison now carried additional plausibility. Both Muhammad and Joseph Smith called themselves prophets. Both, for Bennett, were impostors. Both allowed polygamy. (To conjure up the image of a Turkish harem, Bennett employed the term "seraglio.") Both had political ambitions. Both were willing to use military force. Thus, a simple phrase such as "the Mormon Mahomet" summed up many negative stereotypes.[28]

Bennett granted no sincerity to his foe. Smith was "a consummate knave." He could not be the "dupe of his own imposture"—could not, in other words, have convinced himself that he was telling the truth. Why not? Because "his works plainly show that he is neither fool, nor a fanatic, but a deliberate designer"—and all "for the gratification of his own vanity and selfishness."[29] The awkward interpretation later advanced by biographer Fawn Brodie in 1945 was thus considered and rejected.

If a nineteenth-century reader did not have sufficient reason to dislike Joseph Smith already, one additional charge was hurled in the 1840s: secrecy. Bennett did not participate in the endowment ceremony when it was introduced in 1842, but he may have heard rumors. It was well known that such ceremonies would be performed in the Nauvoo Temple. Under construction during Joseph's lifetime, the temple was sufficiently completed at the end of 1845 for hundreds of people to receive their endowments. In 1847 appeared a pamphlet by Increase and Maria Van Deusen, *The Mormon Endowment*, subtitled *A Secret Drama, or Conspiracy, in the Nauvoo Temple*.[30]

To be sure, this publication appeared after Joseph Smith's death. But the charge of secrecy began earlier, dovetailing into other aspects of the negative image: superstition, immorality, tyranny, and conspiracy. Even Bennett's 1842 book is based on the claim that the real evil of Mormonism and Smith's real character could not be publicly known; one had to become part of the inner circle to gain access to the secret designs.

One accusation from disbelievers might have seemed harmless enough, namely, seeing him as a figure of fun, a clown. The best example comes from the Reverend Henry Caswall, whose *The Prophet of the Nineteenth Century* was published in 1843. Some of Caswall's adjectives are unoriginal. "It is difficult to imagine," he writes, "a human being more corrupt, or more destitute of redeeming qualities. . . . [There is] little in his character besides unscrupulous audacity, reckless falsehood, low cunning, groveling vulgarity, daring blasphemy, and grasping selfishness." Caswall describes an interview in which he asked Smith to identify a psalter. Smith surveyed it in perplexity but confidently answered: "What ain't Greek is Egyptian, and what ain't Egyptian is Greek."[31]

In this account, the sophisticated English visitor has fun at the expense of the naive, rustic Mormon leader, who is both pretentious and ungrammatical. The unlikelihood that any such interchange actually took place did not prevent the story from being published and, one assumes, enjoyed. It was possible, obviously, to see Joseph Smith as a figure of fun. The uncommon humorous portrayal might have seemed a welcome relief from the relentless, unsmiling charges of depravity and criminality. But the humor, such as it was, could easily be harmonized with charges of ignorance and superstition. Leaving no room for affection or even respect, it was perhaps not so harmless after all.

The negative image of Joseph Smith I have sketched with its different component parts was not the only non-Mormon image. Some—one thinks of New York editor James Arlington Bennett—who admired Joseph in many respects. There is the grudging admiration of Josiah Quincy. There were no doubt other non-Mormon friends or admirers of the prophet. But the anti-Smith image I have described was widely recognized. Once circulating, it entered public discourse. One could accept it in whole or in part.

As a postscript, one variation of the negative image requires notice: that Joseph Smith was a "fallen prophet." The label was often used by apostates. With the human desire to preserve consistency, what other choices were there? Those who abandoned the faith could admit to having been taken in, to having been duped, but of course this meant admitting naivete or foolishness. They could, like John C. Bennett, claim to have joined the Mormons simply to expose the fraud—with fingers crossed, so to speak. But this meant they had lied and betrayed the Mormons who had been their friends. If the turncoat had not been sincere when he was a Mormon, was he sincere now or just trying to turn a profit by telling audiences what they wanted to hear?

The usual explanation from apostates was that they had believed the Mormon message as it was originally preached to them but later on discovered something they could not accept. As the new religion developed, they argued, incremental additions were made that were simply unacceptable. In this view, Joseph Smith had been a genuine prophet truthfully proclaiming God's word. But by misbehavior or by adding unacceptable teachings, he had slipped from his pedestal. He was now a fallen prophet. The pattern of disillusioned accusation was voiced at repeated intervals. Some apostates could not accept the ordination of high priests in 1831. As early as 1832, when "the Vision" was published in the *Evening and Morning Star* (now D&C 76), some were offended and left the Church.[32] Then the Book of Commandments, published in 1833, became such a fixed anchor for some that, when further revelations were included in the first edition of the Doctrine and Covenants, published in 1835, they complained. In their view, they were getting teachings and organizational structure they had not bargained for.

With the great financial crisis at Kirtland, Ohio, in 1837, the cry of "fallen prophet" was frequently raised, to be repeated the following year in Missouri.[33] This is a strongly negative image, but it emanated from Latter-day Saints, or apostates, not from outsiders who would never think of accepting Mormonism even in its earliest form. Near the end of Joseph Smith's life, those opponents who "seceded," the publishers of the *Nauvoo Expositor*, explained: "We all verily believe, and many of us know of a surety, that the religion of the Latter-day Saints, as originally taught by Joseph Smith, which is contained in the Old and New Testaments, Book of Covenants, and Book of Mormon, is verily true."[34] But they denounced what they now considered the Prophet's dictatorial pretensions and gross immorality.

Such a conceptualization fell short of denying all validity to Joseph Smith's prophetic status. It enabled the apostates to defend their original conversions while disassociating themselves from later developments. Outside the usual anti-Smith stereotyping, this one tried to strike a middle position. But it was a position difficult to maintain, available only to those who shared the same presuppositions and provocations—likely a small number. While stopping short of rejecting Joseph Smith in his entirety, those who denounced his later teachings and misdeeds, as they saw them, readily resorted to intemperate rhetoric. For Francis Higbee in 1844, for example, Joseph was "one of the blackest and basest scoundrels that has appeared upon the stage of human existence since the days of Nero and Caligula."[35]

Not surprisingly, those seeing Joseph Smith as a fallen prophet were exploited to the hilt by anti-Mormons who did not think he was fallen for the simple reason that for them he had never been a prophet. The two groups of opponents fed on one another.

Among the public at large, among those who had any reaction to the subject at all, the negative image carried the day. This readily mobilized image was not a conclusion coming at the end of a sustained argument. Nor was it necessarily based on accurate information. For Joseph Smith's detractors, it was so obvious as to need no basis in an elaborate lawyer's brief. With a disdainful toss of the head, one simply assumed that all right-thinking people would agree. With presuppositions firmly in place, one might then cite examples of behavior, or rumors, showing Joseph Smith for what he "really was." That the public mind often works in this way is readily demonstrated in contemporary political discourse.

The widely circulated negative image of Smith's lifetime did not die. It has continued to be repeated by anti-Mormons right down to the present. Some later authors repeat the early charges under the trappings of scholarship by the simple device of citing the denunciations that were contemporary with Smith as "primary sources." To be sure, they are primary sources—but of what? Of the negative image of Joseph Smith accepted and promulgated by some of his contemporaries. As we have already established, others, including men and women who knew him very well, saw him quite differently.

Notes

1. Here I use the standard account now published in Joseph Smith et al., *History of the Church of Jesus Christ of Latter-day Saints,* edited by B. H. Roberts, 7 vols., 2d ed. rev. (Salt Lake City: Church of Jesus Christ of Latter-day Saints, 1932-51), 1:1-17, and in the Pearl of Great Price, "Joseph Smith—History." See Hugh Nibley, "Censoring the Joseph Smith Story," in his *Tinkling Cymbals and Sounding Brass* (Salt Lake City: Deseret Book, 1991), 53–101.

2. The issue of money-digging and associated popular superstitions is treated most thoroughly in D. Michael Quinn, *Early Mormonism and the Magic World View,* 2d ed. rev. (Salt Lake City: Signature Books, 1998). See also Richard Lyman Bushman, *Joseph Smith: Rough Stone Rolling* (New York: Alfred A. Knopf, 2005), 48–52; Stephen D. Ricks and Daniel C. Peterson, "Joseph Smith and 'Magic': Methodological Reflections on the Use of a Term," in *"To Be Learned Is Good If. . ."* edited by Robert L. Millet (Salt Lake City: Bookcraft, 1987), 129–47.

3. Gordon A. Madsen, "Joseph Smith's 1826 Trial: The Legal Setting," *BYU Studies* 30 (Spring 1990): 91–108.

4. Quoted in Francis W. Kirkham, *A New Witness for Christ in America,* 2 vols. (Independence, Mo.: Zion's Printing and Publishing, 1942–51), 1:278–79; see also 2:55–56.

5. Abner Cole, Palmyra *Reflector,* excerpted in ibid., 1:283–95; see also 2:63–77. I have sometimes silently dropped capitalization and italics in the original publication. See also Russell R. Rich, "The Dogberry Papers and the Book of Mormon," *BYU Studies* 10 (Spring 1970): 315–19.

6. Ibid.

7. *Painesville [Ohio] Telegraph,* quoted in Kirkham, *A New Witness for Christ in America,* 2:76–77.

8. Thomas Campbell, quoted in ibid., 2:95.

9. Reprinted as Alexander Campbell, *Delusions: An Analysis of the Book of*

Mormon (Boston: Benjamin H. Greene, 1832), passages conveniently reprinted in Kirkham, *A New Witness for Christ in America*, 2:101–9.

10. Ibid., 2:95.

11. David I. Burnett, quoted in Kirkham, *A New Witness for Christ in America*, 2:111–13.

12. The best summary is Lester E. Bush Jr., "The Spaulding Theory Then and Now," *Dialogue: A Journal of Mormon Thought* 10 (Summer 1977): 40–69.

13. Eber D. Howe, *Mormonism Unvailed: A Faithful Account of That Singular Imposition and Delusion* (Painesville, Ohio: Author, 1834).

14. Ezra Booth, quoted in Kirkham, *A New Witness for Christ in America*, 2:132.

15. Ibid., 2:137. See also Hugh Nibley, "Everybody Knew Him When . . . ," in *The Myth Makers* (1969; rpt. in *Collected Works of Hugh Nibley*, Salt Lake City: Deseret Book/Provo, Utah: Foundation for Ancient Research and Mormon Studies, 1991), 11:105–53. The basic treatment is Richard L. Anderson, "Joseph Smith's New York Reputation Reappraised," *BYU Studies* 10 (Spring 1970): 283–314.

16. An attempted rehabilitation of the affidavits is Rodger I. Anderson, *Joseph Smith's New York Reputation Reexamined* (Salt Lake City: Signature Books, 1990), which Richard L. Anderson critically reviews in *Reviews of Books on the Book of Mormon* 3 (1991): 52–80.

17. Andrew F. Smith, *The Saintly Scoundrel: The Life and Times of Dr. John Cook Bennett* (Urbana: University of Illinois Press, 1997).

18. John C. Bennett, *The History of the Saints, or, An Exposé of Joe Smith and the Mormons*, 3d ed. (Boston: Whiting, 1842), 9.

19. Ibid.

20. Ibid., 2.

21. Ibid., 302ff.

22. Paul E. Johnson and Sean Wilentz, *The Kingdom of Matthias* (New York: Oxford University Press, 1994), 150–51, which cites, among other sources, Amariah Brigham, *Observations on the Influence of Religion upon the Health and Physical Welfare of Mankind* (1835); see also Bennett, *The History of the Saints*, 257.

23. Bennett, Letter, *Sangamo Journal*, July 8, 1842.

24. Bennett, *The History of the Saints*, 257.

25. This evaluation rests on Gordon A. Madsen, "Joseph Smith and the Missouri Court of Inquiry," *BYU Studies* 43, no. 4 (2004): 93–136, esp. 99–100.

26. Ibid.

27. Bennett, *The History of the Saints*, 302ff.

28. Arnold H. Green and Lawrence P. Goldrup, "Joseph Smith, an American Muhammad? An Essay on the Parallels of Historical Analogy," *Dialogue: A Journal of Mormon Thought* 6 (Spring 1971): 46–58; Hugh Nibley, *Eduard Meyer's Comparison of Mohammed and Joseph Smith* (Provo, Utah: Foundation for Ancient Research and Mormon Studies, 1989).

29. Bennett, *The History of the Saints*, 57–58.

30. Increase and Maria Van Deusen, *The Mormon Endowment: A Secret Drama, or Conspiracy, in the Nauvoo Temple* (Syracuse, N.Y.: N. M. D. Lathrop

Printer, 1847). For a listing of later editions, including an expanded version in 1854, see Chad J. Flake, ed., *A Mormon Bibliography, 1830–1930* (Salt Lake City: University of Utah Press, 1978). For a context-rich analysis of this and other anti-Mormon works, see Craig L. Foster, *Penny Tracts and Pamphleteering: Anti-Mormon Pamphleteering in Great Britain: 1837–1860* (Salt Lake City: Greg Kofford Books, 2002).

31. Henry Caswall, *The City of the Mormons; or Three Days at Nauvoo in 1842* (London: J. G. E & J., 1842). For a witty dissection, see Nibley, *The Myth Makers*, in *Collected Works of Hugh Nibley*, 11:304–406. For more detail, see Craig J. Foster, "Henry Caswall: Anti-Mormon Extraordinaire," *BYU Studies* 35, no. 4 (1995–96), 144–59.

32. For analysis of the receipt of this vision and reactions to it, both in the Church and among non-members, see Mark Lyman Staker, *Hearken, O Ye People: The Historical Setting of Joseph Smith's Ohio Revelations* (Salt Lake City: Salt Lake City, 2009), chaps. 25–26.

33. For an even-handed discussion of the rise of internal dissent in Missouri and attempts to quell it, see Leland Homer Gentry and Todd M. Compton, *Fire and Sword: A History of the Latter-day Saints in Northern Missouri, 1836–39* (Salt Lake City: Greg Kofford Books, 2010), chap. 4.

34. *Nauvoo Expositor*, June 7, 1844, 1.

35. Ibid., 3.

Chapter 6

The Martyrdom:
Non-Mormons Both Condemn
and Defend the Killings

On June 27, 1844, Joseph Smith was killed, along with his brother Hyrum, by a mob with painted faces. As a continuation of my examination of how different people perceived the Mormon prophet, I shall examine reactions to the murders. But first a quick review of the sad event.

How distasteful does a person have to be to be pronounced unworthy of living? What if you find her physically unattractive? What if he has a body odor problem? What if you don't like the sound of her voice? What if he or she displays bad manners? And on and on. Some people oppose capital punishment under any circumstances, while others justify it for "capital crimes." Murder is universally considered a crime

Yet a group of people in Illinois, in the area surrounding Nauvoo and including several towns, convinced themselves that Joseph Smith must be forcibly removed from the face of the earth. Quite simply, he must be killed, never mind the formalities of due process. This was not the decision of a single deranged individual. The assassinations were not spontaneous. The violent deaths on that day were deliberate—orchestrated and led by specific persons.

Without a narrative account of the events, it is helpful, I think, to recall some specifics. With immigrants continuing to expand the Mormon population, their political domination of Hancock County seemed inevitable. Efforts to punish Joseph Smith legally, by returning him to Missouri to face charges, were nullified by the Nauvoo courts. By this time, Joseph Smith and a few other leaders had introduced polygamy by quietly taking plural wives. In early 1844, he announced his candidacy for president of the United States

The Prophet might have calmed the restive waters by toning down his preaching. A bland repetition of a generalized Christian morality would alarm no one. Instead, perhaps sensing that his remaining days on earth were few, he proclaimed such "advanced" doctrines as eternal marriage to a private circle but publicly, in the King Follett discourse, preached the potential of human beings to become gods in the eternities ahead—not displacing the Almighty Father and Creator but sharing his power and glory.

Opposition arose within the Mormon ranks. A small number of leaders and men of substance organized themselves into a schismatic church. In a provocative newspaper, the *Nauvoo Expositor*, the dissenters minced no words in denouncing Joseph Smith and his new doctrines. Uniting civil, ecclesiastical, and military powers in his single person, attempting to unite church and state, having "almost supreme control" over an anti-republican institution, utilizing force and cruelty reminiscent of the medieval inquisition—such was the Joseph Smith denounced by the seven men who published the *Expositor*. These themes are familiar from Chapter 5.

Feelings ran high. The city council condemned the newspaper as a nuisance and, after consulting the works of the English jurist William Blackstone, voted for its abatement. Pursuant to a court order, the city marshal and his deputies went to the offending press and pied the type. Denunciation now reached a frenzy. Even if it required the use of illegal force, the "good citizens" must do what was necessary to rid the earth of a monster. Such was the message of newspaper editorials and speeches at rallies in neighboring towns

With assurances from Governor Thomas Ford that he would protect them, Joseph and Hyrum Smith reluctantly agreed to submit to the law. They were taken to the county seat of Carthage, Illinois, charged, and imprisoned.[1] With thirteen other individuals, they were charged with "riot," referring to the destruction of the *Nauvoo Expositor* and admitted to bail upon their agreement to appear at the next term of the circuit court.

Then out of the blue, Joseph and Hyrum Smith were charged with another crime—treason. Why was this charge applied, since it in no way applied to the situation? Because treason was a crime for which they could be kept imprisoned. In vain, they repeatedly appealed to the governor.

On June 27, in the late afternoon, some two hundred armed men who had been disbanded from the Warsaw militia excitedly converged on the jail. The prisoners and two friends who had been allowed to stay with them were in a second-floor bedroom. Men charged up the stairs, shouting and shooting.

The prisoners tried to bar the door. Hyrum Smith fell dead when hit in the face and in the back. In quick retaliation, Joseph used a small pistol and got off three shots, wounding but not killing, three of the attackers on the stairs.

Rushing to the window, Joseph looked down upon a sea of hateful, screaming faces. Caught in a crossfire from both inside and outside the jail, he fell from the window to the ground outside the jail. His limp but still living body was dragged to a well where a few of the men fired into him at point-blank. The deed having been accomplished, the group quickly dispersed, returning to their homes.

Whether by word of mouth or through newspaper accounts, it did not take long for the news to spread. *Joseph and Hyrum Smith were dead.* Even today the assassination of a religious leader would be the immediate subject of blaring headlines and excited commentary.

One can imagine the jeering laughs in taverns. "Well, old Joe got what he deserved." Those who had been calling for this use of force, as those who participated in it, were gleeful. As they scattered to their different homes, in subsequent private talk among themselves, there were laughing proclamations: "Now they know who runs this country." It was a common assumption that Mormonism would not last.

But such crowing did not continue long. For one thing, those who had been connected with the incident had reason to fear criminal indictment. They included not only the members of the mob who in painted faces had charged Carthage Jail and emptied their guns into the room occupied by the unfortunate prisoners. There were also those who had encouraged them, including editor Thomas Sharp, who had urged that the Mormon problem be solved "with powder and ball."[2]

One who strongly denounced the murders was Illinois Governor Thomas Ford, who had given his pledge of security to the prisoners. On July 5, 1844, he wrote to the Warsaw Committee of Safety, a vigilante group:

> When I came into your county I announced the policy by which I intended to be governed. The law was to be my guide; and this you well understand. . . . I successively obtained a vote to sustain me in this course from every troop stationed at Carthage, or who was visiting there. From the detachment of your town and vicinity, who visited Carthage the day before the surrender of the Smiths, I obtained a similar pledge. . . . Upon the whole I cannot too strongly express my indignation and abhorrence of the base and profligate act which has disgraced the State and raised

suspicion in the minds of many in regard to my conduct in the matter of the most painful character to my feelings.[3]

Ford refused to assist in driving the Mormons from Illinois. "I am informed that a design is still entertained at Warsaw of attacking Nauvoo," he wrote. "In this you will not be sustained by myself or the people; it is a part of my policy that you remain quiet; and I now announce to you that I will not be thwarted in this policy with impunity."[4]

Another reason for muffling the shouts of triumph became clear as reactions from around the country came in. The killers were not lauded as heroes. Said the *U.S. Democrat*: "We regard these homicides as nothing else than murder in cold blood—murder against the plighted faith of the chief magistrate of Illinois—murder of a character so atrocious and so unjustifiable as to leave the blackest stain on all its perpetrators—their aiders, abettors, and defenders." The *St. Louis Evening Gazette* and all the other newspapers of St. Louis denounced the deed, one of them calling it "unprovoked murder." *The Democrat* in Lee County, Iowa, agreed with the St. Louis press: This was "premeditated murder," the perpetrators of which "ought to be ferreted out and dealt with according to the strict sense of the law."[5]

The *Illinois State Register* called the murders "the most disgraceful and cold blooded ever committed in a christian land" and further promised that "every effort will be made to bring the assassins to punishment." The *Quincy Herald* did not think that the actual murderers would ever be identified but considered the mob's deed "a cold-blooded cowardly act, which will consign the perpetrators if discovered to merited infamy and disgrace." After reporting on several public meetings that passed resolutions in support of Governor Ford, the Quincy editors opined that the general population of Hancock County had not been guilty of the horrendous crime but rather "a few desperate characters." Most Hancock County people would "as heartily condemn the killing of the Smiths as we do."[6]

These editors deplored the incident's effect on the reputation of the state of Illinois. "It will live and be brought up in judgment against us, when the present generation has passed away. . . . The public opinion of the civilized world has been outraged by it, and throughout the United States and in Europe the opprobrium of the transaction will be cast upon our people and State at large. It is a deed that will not soon be forgotten." It was not the Mormons, apparently, who first suggested that the innocent blood of the wronged victims would "stain" the state of Illinois.[7]

The *Bloomington [Iowa] Herald* agreed that "the hitherto fair fame of Illinois has been sullied—blackened—by a deed which casts a stigma upon the whole human family." This editor outdid himself as he tried to find words to express his abhorrence:

> In vain may we search the whole catalogue of crime for an equal to this brutal, cowardly, hellish (yes, hellish is the word, but not half expressive enough to convey a proper idea of its enormity) murder. Assassins may plunge the dagger to the breast of the innocent[,] and unsuspecting savages may torture, kill and slay, but these crimes are virtues in comparison with the heart of the reputed civilized man who in cold blood murders the victim who has voluntarily placed himself in the hands of his enemy, to be tried and dealt with according to law. Only think of it, a man in the nineteenth century, an age of boasted light and reason, voluntarily surrendered as a prisoner ready to suffer for his crimes or misdemeanors overpowered and slain in cold blood. Language is inadequate to paint the outrage in the color it merits. It matters not what may have been the misdeeds of Smith, they cannot be offered in palliation of this horrid crime, nothing can justify such an outrage.[8]

The *[St. Louis] Missouri Republican,* upon hearing the first reports, said: "All our information tends to fix upon the people concerned in the death of the Smiths, the odium of perfidious, black-hearted, cowardly murder—as wanton, as to be without any justification—so inhuman and treacherous, as to find no parallel in savage life under any circumstances."[9] By mid-July the *Lee County [Iowa] Democrat* which had expressed its revulsion earlier, repeated its condemnation of the assassinations at greater length. The murder of the Smiths, the paper asserted, "has caused feelings of deep regret in the breasts of every peaceable and law abiding people; they look upon it as a high handed outrage, and as a cruel, cold blooded, cowardly and contemptible murder."[10]

While condemnation of the murderers was almost universal,[11] it did not represent approval of Joseph Smith or the Mormons. Often the editorial reaction would include disclaimers such as the following from the *Bloomington [Iowa] Herald* "That Smith was an evil disposed man, dangerous in community, we cannot dispute." Or as the *Democrat* put it: "That Jo and his brother were guilty of acts which required the interposition of the law, we are well aware, but after he and his brother had voluntarily surrendered themselves up to justice, under the full assurance that they would receive the protection of Gov. Ford from all violence, they were entitled to all protection against all danger and all enemies."[12] It was not so much the loss of Joseph Smith as the lawless manner of his removal that aroused condemnation.

The Carthage debacle occurred in a season of urban violence and mob disturbances throughout the country.[13] The malady was of the generation, with thirty or more riots in Baltimore, Philadelphia, New York, and Boston from the 1830s to the 1850s, as well as numerous individual lynchings. The assassinations were seen as yet another example of rioting by a lawless mob.

Eighteen-forty-four was a year of intense concern about this rampant lawlessness. The largest outbreak of violence was a series of riots at Philadelphia. The same newspapers that reported the Nauvoo assassinations described the Philadelphia tumult. The two incidents, Philadelphia and Carthage, were often linked. The *New York Daily Tribune*, for example, wrote of the tragedy at Carthage: "Altogether it is a sad and melancholy business, and will leave a dark spot, side by side with the records of the Philadelphia riots, in the history of these times."[14] Wilford Woodruff mentioned this mob spirit in his own journal just days after his first news of the martyrdom: "Mob spirit is rising through out the Country. Philadelphia is full of it."[15]

In the face of all the indignation about rampant violence, was anyone willing to defend the assassinations? One newspaper reported revealingly, "A man was assailed and knocked down with a musket in Warsaw yesterday, for presuming to express disapprobation at the murder of the Smiths."[16] How many such altercations occurred we have no way of knowing, but it is apparent that Warsaw continued to be a center of anti-Mormon sentiment.

It was in Warsaw especially that the rationale for using violence against the Mormons was most fully articulated and expressed in meetings, resolutions, newspaper articles, and letters. It was the same argument used to justify vigilante or regulator activity elsewhere in the country: (1) The perceived offense was so serious that it could not be allowed to continue; (2) The law had proved itself powerless; and (3) The extralegal, vigilante organization represented the popular will. This was the claim. Such had been the basis of editor Thomas Sharp's inflammatory demand, mentioned earlier, that the Mormon problem must be solved "by powder and ball."

Sharp now continued hammering the Mormons in the pages of the *Warsaw Signal*. Stung by the nearly universal condemnation of the murders, he published a lengthy article entitled "The Act and the Apology" on July 10, 1844. To understand his line of reasoning it will help to itemize the main points:

1. Above the strict law of the land is something higher, variously called the law of God, the law of nature, or "reserved rights." Admitting that the assassinations were outside the law of the land, Sharp appealed to the higher law of self-defense.

2. Joseph Smith "and his minions," in Sharp's description, had been guilty of theft, counterfeiting, and physical and verbal abuse.

3. The law had proven itself incapable of bringing Joseph Smith to justice: "The Mormon community were leagued together, and judging from their acts, it appeared to be a part of their religion to fleece, insult and rob the Gentiles, as non-believers are by them called, and then to stand by and protect each other from legal punishment."

4. Smith's actions had become increasingly presumptuous. Sharp, a newspaper editor, was especially incensed by the destruction of the *Nauvoo Expositor*.

5. Though the Smiths had been arrested, their just condemnation by a verdict of the court was not assured. Answering those who insisted that the law should have been allowed to run its course, Sharp argued that "the course of the law in the case of these wretches would have been a mere mockery." This argument was twofold. First, the prisoners would probably have escaped. Second, even if they had not escaped, they would have gone free. This was explained quite simply by the fact that Mormons were a majority in the county. "Last year he [Smith] selected one of his miserable cat's paws for County Commissioner; at the next August election, he would have selected another, which would have given him the complete control of the County Commissioner's Court. This Court selects the Grand and Petit Jurors; or in other words Joe Smith would through them have chosen first the men who could alone bring him to trial, and secondly, the jury before whom he would be arraigned."

6. It was better that these two leaders, "the instigators and authors of all our troubles," be killed than to have a war in which many would suffer. Sharp asked: "Is it not better that the blood of two guilty wretches, whose crimes had long awaited the vengeance of Heaven, has been shed and thus by cutting off the fountain head to dry up the stream of corruption; or would it have been better that they had escaped, as they inevitably would have done through the meshes of the law, and thus brought on a conflict, in which not only hundreds of valuable lives would have been lost, but the blood of the innocent mingled with that of the guilty?"

Sharp compared himself and his associates to the freedom fighters of the American Revolution. "No man through whose veins courses one drop of that noble blood, which prompted our forefathers to throw off the yoke of British oppression, will ask his fellow freemen to kneel at the nod of any tyrant, nor condemn him for asserting his liberty, even if in so doing he is obliged to commit a daring violation of law."

Incredibly, Sharp concluded by claiming that "the community in which we live, is a law abiding community, and . . . it will go as far to maintain the supremacy of the law as any other in the nation. Our citizens have regretted, and still regret the necessity that existed for taking the law in this particular instance, into their own hands."[17]

One week later, on July 17, 1844, a lengthy article by Sharp reviewed the whole sequence once again. Regarding the promise made to Joseph and Hyrum Smith that they would be safe, Sharp wrote: "They had the promise of the Governor's protection; this was not well, and we think was not generally known, until his Excellency proclaimed it after the catastrophe." Sharp put himself in the minds of "the old citizens" of Hancock County. What satisfaction could they have in knowing that Joseph Smith was in jail? Didn't Joseph and Hyrum deserve to die? "Evidence enough to damn them forty times over, has been published. Read the history of the Missouri investigation—[John C.] Bennet[t]'s, [George W.] Harris, Eber D. Howe's and [Pomeroy] Tucker's words, the multitudes of affidavits which have been published." Sharp obviously accepted these anti-Mormon works without question. Knowing that "the law could not reach" the Smiths, what would the "old citizens" naturally conclude? "They chose a bitter alternative—one revolting to their own sensibilities, but prompted by a high sense of duty to themselves and their Country. . . . It had to be done then and there or not at all." In a ringing declaration, Sharp proclaimed, "We plead the necessity of the case."[18]

Although the overwhelming weight of newspaper opinion denounced the murderers, the Warsaw anti-Mormons did gain some support. George T. M. Davis, editor of the *Alton [Illinois] Telegraph*, wrote that he could not approve of mob violence; but if ever there was a justification for such behavior, Mormonism was it. The Mormons had been disliked wherever they had lived. They had become numerous, threatening to control the state at the ballot box. The Mormon community was "a compound of ignorance and villainy—the mass falling under the class of ignorance; while nine tenths of all the principal men, and their immediate instruments, are most justly to be enumerated as villains and desperadoes of the deepest dye." Nauvoo was a refuge for criminals. The Mormons controlled Hancock County offices and thus could prevent the execution of justice through the courts. Editor Davis had bought Sharp's argument. Noticing the frequency of mob violence in American cities, Davis drew this conclusion: The cities where riots have occurred "should seal their lips against condemning the citizens of Carthage and Warsaw." In the fall of 1844, Davis expanded his article into a pamphlet.[19]

Another editor at the *Alton Telegraph,* a Mr. Bailhache, condemned the assassins. Mob violence was never excusable, he wrote. A pledge of honor had been given for the protection of the prisoners. If guilty, they would have been duly convicted and punished. While acknowledging this argument, Sharp countered, "If you are so scrupulously good as to suffer a bloody villain to cut your own throat, or the throats of your friends, and for fear of violating the law will not consent to resort to the only means left you to prevent such a state of things, and seize the only opportunity that probably ever would have been presented, to remove the wretches who would inevitably bring about all these evils, we can only say, that you are a better christian than we ever expect or desire to be."[20]

Few accepted Sharp's rationalization of vigilante lynching. The Mormons proclaimed that killing the two prisoners was murder and demanded punishment.[21] But almost all other newspapers reacted with the same insistence. The *New York Herald* considered Sharp's defense of the murders "a gratuitous justification of cold-blooded murder." Even granting all his premises, the fact remained, said the *Herald,* that Sharp was appealing to violence instead of the law.[22]

The *New York True Sun* again raised the question of what the murders would mean for the reputation of Illinois. "The honor of the State of Illinois, already equivocal in pecuniary affairs, will have the stain of blood upon it, if the murderers be not brought to condign punishment." In the eyes of this editor, the perpetrators were "a gang of cowardly cut-throats, every one of whom is as worthy of the gallows as any pirate that ever swung."[23]

Whether the murderers would be brought to justice would be determined in the Illinois courts. In *Carthage Conspiracy,* modern scholars Dallin H. Oaks and Marvin S. Hill describe "the trial of the accused assassins of Joseph Smith."[24] They give evidence of efforts to prevent Sheriff Minor Deming from arresting the murderers; the "deal" made by Governor Ford with two of the accused, Thomas Sharp and Levi Williams; the selection of a grand jury with no Mormons (despite their predominance in the population); the indictments of nine men, four of whom never appeared for trial; the selection of a jury that again excluded all Mormons; and the subsequent trial of the remaining five before a crowd of anti-Mormon spectators. When the prosecuting attorney excluded the testimony of his three most telling witnesses, and when defense attorneys emphasized the widespread sentiment against the Smiths and the need of an acquittal in order to preserve the peace, the verdict was a foregone conclusion. In essence, the anti-Mormon rationale already spelled out in Thomas Sharp's newspaper—popular sovereignty and reserved rights—was accepted in the court.

The killers succeeded in escaping justice for the murders of Joseph and Hyrum. However, if they thought the end of the Prophet Joseph meant the end of Mormonism, they were wrong. "Thus Ends Mormonism!" was the headline of an article in the *New York Herald*.[25] But it quickly became obvious that the loss of their leader would not cause the Mormons to give up or scatter.

The editor of the *Philadelphia Sun* made the inevitable comparison with Muhammad:

> Since the time of the Arabian Mahomet, there never were circumstances in the history of a religious sect, so propitious to the establishment and wide spread increase of its votaries, as there are now exhibited in the history of the Mormon sect. The manner and circumstances of Mr. Smith's death, have invested his cause with a dignity, and have infused an element of success, greater than its most devoted friends could have anticipated.
>
> There wants nothing but a deep conviction of the truth of the Mormon doctrine to animate a dozen of Smith's adherents to set out on a mission from the scene of their prophet's martyrdom, and effects of the most astounding character in the religious world must necessarily follow.
>
> Nauvoo and Carthage will become the Mecca and Medina of the Mormon Prophet, and thousands of devotees may be drawn to make holy pilgrimages to the scenes of the prophet's labors and of his death.[26]

This non-Mormon editor was not reluctant to look to the future. "Mormonism has just commenced its career," he wrote. "It will date its greatest triumphs from the massacre at Carthage Prison."[27]

That the assassinations had produced martyrs was also recognized by the *Plough-boy* of Mount Carmel, Illinois: "Who knows but what Carthage of Illinois, will yet become as noted in history as is its ancient namesake, of Punic memory. Joe and his brother Hyrum, will be looked upon as martyrs, by the Latter day Saints; and in their future church history, Carthage will figure, as the place where died the Prophet by the hands of the ungodly."[28]

A similar analysis appeared in the pages of the *Tompkins Democrat* in New York:

> "This is the end of Mormonism," is the exclamation of many editors on announcing the death of Joseph Smith. We differ with them. The doctrines inculcated by him would soon have yielded to the light of reason, had he lived; but now that he has sealed them with his blood, he will be looked upon as a martyr; and how feeble a thing is reason, to combat religious error, when it has become impossible for the prophet and high

priest of that error to recant and acknowledge its falsity—when, indeed, he has laid down his life in the defence of it.[29]

This editor was one of the few who had positive words to say about the dead prophet: "Disguise it how we may, a great man has fallen; and among the extraordinary characters of the age—those who have risen from the lowest walks of life, to be 'rulers among men,' history will record the name of JOSEPH SMITH."[30]

This same editor did not hold the press guiltless. He noted that the *Inquirer*, also a New York paper, "after contributing its efforts to bring about these appalling murders by publishing every lie that has been promulgated against the Mormons, cries out 'Horrible! We can scarce credit the account.'"[31]

Horace Greeley, editor of the *New York Tribune*, who would go on to become a prominent Republican leader, made the following comments about the Carthage tragedy and its long-range implications for Mormonism:

> Gross and monstrous as the delusions and perhaps the abominations practiced in the name of that faith, yet it is a vital, living thing. Men and women made of the same sort of flesh and blood and actuated by similar sensations and passions, as Protestants, Catholics, Mohammedans, or whatsoever creed or worship the sun shines upon, do actually believe in this Mormonism—are content to live and die by it—to yield up worldly wealth, domestic ties, and the strong bonds of love of Native land, for it and thus feeling and thus believing, to their damned and distorted spiritual vision Joe Smith is as much the Martyr Hero as any whose shadow has ever fallen upon the world. The blood of Joe Smith, spilled by murderous hands, will be like the fabled dragon's teeth sown broadcast, that everywhere sprang up [as] armed men.[32]

He counseled the Saints to "bide their time," to which the Mormon editor of the *Nauvoo Neighbor* responded: "Well said, Mr. Greeley. Pure religion always did 'bide its time.'"[33]

In short, among the militant anti-Mormons in Illinois, the killings were justified by the exigencies of the situation. The rationalization would next be used to justify the continued persecution of the Mormons and their expulsion from the state. For others in Illinois and the rest of the country, the murders were a cowardly, lawless act. A few writers, even while disdainful of the Mormon religion, had the acuity to recognize that the assassinations at Carthage had made two martyrs.

Notes

1. For a detailed account of the events preceding the imprisonment as well as the dénouement, see, in addition to standard biographies, B. H. Roberts, *Comprehensive History of the Church of Jesus Christ of Latter-day Saints* (1930; rpt., Provo, Utah: BYU Press, 1965), 2:254–87; Henry H. Smith, *The Day They Martyred the Prophet* (Salt Lake City: Bookcraft, 1964); Reed H. Blake, *24 Hours to Martyrdom* (Salt Lake City: Bookcraft, 1973); and Glen M. Leonard, *Nauvoo: A Place of Peace, A People of Promise* (Salt Lake City: Deseret Book, 2002), 380–98.

2. Thomas Sharp, *Warsaw Signal,* June 12, 1844.

3. Thomas Ford, Letter to the Warsaw Committee, July 10, 1844, in Journal History of the Church of Jesus Christ of Latter-day Saints, chronological scrapbook of typed entries and newspaper clippings, 1830-present, July 3, 1844, LDS Church History Library.

4. Ibid.

5. These newspaper reactions are drawn from the *Nauvoo Neighbor*, July 10, 1844, which made an effort to publish all such sentiments. Another summary of many newspaper reactions was published in *Lee County Democrat*, June 29, 1844. See also Larry C. Porter, "How did the U.S. Press React When Joseph and Hyrum Were Murdered?" *Ensign,* April 1984, 22–23.

6. Quoted in *Nauvoo Neighbor*, July 10, 1844.

7. That honor might belong to Governor Thomas Ford, whose letter immediately after the martyrdom reviewed his guarantee of protection: "The pledge of security of the Smiths, was not given upon my individual responsibility. Before I gave it, I obtained a pledge of honor by an unanimous vote from the officers and men under my command, to sustain me in performing it. If the assassination of the Smiths was committed by any portion of them, they have added treachery to murder, and have done all they could do to disgrace the State, and sully the public honor!" *Nauvoo Neighbor*, August 14, 1844. The phrase, "long shall his blood which was shed by assassins stain Illinois . . . ," appeared in W. W. Phelps's hymn, "Praise to the Man." In the recent edition, this line reads: "long shall his blood which was shed by assassins plead unto heaven . . . " *Hymns* (Salt Lake City: Church of Jesus Christ of Latter-day Saints, 1985), No. 27.

8. Quoted in *Nauvoo Neighbor*, 10 July 1844.

9. Quoted in ibid.

10. Quoted in *Nauvoo Neighbor*, July 17, 1844.

11. "Most of the newspaper press of our country has condemned the assassination of General Joseph and Hyrum Smith as a cowardly, cold blooded murder." *Nauvoo Neighbor*, August 7, 1844. The best evidence comes from Thomas Sharp's acknowledgment that "the summary execution" of the Mormon leaders "has brought upon us the severest censure of nearly the whole newspaper press, as far as we have yet heard. From the almost unanimous expression, of the papers that have reached us, we doubt not, that the same indignant cry of 'cold blooded

murder,' will be echoed from one extreme of our wide spread Union to the other." *Warsaw Signal*, July 10, 1844.

12. Both reprinted in *Nauvoo Neighbor*, July 10, 1844.

13. Paul D. Ellsworth, "Mobocracy and the Rule of Law: American Press Reaction to the Murder of Joseph Smith," *BYU Studies* 20, no. 1 (Fall 1979): 71–82.

14. Quoted in ibid., 78.

15. Scott G. Kenney, ed., *Wilford Woodruff's Journal, 1833–1898*, typescript, 9 vols. (Midvale, Utah: Signature Books, 1983–85).

16. *Warsaw Signal,* July 10, 1844.

17. Thomas Sharp, "The Act and the Apology," reprinted in *Nauvoo Neighbor*, August 7, 1844.

18. Thomas Sharp, *Warsaw Signal*, July 17, 1844.

19. George T. M. Davis, *An Authentic Account of the Massacre of Joseph Smith, the Mormon Prophet and Hyrum Smith, His Brother, Together with a Brief History of the Rise and Progress of Mormonism and All the Circumstances Which Led to Their Death* (St. Louis: Chambers and Knoff, 1844).

20. Thomas Sharp, *Warsaw Signal,* July 10, 1844.

21. *Nauvoo Neighbor*, August 7, 1844.

22. *Nauvoo Neighbor*, September 25, 1844.

23. *Nauvoo Neighbor*, August 7, 1844.

24. Dallin H. Oaks and Marvin S. Hill, *Carthage Conspiracy: The Trial of the Accused Assassins of Joseph Smith* (Urbana: University of Illinois Press, 1975).

25. *Nauvoo Neighbor*, August 14, 1844.

26. Ibid.

27. Ibid.

28. *Nauvoo Neighbor*, July 31, 1844.

29. *Nauvoo Neighbor*, August 7, 1844.

30. Ibid.

31. *Nauvoo Neighbor*, August 14, 1844.

32. Horace Greeley, in *Nauvoo Neighbor*, July 24, 1844.

33. Ibid.

Chapter 7

The Saints Mourn: Diaries and Letters

The news of the assassinations at Carthage spread quickly to Nauvoo, then more slowly to Latter-day Saints in branches abroad and to missionaries laboring in the field. The immediate reactions were stunned surprise and grief that seemed too great to bear. Joseph Smith had been their prophet, God's instrument to restore Christ's gospel and church. Joseph had been their champion, their townsman, their friend. Along with expressions of outrage came affirmations of Joseph's and Hyrum's innocence and greatness—and a mighty declaration that the restored gospel had not been defeated but would continue its triumphant march.

Warren Foote's journal entry of June 28, 1844, captures the shock of the Saints as the news reached Nauvoo:

Elihu Allen and I were working in the harvest field cutting his wheat when about three o'clock P.M. my wife came out and told us that word had just come that Joseph Smith and his brother Hirum was shot in Carthage Jail yesterday afternoon. I said at once, "that it cannot be so." Yet it so affected us that we dropped the cradle and rake and went home. We found that the word had come so straight that we could no longer doubt the truth of it. We all felt as though the powers of darkness had overcome, and that the Lord had forsaken His people. Our Prophet and Patriarch were gone! Who now is to lead the Saints! In fact we mourned "as one mourneth for his only son." Yet after all the anguish of our hearts, and deep mourning of our souls a spirit seemed to whisper, "All is well. Zion shall yet arise and spread abroad upon the earth, and the kingdoms of this world shall become the Kingdom of our God and his Christ." So we felt to trust in God.[1]

Jacob Gibson observed the "distress and many tears and weeping" found throughout Nauvoo. At a meeting in the public square, he notes, "the first murmurs, were revenge from almost every quarter." However, the speaker—probably Willard Richards—admonished the crowd to "'be still and know that God raineth, [sic] be composed and return to your homes.'" Later in the day, the bodies of the dead prophets were brought to Nauvoo for viewing. Gibson's emotions overcame him. With unrefined eloquence, he wrote: "but I cant describe the Sean no, no, no."[2]

"In vain would it be for me to attempt to describe the feeling of consternation, dismay, and anguish that the sad intelligence produced," said Benjamin F. Cummings. "Never did man feel a greater sorrow for the loss of human friends tha[n] was felt for these two men."[3] Aroet L. Hale, who later played the snare drums at the funeral ceremony, noted: "To See Stout men & Women Standing around in groops Crying & morning for the Loss of their Dear Prophet & Patriarch was Enough to break the hart of a Stone."[4] Sixteen-year-old John Lyman Smith, a cousin of the Prophet, said, "I could not weep for the fountain was dried up, for I would gladly have given my life for them, but so it was & it is not for me to judge for God Doeth all things well."[5]

Newel Knight, who had been a close friend of the Prophet even before the Church was organized, attended the public viewing of the bodies on June 29, the funeral services, and then a mock burial. After the bodies had been laid out for public viewing, they were hidden in the Mansion House while sand and gravel were placed inside the coffins. These two coffins were then placed inside plainer ones, nailed shut, and buried in a cave near the Nauvoo Temple. The primary fear was that someone would secretly dig up the bodies and take them to Missouri, where a reward had been offered for the return of Joseph Smith, dead or alive.[6] Knight filled pages of his journal with his witness of the character of both Joseph and Hyrum Smith: "In the hour of prosperity they taught the people humility and meekness, in the hour of persecution they practised these virtues and no men have done a greater work on earth since the days of the Savior." Knight's feelings overflowed:

> O how I loved those men, and rejoiced under their teachings! it seems as if *all* is gone, and as if my very heart strings will break, and were it not for my beloved wife and dear children I feel as if I have nothing to live for, and would rejoice to be with them in the Courts of Glory. But I must live, and labor, and try to do good, and help to build up the kingdom of our God here on the earth. And I pray God my Father that I may be

reconciled unto my lot, and live and die a faithful follower of the teachings of our *Murdered Prophet and Patriarch.*[7]

By simultaneously grieving and resolving to continue Joseph's work, Knight was expressing the feelings of all Saints. Their grief tempered by faith, the Latter-day Saints looked to the God and to the gospel as taught to them by Joseph Smith for some measure of comfort.

Mail sent from Nauvoo expressed the same sentiments. On June 30, Vilate Kimball wrote to her "Dear Dear Companion," Heber C. Kimball, who was preaching in the East: "I saw the lifeless corpses of our beloved brethren when they were brought to their almost distracted families. Yea I witnessed their tears, and groans, which was enough to rend the heart of an adamant. Every brother and sister that witnessed the scene felt deeply to sympathyze with them. Yea, every heart is filled with sorrow, and the very streets of Nauvoo seem to mourn. Where it will end the Lord only knows."[8]

When the Nauvoo Legion was called out, Vilate continued, ten drums were found with blood on them. "No one could account for it," she wrote. "While they were examining the eleventh there came a large drop on that." Vilate saw these manifestations as grim omens and gave her interpretation: William Law had apostatized, had now brought about the death of Joseph and Hyrum through his traitorous actions, and would not be satisfied, Vilate concluded, until nine more were murdered. Blood on the drums—it was an omen one might expect from Elizabethan tragedy.

On July 18, Almira Mack, niece of Lucy Mack Smith, wrote to her sister, who had just lost a little son:

> Your trouble, you think, is as much as you can bear; but it is not like Aunt Lucy's. What must have been her feelings at seeing two of her sons brought into the house dead? Murdered by wicked men. When your little boy was sick, you could be with him and administer to his wants, and when he was gone, you could bury him with decency. But this privilege she could not have. . . . These two of the noblest men on earth were slain, and for what? Was it for crimes they had committed? I answer NO, but it was because they professed the religion of Jesus Christ. They were Prophets of the Lord, and they laid down their lives as did the Prophets in ancient days.[9]

The sense of outrage still burned strong. The deaths were cruel and undeserved; the righteous had been slain by the hands of the wicked. Almira's testimony elevates the Prophet and his brother to the status of martyrs.

Lucy Walker Kimball later recalled her own shock at hearing the news. She had been living with Agnes Coolbrith Smith, widow of Don Carlos Smith, Joseph's brother, and both had been sealed to Joseph as his plural wives:

> We had just retired on the night of 27th June, when there came a loud rap at the door below. News, I cried, and fled down stairs, opened the door. A messenger quietly said Joseph and Hyrum have been murdered. I seemed paralized with terror, had no power to speak or move. Agnes, called out what is the news, receiving no answer, came rushing down to learn the awful truth. When at length we returned to our chamber and on our bended knees poured out the anguish of our souls to that God who holds the destinies of his children in his own hands, for a time it seemed utterly impossible that he would allow his prophet to be slain by his foes. . . .
>
> The Dogs howled and barked, the cattle bellowed and all creation was astir. We kept by the open window with our arms around each other, untill the dawn, witnessing the terrible commotion and calling to mind his profetic words. My soul sikens as I recall the anguish of the whole people as they crowded around his lifeless body and that of his noble brother Hyrum who was so true to him.[10]

Zina Diantha Huntington, also one of Joseph's plural wives, later described her reaction in similar detail:

> It was June 27th, 1844, and it was rumored that Joseph was expected in from Carthage. I did not know to the contrary until I saw the governor and his guards descending the hill by the temple, a short distance from my house. Their swords glistened in the sun, and their appearance startled me, though I knew not what it foreboded. I exclaimed to a neighbor who was with me, "What is the trouble! It seems to me that the trees and the grass are in mourning!" A fearful silence pervaded the city, and after the shades of night gathered around us it was thick darkness. The lightning flashed, the cattle bellowed, the dogs barked, and the elements wailed. What a terrible night that was to the Saints, yet we knew nothing of the dark tragedy which had been enacted by the assassins at Carthage.
>
> The morning dawned; the sad news came; but as yet I had not heard of the terrible event. I started to go to Mother Smith's, on an errand. As I approached I saw men gathered around the door of the mansion. A few rods from the house I met Jesse P. Harmon. "Have you heard the news?" he asked. "What news?" I inquired. "Joseph and Hyrum are dead!" Had I believed it, I could not have walked any farther. I hastened to my brother Dimick. He was sitting in his house, mourning and weeping aloud as

only strong men can weep. All was confirmed in a moment. My pen cannot utter my grief nor describe my horror.[11]

Harvey Harris Cluff was a child of eight at the time. Writing in his journal later, he still remembered first hearing the woeful news: "I shall never, no never! eradicate from my mind the crushed feeling that fell upon me."[12]

John Loveless was on a Mississippi river boat when the announcement of the murders was made. Incredibly, to Loveless, the passengers cheered. "Had I possessed the strength of Sampson," he wrote, "I would, like him, have sunk the whole mass in one gulf of oblivion and sent them to their congenial spirits, howling devils of the infernal regions."[13]

Many of the journal references, like John Loveless's, were recorded by people who were not in Nauvoo at the time of the tragedy. To help promote Joseph Smith's candidacy for the presidency of the United States, many Mormon men, including all but three of the apostles, had left on preaching tours. They were widely scattered. Because news traveled slowly in the pre-telegraph era, the murders were not reliably reported in some places for a week or two or even longer.

Some of those who were away from Nauvoo told of experiencing dark premonitions on June 27, only to discover later that this was the date of the awful event. Erastus Snow wrote in his "Autobiography": "Although at that time I was ignorant of the awful tragedy which had occurred, I felt resting down upon me a more dreadful pressure of sorrow and grief and sense of mourning, than I had ever before felt, but knew not why."[14]

Parley P. Pratt recalled something similar. A day or two before the murder, he was "constrained by the Spirit to start prematurely for home." On a canal boat in New York state, traveling with his brother William, he had an ominous experience:

As we conversed together on the deck, a strange and solemn awe came over me, as if the powers of hell were let loose. I was so overwhelmed with sorrow I could hardly speak; and after pacing the deck for some time in silence, I turned to my brother William and exclaimed—"Brother William, this is a dark hour; the powers of darkness seem to triumph, and the spirit of murder is abroad in the land; and it controls the hearts of the American people, and a vast majority of them sanction the killing of the innocent. My brother, let us keep silence and not open our mouths."

According to Parley's later calculations, "It was the same hour that the Carthage mob were shedding the blood of Joseph and Hyrum Smith, and John Taylor, near one thousand miles distant."[15]

On July 6, John D. Lee, preaching in Kentucky, first heard rumors of the murder. That night, as explained in his journal, a heavenly messenger appeared and uttered these words: "Instead of electing your leader the chief magistrate of the Nation—they have Martyrd him in prison—which has hasten[ed] his exaltation to the exutive [executive] chair over this generation." When Lee received a confirming letter from Nauvoo, Lee gave vent to his emotions. "The feeling of grief and anguish operated so powerful upon my natural affections," he wrote, "as to destroy the strength of mind & rendered it almost impossible for me to fill my appointments."[16]

"That awful night" of June 27, said Orson Hyde, "there was an unspeakable something, a portentous significancy in the firmament" and "multitudes felt the whisperings of woe and grief." Hundreds of miles from the scene of the crime, he says, two unnamed apostles became "unaccountably sad" and filled with "unspeakable anguish of heart." A president of the high priests in Kentucky, said Hyde, had a vision of the bodies of the two martyrs.[17]

How many of these incidents were truly noted on the night of June 27 and how much of gloom and depression were refracted through the lens of later reflection? We will probably never know for sure. Whatever feelings people had—or remembered having—on that night, it was easy to project back onto them an extraordinary significance.

In the multi-volume history of the Church that reproduces documents from the period, Church historians of the mid-nineteenth century inserted a note crediting the following with "depression" or sadness on the "memorable day" of June 27: Brigham Young, Wilford Woodruff, Heber C. Kimball, Orson Hyde, Parley P. Pratt, George A. Smith, and Amasa Lyman.[18]

James Holt, preaching in Lebanon, Tennessee, on June 27, was just concluding a sermon when "the spirit of revelation" came upon him. He told the crowd "that the enemies of the Church had taken the Prophet of God [that] day and put him to death, as they had all the prophets of God in all dispensations of the world." "'Now,'" he told his audience, "'you may have this for a testimony of the Gospel, for that is true Mormonism.'" He offered to answer any questions, but there were none. "All seemed struck with amazement, and their eyes were full of tears." He looked out the window at the setting sun.

The next day he told his father about Joseph Smith's death. "He said he did not believe anyone could know anything for a certainty at such a distance. I told him that the spirit of God could reveal anything to man that was going on in any part of the world, and I knew that God had revealed the truth to me, and that I should start for home right away."[19]

Although written thirty-seven years after the fact, the description of the exact setting and the names of those who, in principle, could confirm this testimony lend credence to Holt's testimony.

For many months, threats and efforts to take Joseph Smith back to Missouri for trial had been hanging over the Prophet's head. Anti-Mormons in Illinois were threatening to use whatever force was necessary to rid themselves of the Mormons and their leaders. The possibility of violent attacks and murders had to be in the minds of many Mormons. It does not stretch credibility to think that some were brooding about such things at about the time the assassinations occurred.[20]

In, Massachusetts, Wilford Woodruff had been hearing rumors of the Prophet's death for several days when, on July 9, he found a detailed report of the murders in the Boston *Times*: "My prayer," he wrote in his journal, "is that God will prepare our minds for the worst & that we may maintain our integrity untill death, that we may overcome as Jesus has overcome."[21]

The news from Nauvoo was fragmentary. "We do not obtain one word from any of our friends so that we can obtain any thing correct upon the subject," Woodruff wrote. "I hope we may get something soon." He noted the mob spirit in the country and the outbreak of war between Texas and Mexico, concluding that "the world is sheding the blood of prophets Patriarch & Saints in order to fill up their cup."[22]

On July 17, Brigham Young arrived in Boston. He and Woodruff walked to the home of a Church member, where they could have some privacy. No longer able to deny the Prophet's death, Woodruff gave himself up to his feelings of sorrow:

> I have never shed a tear since I heard of the death of the prophet untill this morning but my whole soul has felt nerved up like steel.
>
> Br Young took the bed and I the big Chair, and I here veiled my face and for the first time gave vent to my grief and mourning for the Prophet and Patriarch of the Church Joseph and Hiram Smith who were murdered by a gentile mob. After being bathed in a flood of tears I felt composed.[23]

Heber C. Kimball first heard the news on July 9. "The papers were full of News of the death of our Prophet," he wrote. "I was not willen to believe it, for it was to much to bare. [T]he first news I got of his death was on Tuesday morning . . . it struck me at the heart.[24] Reluctant to believe the reports, Kimball traveled to Baltimore, where he was scheduled to hold a nominating convention for Joseph Smith. On July 12, he and Lyman Wight picked up mail that told of events in Nauvoo up to June

19, at which time the Prophet was still alive and free. Kimball and Wight prayed fervently "that we might get some definite news." In the evening they received a letter that told of events up to June 24, when Joseph and Hyrum Smith were incarcerated in Carthage Jail. "This letter satisfied us that the Brethren ware dead O Lord what feelings we had."[25]

On Sunday, July 14, Kimball broke the news to a congregation of Saints in Philadelphia. He reported, "Great sorrow prevailed and agreed to dress in morning. O Lord How can we part with our dear Br, O Lord save the Twelve." The next day he left for New York and from there went on to Boston, arriving on July 18. There he found Brigham Young, Orson Hyde, Orson Pratt, and Wilford Woodruff, all of whom "felt Sorrifull for the Loss of our Prophet and Patriarch."[26]

Preaching in Canada and upper New York, Alfred Cordon also heard the sad news on July 9. At first he did not believe the statement "as we had heard of their death so many times." Finally, on July 26, Cordon and his missionary companion read a newspaper account that convinced them: "We returned to Mr. Parkhurst's very sorrowfull, we did not fully credit the report till now."[27]

James Madison Fisher remarked that "everything seemed black as ink."[28] William Hyde said, "My soul sickened and I wept before the Lord and for a time it seemed that the very Heavens were clad in mourning."[29] In Pennsylvania, William I. Appleby noted in his diary on July 10: "Heard of the murder of Br. Joseph & Hyrum Smith by a Mob at Carthage, Illinois. . . . I could not credit the Report of their deaths at first, indeed I did not want to believe it, and almost hoped against hope!"[30]

More than a month after the assassinations, on August 11, Brigham Young was still moved by accounts of how the news had been received in Nauvoo. "It has ben a time of morning," he wrote to his daughter Vilate. "The day that Joseph and Hyrum ware braught from Cartheg to Nauvoo it was judged by manny boath in and out of the church that there was more than 5 barels of tears shead. I cannot bare to think enny thing about it."[31]

Jane Manning James, a young free black woman employed as a servant in the Smith household, gave her testimony many years later: "When he was killed, I liked to a died myself, if it had not been for the teachers, I felt so bad. I could have died, jus laid down and died; and I was sick abed, and the teachers told me, 'You don't want to die because he did. He died for us, and now we all want to live and do all the good we can.'"[32]

The news eventually reached Church members in other parts of the world. One of the last to hear of the martyrdom, was Benjamin F. Grouard, who was preaching Mormonism in the Society Islands. Taking passage on a ship to Tahiti on February 1, 1845, Grouard found newspapers telling of the event, but the account was "so contradictory & improbable that I did not know what to believe." He then remembered a dream in which he had seen the bodies of Joseph and Hyrum; but not until February 25, 1845, did Grouard receive reliable news, which led to the following journal entry:

> Tuesday Feb 25th the sad news came fully confirmed. The whale ship Averic had been cast away on Raitea, an Island one hundred miles to the leaward, & consiquenty her papers &c came to Tahiti & among the rest was the governors letter addressed to the citizens of Illinois stating the particulars of the assasination of "Joseph & Hyrum Smith." Though we had been looking for & partialy expecting such news from the many flying reports which had already come, yet when we were thus fully convinced of its truth it was a dreadful shock to us—one which we were illy prepared to receive. The heartrending anguish it caused us I will not attempt to discribe—: that our beloved prophet & patriarch were gone—gone to return no more to rejoyce—that we must return to the church & find their places vacant who had blessed us in the name of the Lord & told us to go in peace & prosper, those who held the cause of Zion so close to their hearts, who lived for it, laboured for it, & died for it—that we could see them no more, no more hear their voices till we meet them in the celestial kingdom of God it was bitter, bitter, more than words can tell.[33]

Expressing his indignation toward the murderers, the state of Illinois, and even the United States, Grouard concluded, "You have accomplished what you have sought for these last 14 years, & now look out for the judgements of God."[34]

That the Prophet's death was but one scene in the great latter-day drama of the last days was suggested by more than one writer. On July 24, 1844, the *Nauvoo Neighbor* reported not only on the martyrdom but also on the latest outbreak of mob violence in Philadelphia. The *Neighbor* then editorialized: "O Liberty where hast thou fled? Has the Lamb opened the second seal, spoke of by John the Revelator, and given the rider on the red horse the great sword, and power to take peace from the earth?"[35]

Lucy Walker Kimball, in her account of the night in which she heard the news, records that, after the shock, she and Agnes Coolbrith Smith wondered why God would allow such a thing to happen:

> Why not? His only begotten Son offered his life as a sacrifice. What did Joseph say when he gave himself up, at the solicitation of those who plead he would not forsake his flock, "If my life is worth nothing to you it is worth nothing to me." He well knew what his destiny was when he

gave up the plan of flying to the "Rocky Mountains." How we plead that Father would, as he had done fifty times before, save him from his foes. But he gave his life cheerfully to save the people. He had often said he would not die a natural death but by the hands of his enemies. That he made every preparation for this great sacrifice we well knew, as we called to mind his own words and yet felt unprepared for the blow, when it came. . . . We kept by the open window with our arms around each other, untill the dawn, witnessing the terrible commotion and calling to mind his profetic words.[36]

In the midst of massive shock and grief, the Saints groped for an explanation that would leave their faith intact. Their early statements laid the groundwork for what the story of the martyrdom would become for them—a powerful testimony to the character and mission of the Prophet-martyr of the Restoration.

Notes

1. Warren Foote, Journal, June 28, 1844, LDS Church History Library. Descriptions and synopses of unpublished diaries and journals cited here can be found in my *Guide to Mormon Diaries and Autobiographies* (Provo, Utah: Brigham Young University Press, 1977). When exact dates are not given, the relevant passages can readily be found in the entries for late June or early July 1844.

2. Jacob Gibson, Journal, LDS Church History Library.

3. Benjamin Franklin Cummings, Journal, L. Tom Perry Special Collections, Harold B. Lee Library, Brigham Young University, Provo, Utah.

4. Aroet Lucius Hale, Journal, LDS Church History Library.

5. John Lyman Smith, Journal, LDS Church History Library.

6. Barbara Hands Bernauer, "Still 'Side by Side': The Final Burial of Joseph and Hyrum Smith," *John Whitmer Historical Association Journal* 11 (1991): 17–33.

7. Newel G. Knight, quoted in William G. Hartley, *"Stand by My Servant Joseph": The Story of the Joseph Knight Family and the Restoration* (Salt Lake City: Deseret Book, 2003), 349–50.

8. Vilate Kimball, Letter to Heber C. Kimball, June 30, 1844, quoted in Stanley B. Kimball, *Heber C. Kimball: Mormon Patriarch and Pioneer* (Urbana: University of Illinois Press, 1981), 108.

9. Almira Mack Covey, Letter to Temperance Mack, July 18, 1844, quoted in John C. Cumming, *The Pilgrimage of Temperance Mack* (Mount Pleasant, Mich.: privately printed, 1967), 41–47.

10. Lucy Walker Kimball, Letter quoted in Kimball, *Heber C. Kimball*, 314. Lucy married Heber C. Kimball on February 8, 1845, and was sealed to him for time on January 15, 1846.

11. Zina Diantha Huntington, Autobiographical sketch, in Edward W. Tullidge, *Women of Mormondom* (New York: Tullidge and Crandall, 1877), 326.

12. Harvey Harris Cluff, Journal, quoted in Bitton, *Guide to Mormon Diaries and Autobiographies*, 71.

13. John Loveless, Autobiography, in *Our Pioneer Heritage,* compiled by Kate B. Carter, 20 vols. (Salt Lake City: Daughters of Utah Pioneers, 1958–77), 12:221–26.

14. Erastus Snow, "Autobiography," *Utah Genealogical and Historical Magazine* 14 (1923): 110.

15. Parley P. Pratt, *Autobiography of Parley Parker Pratt*, edited by Parley P. Pratt Jr. (New York: Russell Brothers, 1874), 331–34.

16. John D. Lee, Diary, July 6, 1844, LDS Church History Library.

17. Orson Hyde quoted in Joseph Smith et al., *History of the Church of Jesus Christ of Latter-day Saints,* edited by B. H. Roberts, 2d ed. rev., 7 vols. (Salt Lake City: Deseret News Press, 1902–32), 7:132; hereafter cited as *History of the Church.* When the account first appeared in the *Millennial Star*, it was unsigned except for "Ed." The editor of the *Millennial Star* at the time was Orson Spencer. When it appeared later in the *Frontier Guardian*, again there was no byline. When it was published later still in the *Elders' Journal*, it appeared under Orson Hyde's byline.

18. *History of the Church*, 7:132–33.

19. Dale L. Morgan, ed., "The Reminiscences of James Holt: A Narrative of the Emmett Company," *Utah Historical Quarterly* 23 (January–April 1955): 19–20.

20. After noting the lack of contemporary diary evidence, Dale L. Morgan writes: "It would seem that memories were afterwards distorted by the emotional need for personal participation in an overwhelming tragedy." Ibid., 20 note.

21. Scott G. Kenney, ed., *Wilford Woodruff's Journal, 1833–1898,* typescript, 9 vols. (Midvale, Utah: Signature Books, 1983–85), July 17, 1844.

22. Ibid.

23. Ibid., July 17, 2844.

24. Stanley B. Kimball, ed., *On the Potter's Wheel: The Diaries of Heber C. Kimball* (Salt Lake City: Signature Books, 1987), July 9, 1844.

25. Ibid.

26. Ibid., July 14 and 18, 1844,

27. Alfred Cordon, Journal, July 26, 1844, LDS Church History Library.

28. James Madison Fisher, Journal, LDS Church History Library.

29. William Hyde, Journal, LDS Church History Library.

30. William I. Appleby, Journal, July 10, 1844, LDS Church History Library.

31. Brigham Young, Letter to Vilate Young, August 11, 1844, LDS Church History Library.

32. Jane Manning James, "Reminiscence," *Young Woman's Journal* 16 (December 1905): 553.

33. Benjamin F. Grouard, Journal, February 1 and 25, 1845, microfilm, LDS Church History Library.

34. Ibid.

35. *Nauvoo Neighbor*, July 24, 1844. The same issue contained a report on "Millerism." Miller's prophecies of Christ's second coming had failed, but he had now recalculated. The Mormon newspaper ridicules Miller, refrains from being too specific about dates, and yet is still willing to see the riots and assassinations in the context of apocalypse.

36. Lucy Walker Kimball, Letter, quoted in Kimball, *Heber C. Kimball*, 314.

Chapter 8

The Saints Mourn: Martyrdom Poetry

In the aftermath of the killings, Mormon poets and versifiers struggled to convey their grief and sense of loss. Unlike the letters and diaries, the poems sought a higher level of understanding for the Saints and for the world. Two exceptions expressing a personal reaction were both unpublished: William Hyde's "On the Death of Joseph and Hyrum Smith" and William I. Appleby's "Lines Suggested by the Reflections of the Call and Martyrdom of the Prophet and Patriarch." Hyde, preaching the gospel in Vermont in June 1844, had heard the news from a stranger:

> I listened to this stranger's tale
> Until my strength did almost fail;
> My blood did chill within my vein,
> From weeping I could not refrain.[1]

The more general grief of the Saints was conveyed by the "Lamentation of a Jew among the Afflicted and Mourning Sons and Daughters of Zion, at the Assassination of the Two Chieftains in Israel," apparently penned by Alexander Neibaur and published on July 15:

> How can we, a people in sackcloth,
> Open our lips before thee?
>
> . . .
>
> Our eyes are dim, our hearts heavy;
> No place of refuge being left.[2]

Charles Rogers, addressing Joseph Smith in his "On the Death of the Prophet," wrote:

> We feel thy loss, yea, tears of sadness
> Fill every eye in Zion's land;
> We would have met thy fate with gladness,
> Could we have staid thy murderers hand.[3]

Beyond expressions of grief, the poems expressed other ideas, as, for example, the despicableness of the assassins. Eliza R. Snow sees the dead martyrs as a sacrifice "t'appease the ragings of a brutish clan, / That has defied the laws of God and man!"[4] Sylvester Hulet's "O Earth Attend" calls on the Saints to "weep o'er the deeds just done by wicked hands."[5] William Hyde describes the Carthage mob as "those hellish fiends, in hellish form, / Out from their coverts they did swarm."[6] In Nelson W. Whipple's unpublished "The Two Martyrs," the assassins are "mobers vile . . . feindish [sic] men / Who left them bleeding on the plain."[7]

In Eliza R. Snow's words, the mob's crime was "the blackest deed that men or devils know / Since Calv'ry's scene."[8] For Sylvester Hulet, "ne'er transpir'd on earth, (nor yet in hell) / A scene more tragic since the Savior fell."[9]

These writers did not see the assassinations of two ordinary men. The prophet had been slain of whom Christ had said: "His word ye shall receive, as if from mine own mouth" (D&C 21:5). The Saints groped for words to express how important, how tragic, the event really was. For them, it had cosmic importance.

In the tradition of eulogy, the Mormon poets paid tribute to the character of the departed leaders. In "O Give Me Back My Prophet Dear," printed a year after the murders at Carthage, John Taylor cried out:

> O give me back my Prophet dear,
> And Patriarch, O give them back;
> The Saints of latter days to cheer,
> And lead them in the gospel track.
> But ah! they're gone from my embrace,
> From earthly scenes their spirits fled;
> These two, the best of Adam's race,
> Now lie entombed among the dead.[10]

In "The Seer," also written by Taylor, Joseph was "of noble seed—of heavenly birth," and "His equal now cannot be found / By searching the wide world around."[11] Eliza R. Snow put it this way in her commemorative poem:

> For never, since the Son of God was slain
> Has blood so noble, flow'd from human vein
> As that which now, on God for vengeance calls
> From "freedom's ground"—from Carthage prison walls![12]

Not only were the martyrs great and noble, but they were also *innocent*. Sylvester Hulet insists that it was "righteous blood that now stains this guilty land." In "O Give Me Back My Prophet Dear," John Taylor pleads:

> Ye men of wisdom tell me why,
> When guilt nor crime in them were found,
> Why now their blood doth loudly cry,
> From prison walls, and Carthage ground.[13]

Eliza R. Snow expressed the same idea:

> Once lov'd America! what can atone
> For the pure blood of innocence, thou'st sown?
>
> . . .
>
> Yes, blameless men, defam'd by hellish lies
> Have thus been offer'd as a sacrifice.[14]

Such protestations of blamelessness answered Thomas Sharp and the anti-Mormon press, who had loudly denounced Joseph and Hyrum as criminals.[15] (See chap. 5.)

The martyrs' sacrifice required the spilling of their blood, which becomes a powerful symbol in these poems. It was "innocent blood" that would "stain Illinois" (or "plead unto heaven") and call upon God for vengeance. In her poem on the assassinations dated July 1, 1844, Eliza R. Snow tells how the murdered brothers "seal'd their testimony with their blood."[16] (Coincidentally, on the very same day, July 1, Sally Randall wrote a letter expressing the same idea in prose: "The earth is deprived of the two best men there was on it. They have sealed thare testimony with thare blood."[17]) John Taylor's well-known tribute stated that Joseph Smith, "like most of the Lord's anointed in ancient times, has sealed his mission and his works with his own blood; and so has his brother Hyrum" (D&C 135:3).

In the poetry, the ultimate sacrifice was also made by choice: With full knowledge of their impending fate, the brothers voluntarily returned to give their lives. As the "Lamentation of a Jew" put it:

> O look in righteousness upon thy faithful servants,
> Who have laid bare their lives unto death,

> Not withholding their bodies:
> Being betrayed by false brethren and their lives cut off,
> Forbidding their will before thine:
> Having sanctified thy great name,
> Never polluting it;
>
> Ready for a sacrifice;—standing in the breach,
> Tried, proved and found perfect.
> To save the blood of the fathers;
> Their children, brothers, and sisters.[18]

John Taylor, in "The Seer," wrote of the Prophet Joseph: "The saints;—the saints; his only pride, / For them he liv'd, for them he died!"[19]

Joseph's own words about his sacrifice have been held in remembrance by the Saints through the ages: "I am going like a lamb to the slaughter; but I am calm as a summer's morning; . . . I shall die innocent, and it shall be said of me—He was murdered in cold blood."[20]

It is evident that the Mormon martyrdom literature was attempting to do several things. It was an expression of grief, both in prose and poetry. It condemned the assassins and heaped shame on the country that had allowed such a thing to occur. It proclaimed in ringing words the greatness, the nobility, and the innocence of the martyrs, who had sealed their testimony with their blood and whose work would continue in the courts on high while the Church would continue its onward course below.

The poets also sought to articulate the significance of the mission of Joseph Smith. What had he done that was so great? What was his real contribution that deserved such memorials? It went far beyond being innocent or noble or even dying for his cause and his people. The martyrdom poems contain succinct statements of the profound and far-reaching works of this prophet of God. Eliza R. Snow proclaims:

> Oh wretched murd'rers! fierce for human blood!
> You've slain the prophets of the living God,
> Who've borne oppression from their early youth,
> To plant on earth, the principles of truth.
>
> . . . .
>
> We mourn thy Prophet, from whose lips have flow'd
> The words of life, thy spirit has bestow'd—
> A depth of thought, no human art could reach
> From time to time, roll'd in sublimest speech,
> From the celestial fountain, through his mind,
> To purify and elevate mankind:

> The rich intelligence by him brought forth,
> Is like the sun-beam, spreading o'er the earth.[21]

In "Praise to the Man," by W. W. Phelps, published on August 1, 1844, Joseph was "anointed" by Jesus, "communed with Jehovah," and opened "the last dispensation."[22] John Taylor described Joseph the Seer in these terms:

> With Gods he soared, in the realms of day;
> And men he taught the heavenly way.
>
> . . .
>
> The chosen of God, and the friend of men,
> He brought the priesthood back again,
> He gazed on the past, on the present too;—
> And ope'd the heav'nly world to view.[23]

Such efforts to capture in poetic form the greatness and significance of Joseph Smith's mission did not end in 1844–45. Three years after the event, William I. Appleby brought together several of the themes in his own poetic effort:

> Joseph, the Prophet of the Lord,—thy name to me is dear,—
> And to thy mem'ry now, I often drop the tender tear;
> Call'd thou wast, when young, thy faithfulness to prove
> To do the work agreed by thee e'er thou left the courts above.
>
> On this terrestrial ball thou came, at the appointed time,
> To do those works of might and power, and let thy wisdom shine.
> To break the spell of darkness—the time had arriv'n
> To bring to light the truth, the way and plan of heav'n.

Appleby lists the signal achievements of his prophetic hero, starting with the Book of Mormon. Then:

> Again the Priesthood is restor'd the Church is organized,
> According to Revelation but by the world, despis'd—.
> Built on the ancient pattern, (a dispensation new)
> Of "Apostles, and Prophets," and inspiration too—

The poem goes on to list the appearances of John the Baptist, Peter, James, John, Elias, Elijah, and Moses. As for Smith's present role, here is Appleby's conception:

> Thou'st only pass'd behind the veil, to plead the cause above,
> Of Mourning, bleeding Zion, which was thy daily love.—

Appleby has no doubt of Joseph Smith's continuing prophetic calling:

> Thou art the "Angel of the Church" under Christ thy head—
> Thou has minister'd to it since thy death, by thy counsels it is led.

> Thou wilt stand in thy place and lot, in the Resurrection morn,
> With all the ancient worthies, whose brows a crown adorns—.
> At the head of thy dispensation thou ever thus will stand,
> While less inferior spirits, shall bow at thy command.[24]

Such themes and sentiments are common to those who tried to capture the greatness of their prophet in verse.

With their prophet and patriarch gone, what should the Saints do? The poetry might well have fanned the flames of anger. Instead it counseled patience while at the same time calling for divine retribution or vengeance. In "The Assassination of Gen'ls Joseph Smith and Hyrum Smith," Eliza R. Snow admonished: "Ye Saints! be still and know that God is just."[25] In Parley P. Pratt's "Cry of the Martyrs," the victims themselves petition the Lord:

> "How long, O Lord! holy and true, dost thou
> Not judge and avenge our blood on them that
> Dwell on the earth?"

The Lord, in turn, replies: "BE PATIENT—O ye martyred souls and wait."[26]

One Mormon woman close to the event, Sarah Griffith Richards, found that the poetic words that came to her again and again were those of John Milton in "On the Late Massacre in Piedmont":

> Avenge, O Lord, thy slaughtered saints, whose bones
> Lie scattered on the Alpine mountains cold,
> Even them who kept thy truth so pure of old
> When all our fathers worshiped stock and stones.[27]

Powerful religious faith does not in itself assure great art. If we compare any of the Mormon poetry with, say, the moving tribute to Abraham Lincoln "When Lilacs Last in the Dooryard Bloom'd," it is apparent that the Mormons had no Walt Whitman. By academic standards, the Mormon martyrdom poetry may be deficient in tone and concreteness, uninteresting in rhythm and rhyme, and so forth. But the sincerity of the Saints' emotion is unquestionable. Without doubt the poems represented, in Wordsworth's phrase, "the spontaneous overflow of powerful emotions."

Of the thousands of poems written to pay tribute to departed loved ones, not many are truly memorable. At the deaths of Abraham Lincoln and John F. Kennedy, great quantities of verse were penned, some tasteful and eloquent but much of it mediocre. Yet good or bad, the poetic outpouring expressed provided catharsis for the emotions of the survivors.

The Mormon martyrdom poetry did this, too. If the diaries and letters were unsurpassed in enunciating individual reactions to the sad news, the poetry did something more. It not only expressed grief but spelled out *meaning*. It denounced the assassins, proclaimed the greatness of Joseph and Hyrum Smith in the economy of heaven, explained how their testimony gained in force by their death, placed them alongside the biblical prophets and martyrs, and portrayed them still laboring for the salvation of men in the councils on high. A literature that does this does not necessarily achieve greatness, but it accomplishes something very important for a community of believers, defining not only their loss, but also themselves.

Notes

1. William Hyde, Journal, late June, holograph, LDS Church History Library.

2. [Attributed to Alexander Neibaur], "Lamentation of a Jew among the Afflicted and Mourning Sons and Daughters of Zion, at the Assassination of the Two Chieftains in Israel," *Times and Seasons*, July 15, 1844, 591. Neibaur, a German Jew, was converted to Mormonism in England. He lived in Nauvoo from 1841 to 1846 and later moved to Utah with the Saints. His diary entry of a conversation with Joseph Smith is one of the early accounts of the First Vision. A direct descendant of Alexander Neibaur states unequivocally that he authored the "Lamentation." See Theda Lucille Bassett, *Grandpa Was a Pioneer* (Salt Lake City: privately published, 1988), 26–27.

3. Charles Rogers, *The Prophet*, August 10, 1844.

4. Eliza R. Snow, "The Assassination of Gen'ls Joseph Smith and Hyrum Smith," *Times and Seasons*, July 1, 1844, 575, rpt., in *Nauvoo Neighbor*, July 17, 1844; in a broadside, published in Nauvoo, August 17, 1844; in the *Millennial Star* 5 (September 1844): 53; in *Frontier Guardian*, July 25, 1849; and in the *Deseret News*, December 16, 1857. Two other poems by Eliza R. Snow which touch on the martyrdom include "To Elder John Taylor," *Times and Seasons*, August 1, 1844; rpt. in the *Nauvoo Neighbor*, August 14, 1844; and "Lines Written on the Birth of

the Infant Son of Mrs. Emma, Widow of the Late General Joseph Smith," *Times and Seasons*, December 1, 1844; and rpt. in *Nauvoo Neighbor*, December 4, 1844; *The Prophet*, December 28, 1844; *Frontier Guardian*, March 7, 1849. All of these poems also appeared in Eliza R. Snow, *Poems: Religious, Historical, and Political* (Liverpool, England: Millennial Star, 1856). My thanks to Jill Mulvay Derr and Karen Lynn Davidson, who have compiled a detailed list of Snow's works. For their critical edition of all these poems, see *Eliza R. Snow: The Complete Poems* (Provo, Utah: BYU Studies, 2009).

5. Sylvester Hulet, *Times and Seasons*, December 15, 1844, 751.

6. William Hyde, Journal, June 1844.

7. Nelson W. Whipple, Journal, holograph, LDS Church History Library.

8. Snow, "The Assassination of Gen'ls Joseph Smith and Hyrum Smith," 575.

9. Hulet, Poem, 751.

10. John Taylor, "O Give Me Back My Prophet Dear," *Times and Seasons*, August 1, 1845, 991.

11. John Taylor, "The Seer," *Times and Seasons*, January 1, 1845, 767.

12. Snow, "The Assassination of Gen'ls Joseph Smith and Hyrum Smith," 575.

13. Hulet, Poem, 751; Taylor, "O Give Me Back My Prophet Dear," 991.

14. Snow, "The Assassination of Gen'ls Joseph Smith and Hyrum Smith," 575.

15. Annette P. Hampshire, "Thomas Sharp and Anti-Mormon Sentiment in Illinois, 1842–1845," *Journal of the Illinois State Historical Society* 72 (May 1979): 82–100.

16. Snow, "The Assassination of Gen'ls Joseph Smith and Hyrum Smith," 575.

17. Sally Randall, quoted in Kenneth W. Godfrey, Audrey M. Godfrey, and Jill Mulvay Derr, eds., *Women's Voices: An Untold Story of the Latter-day Saints, 1830–1900* (Salt Lake City: Deseret Book, 1982), 140–42.

18. [Neibaur], "Lamentation of a Jew," 591.

19. Taylor, "The Seer," 767.

20. It alludes to the familiar messianic references in Isaiah 53:7 and Jeremiah 11:19.

21. Snow, "The Assassination of Gen'ls Joseph Smith and Hyrum Smith," 575.

22. W. W. Phelps, "Praise to the Man," *Times and Seasons*, August 1, 1844, 607. Phelps also penned "A Voice from the Prophet," which touches on the martyrdom theme.

23. Taylor, "The Seer," 767.

24. William I. Appleby, "Lines Suggested by the Reflections of the Call and Martyrdom of the Prophet and Patriarch of the 'Church of Jesus Christ of Latter Day Saints'—Joseph and Hyrum Smith, (Murdered in Carthage Jail, Hancock, Illinois, by a Mob etc. June 27th AD. 1844)," in Appleby, Journal, 224.

25. Snow, "The Assassination of Gen'ls Joseph Smith and Hyrum Smith," 575.

26. Parley P. Pratt, "Cry of the Martyrs," *Times and Seasons*, September 2, 1844, 639.

27. Sarah D. Griffith, Diary and Papers, LDS Church History Library.

Chapter 9

Apotheosis

Joseph Smith was a human being. Latter-day Saints do not place him on the same level as Jesus Christ, do not address prayers to him, and do not worship him. Strictly speaking, therefore, apotheosis (meaning exaltation to the status of a god) may not be an accurate description of his final trajectory. But in light of the fact that this volume is concerned with image—with what people thought or now think about Joseph Smith—the term is pretty close.

During his life, as we have seen, Joseph Smith was described as a prophet. But he was not just *a* prophet, certainly not one of the minor, relatively insignificant prophets. He was on the level of the greatest of the Old Testament prophets—Isaiah, Jeremiah, Ezekiel. More than this, as we have seen, he was "like unto" Enoch, Joseph, Moses, John the Baptist, Paul, and Jesus. The external similarities are there, but the more important point here is that these role comparisons were in the minds of Joseph Smith and his followers.

Unbelieving contemporaries jeered at such claims, which must have seemed not merely presumptuous but wildly incongruous. His followers were not impressed by such scoffing. They considered themselves better judges of Joseph Smith's true value, and they often put their lives on the line for him and for what he taught.

Who else had been prefigured by the earlier biblical figures? Who else was like unto Moses? Why, Jesus Christ, of course. Almost any Christian biblical commentary on Deuteronomy 18 will explain that the future prophet "like unto me [Moses]" was Jesus of Nazareth, which coincides with the New Testament gloss (Acts 7:37) and even with the Book of Mormon (3 Ne. 20:23). When Joseph Smith was also said to be like unto Moses, therefore, he became not just another prophet but one who shared that connection with Jesus Christ. Can we appreciate the breathtaking audacity, or fearsome responsibility, of being thus placed in the company of those towering figures: Moses and Jesus Christ?

The juxtaposition of the three names could mean not much more than a claim for greatness: Moses was great, so was Jesus, and so was Joseph Smith. The precise role of each would remain to be spelled out. Chapter 3 delineates some of the remarkable ways, beyond a generalized greatness, in which these lives were similar.

In Liberty Jail in 1839, Joseph Smith cried out: "O God, where art thou? And where is the pavilion that covereth thy hiding place?" (D&C 121:1). We do not need the cross-reference to be reminded of Jesus at the ninth hour saying "Eli, Eli, lama sabachthani? that is to say, My God, my God, why hast thou forsaken me?" (Matt. 27:46). Psalm 22 may well have had many other applications by persons who felt abandoned, but here, within limits, was a psychological sharing. Writing from the jail, Joseph recorded God's answer:

> And if thou shouldst be cast into the pit, or into the hands of murderers, and the sentence of death passed upon thee; if thou be cast into the deep; if the billowing surge conspire against thee; if fierce winds become thine enemy; if the heavens gather blackness, and all the elements combine to hedge up the way; and above all, if the very jaws of hell shall gape open the mouth wide after thee, know thou, my son, that all these things shall give thee experience, and shall be for thy good.
>
> The Son of Man hath descended below them all. Art thou greater than he? (D&C 122:7–8)

The very point here is that Joseph was not Jesus and had not done what Jesus had done, but it is worth noting that the comparison was going through Joseph Smith's mind.

Coming out of Liberty Jail, he made his way to Illinois, where his beleaguered followers were waiting on the banks of the Mississippi. During the busy months that followed, he exerted enormous leadership strength by such dramatic measures as sending most of the Twelve Apostles to England and purchasing land for the founding of the new city of Nauvoo. In the midst of all this, disease attacked the weakened people. In July and August he administered to the sick.

Here is B. H. Roberts's description of the events of July 22:

> President Smith's house was crowded with sick whom he was trying to nurse back to health. In his dooryard were a number of people camped in tents, who had newly arrived, but upon whom the fever had seized. Joseph himself was prostrate with sickness, and the general distress of the saints weighed down his spirit with sadness. While still thinking of the trials of his people in the past, and the gloom that then overshadowed them, the Spirit of God rested upon him and he was immediately healed. He arose and began to administer to the sick in his house, all of whom immediately recovered. He then healed those encamped in his dooryard, and from thence went from house to house calling on the sick to arise from their beds of affliction, and they obeyed and were healed.[2]

The dramatic description continues and is verified by several eyewitnesses.

Several reactions are possible. For the moment, let us restrict ourselves to asking which comparisons would come to mind. For Roberts, it was nothing less than a modern fulfillment of New Testament promises (James 5:14–15; Mark 16:17), the power of healing having been restored to earth (D&C 84:65–70). A Catholic might think of Charles Borromeo administering to the plague victims in Milan, later canonized as a saint and venerated as a modern version of New Testament apostolic power. But who in the New Testament was the great Healer if not Christ himself?

Let us consider some of the titles that were used to describe Smith's role. That of "prophet," already mentioned, is closely related to seer and revelator. He was also a priest, technically a high priest, referring to his priesthood authority. And he was "king," meaning his role of rulership over the kingdom of God on earth.[3] It will immediately occur to the perceptive reader that it is Jesus Christ who is traditionally described as bringing together the three titles of prophet, priest, and king. Latter-day Saints join other Christians in singing about Jesus Christ "He lives, my prophet, priest, and king."[4]

At the end of his life, as he was taken to Carthage Jail in June 1844, Joseph said, "I am going like a lamb to the slaughter; but I am calm as a summer's morning; I have a conscience void of offense towards God, and towards all men" (D&C 135:4). I wonder if Mormons reading these famous words have remembered that the prime example of the spotless lamb being led to the slaughter is Jesus Christ. Specifically in Isaiah 53:7, the Suffering Servant, the man of sorrow who was bruised for our iniquities, "is brought as a lamb to the slaughter."

Did Joseph Smith voluntarily give up his life for his people? Instead of escaping, he, with strong premonitions of impending death, voluntarily turned himself in to the authorities. Not that he wanted to die. He went to Carthage because he had to, having abandoned the idea of escape. The important point here is that some people perceived him as going to Carthage in order to prevent an attack on Nauvoo. For Heber C. Kimball even a reluctant submission called up the following comparison: "Judas, when he lost the faith, received the power of the devil, and betrayed the Son of God into the hands of murderers. Joseph Smith in like manner was betrayed into the hands of wicked men, who took his life."[5]

Immediately after the martyrdom, the language of his sorrowing friends sometimes came close to traditional Christian language about Christ. Here, for example, is Joseph Smith the intercessor:

> Unchanged in death, with a Savior's love
> He pleads their cause in the courts above.

And again:

> He died; he died—for those he lov'd,
> He reigns; he reigns in the realms above.[6]

Mormons never claimed that Joseph Smith atoned for the sins of humankind, but they did not always use restraint when making these comparisons. Here is a recollection of Brigham Young:

> When Martin [Harris] was with Joseph Smith, he was continually trying to make the people believe that he (Joseph) was the Shepherd, the Stone of Israel. I have heard Joseph chastise him severely for it, and he told me that such a course, if persisted in, would destroy the kingdom of God. . . . This people never professed that Joseph Smith was anything more than a Prophet given to them of the Lord, and to whom the Lord gave the keys of the last days, which were not to be taken from him in time, neither will they be in eternity.[7]

In describing Joseph's death, Apostle John Taylor wrote: "Joseph Smith, the Prophet and Seer of the Lord, has done more, save Jesus only, for the salvation of men in this world, than any other man that ever lived in it" (D&C 135:3). Once again the two are placed in conjunction. The superior, unique contribution of Jesus Christ is recognized, but it is not trivial that here Joseph Smith is placed second only to Jesus Christ.

How did the Saints picture Joseph Smith after his death? Did they consider that he had simply joined the great mass of humanity in the grave or in the spirit world awaiting the resurrection and final judgment? No. They could not help but think of him as occupying a status of elevated significance. Three aspects of how Joseph's people envisioned his postmortal activity are noteworthy.

First, he ascended to the highest levels and continued to observe the experiences of his people on earth. This idea was expressed most memorably in W. W. Phelps's hymn "Praise to the Man," mentioned earlier in other connections. The closing words of its first verse are:

> Mingling with Gods, he can plan for his brethren.
> Death cannot conquer the hero again.[8]

I have already commented on the word "hero" in the last line. (See chap. 1.) In the penultimate line, Joseph is not languishing in a spirit prison, not even preaching the gospel to the departed spirits, but is "mingling with Gods" and planning for those on earth.

Second, Joseph communicated to Church leaders, thus performing the role of intermediary. In a sense, this activity began on August 8, 1844, when in a great showdown, the body of Saints gathered at Nauvoo rejected Sidney Rigdon's bid to lead the Church as its "guardian." When Brigham Young spoke, a manifestation occurred: "It did not appear to be Brigham Young; it appeared to be Joseph Smith that spoke to the people—Joseph in his looks, in his manner, and in his voice; even his figure was transformed so that it looked like that of Joseph, and everybody present who had the Spirit of God, saw that he was the man whom God had chosen to hold the keys now that the Prophet Joseph had gone behind the veil, and that he had given him power to exercise them."[9] Just what happened we do not know except that many present on the occasion were satisfied that Brigham Young now rightfully assumed the leadership role previously held by Joseph Smith.

During the journey west, Brigham Young had dreams in which Joseph Smith appeared to him. On February 17, 1847, for example, Joseph appeared in a dream and said, "Tell the people to be sure to keep the Spirit of the Lord and follow it, and it will lead them just right."[10] Brigham accepted the dream as a genuine communication, proving that Joseph Smith was still interested in his people, still, under God, able to convey the divine will.

Third, Joseph Smith would participate in the final judgment, not as an ordinary mortal standing in the dock, but as a judge. Here is Brigham Young, speaking in 1859: "No man or woman in this dispensation will ever enter into the celestial kingdom of God without the consent of Joseph Smith."[11] In 1882 George Q. Cannon delivered an important discourse on the keys of presiding over the last generation, explaining about Joseph Smith: "He will sit as a judge to judge those who have received or those who have rejected his testimony. He will stand as a swift witness before the judgment seat of God against this generation."[12] In context, it is clear enough that Joseph is subordinate to Christ, but the fact remains that he would, in the Mormon view, perform the role of judge in the last judgment.

If this does not add up to apotheosis in the complete sense, it is something close to it. Joseph Smith was not your ordinary human being, not even your ordinary prophet.

After describing the murders at Carthage Jail, Edward W. Tullidge, one of the first Mormon biographers of Joseph Smith, wrote the following:

> Thus lived, and labored, and loved, and died the martyr prophet of the nineteenth century. Thus flashed athwart the black midnight of his age the light of the latter-days. But the darkness comprehended it not; and even as one of old was he betrayed and sacrificed. Back to that scene on Calvary leaps the thought of man. Instinctively are associated the tragedy of that day and the tragedy of this. Across the ages stride the footsteps of the self-same genius. In the agony of death appears the self-same spirit. Nay, from out the agony of Calvary and of Carthage comes the self-same voice: "Lama Sabacthana!"—"Oh, Lord, my God!"
>
> America, thou land of promise!
>
> O, Jerusalem, Jerusalem![13]

Such expressions may scandalize nonbelievers. It was bad enough, they would say, that Joseph Smith claimed revelations. These further claims are simply beyond the pale. He should be roundly condemned for blasphemy. But to find something offensive does not make it disappear. I leave to others the denunciation of this nineteenth-century American for his outrageous self-dramatization, if that is the way they wish to see it. Heaven knows he received an abundance of such condemnation during his lifetime.

To avoid misunderstanding, however, two mitigating considerations should be mentioned. First, when all is said and done, Joseph Smith did not claim that he was God or Christ. Indeed, the scriptures he brought forth—the Book of Mormon, Doctrine and Covenants, and Pearl of Great Price—are altogether Christocentric. It was Jesus Christ, firstborn in the spirit and the Only Begotten Son in the flesh, who atoned for the sins of humankind.

Furthermore, and this may surprise some readers, if Joseph Smith anticipated an exalted status for himself, he presented an almost equally attractive prospect for all human beings who were willing to qualify. If he could receive revelations from God, so could they. He did not claim a monopoly. If he was a prophet, priest, and king, so might they be. Their status of prophet, bearing the testimony of Jesus, or receiving divine guidance for their own callings would not conflict with his. Priesthood authority was dispersed among all worthy males (and, as often explained, among women in that they shared it with their husbands)—truly a "priesthood of all believers." If their status as kings and queens, as expressed in temple ceremonies, took effect only after death, the same was true for Joseph. Whatever these prerogatives might mean, Joseph Smith did not selfishly grasp exclusively to himself.

Those shocked by the audacity of the concept must at least acknowledge the presence of a similar soteriology in early Christianity and in the later Greek Orthodox tradition.[14] It was thus that Joseph Smith elucidated the full meaning of being "heirs of God, and joint-heirs with Christ" (Rom. 8:17).

In Catholic usage the term used to describe the special respect given to the Blessed Virgin and the saints is *veneration*. This same term might appropriately be used to describe Mormons' feelings towards Joseph Smith, except that they do not address prayers to him, as Catholics do to Mary and the saints. "We admire and thank Joseph Smith," a recent speaker said, "but we worship and adore Jesus Christ."

In the hearts and minds of his followers, Joseph Smith had rejoined the great prophets and patriarchs who stood at the head of other dispensations. With them in the heavenly council, he mingled with Gods and planned for his people.

Notes

1. John Taylor, "The Seer," *Times and Seasons*, January 1, 1845, 767.

2. B. H. Roberts, *Comprehensive History of the Church of Jesus Christ of Latter-day Saints*, 6 vols. (Salt Lake City: Deseret News, 1930), 2:19.

3. Melodie Moench [Charles], *Joseph Smith: Prophet, Priest, and King*, Historical Department Task Paper, No. 25 (Salt Lake City: LDS Historical Department, 1978).

4. Samuel Medley, "I Know That My Redeemer Lives," *Hymns* (Salt Lake City: Church of Jesus Christ of Latter-day Saints, 1985), no. 136.

5. Heber C. Kimball, August 13, 1853, *Journal of Discourses*, 26 vols. (Liverpool and London: Latter-day Saints' Book Depot, 1854–86), 2:107.

6. Taylor, "The Seer," 767.

7. Brigham Young, April 17, 1853, *Journal of Discourses*, 2:127.

8. W. W. Phelps, "Praise to the Man," *Hymns* (Salt Lake City: Church of Jesus Christ of Latter-day Saints, 1985), no. 27.

9. Brigham Young, *Journal of Discourses,* 23:364. See also Lynne Watkins Jorgensen, "The Mantle of the Prophet Joseph Passes to Brother Brigham: One Hundred Twenty-one Testimonies of a Collective Spiritual Witness," in *Opening the Heavens: Accounts of Divine Manifestations, 1820-1844,* edited by John W. Welch with Erick B. Carlson (Provo, Utah: BYU Press/Salt Lake City: Deseret Book, 2005), 373–480.

10. Elden J. Watson, ed., *Manuscript History of Brigham Young, 1846–1847* (Salt Lake City: Privately published, 1971), 530.

11. Brigham Young, 1859, *Journal of Discourses,* 7:289.

12. George Q. Cannon, 1882, *Journal of Discourses,* 23:361.

13. Edward W. Tullidge, *Life of Joseph the Prophet* (New York: Tullidge & Crandall, 1878), 545.

14. Keith E. Norman, *Deification: The Content of Athanasian Soteriology* (Provo, Utah: FARMS, 2000).

Chapter 10

Joseph Smith and the Scholars

It is the vice of scholars to suppose that there is no knowledge in the world but that of books. —William Hazlitt

Not contemporary with Joseph Smith were the later scholarly works published about him. Each of these, however elaborate the scholarly apparatus, portrayed an additional image of the Mormon leader.

Most people whose lives would be worthy biographical subjects are never discovered by scholars. Typically, even those whose lives have been the subject of research and writing wait a generation or more for their biographer. It is an indication of the interest in Joseph Smith, therefore, that only eight years after his death Charles Mackay's *The Mormons* (1852) appeared, with the subtitle *With Memoirs of the Life and Death of Joseph Smith, the "American Mahomet."*[1] Mackay's work was based on primary sources, and he tried to be evenhanded. It was not a bad beginning.

A year later, Lucy Mack Smith's *Biographical Sketches of Joseph Smith the Prophet, and His Progenitors for Many Generations* (1853) was published in Liverpool.[2] Dictated by the Prophet's mother, this work is a strange amalgam of self-serving recollections, informative details, and unacknowledged quotations from what had by then become the official history. Not so much a biography as a primary source that later biographers would use, it is nevertheless a landmark.[3]

In 1878 Edward Tullidge brought out his *Life of Joseph the Prophet*. Published first in New York, then in 1880 in Independence, Missouri, this book became entangled in the rivalry between the Utah Mormons and the still young Reorganized Church of Jesus Christ of Latter Day Saints, to which Tullidge temporarily gravitated.[4] It is a favorable account of its subject that would not alienate believers, but it is not only that. Examples of Joseph's human frailties are in evidence throughout. Most interestingly, Tullidge used a new model for explaining the Mormon prophet—that of spiritualism. This faddish movement, which had been going for about thirty years, was attracting many Americans. Some Mormon apostates found it appealing.[5] Tullidge thought he was paying Joseph Smith a compliment by describing him as a medium able to establish contact with the unseen world.

In 1888 George Q. Cannon published *The Life of Joseph Smith, the Prophet* in Salt Lake City.[6] A journalist and publisher as well as a counselor in the Church's First Presidency, Cannon was a leader in the Sunday School movement and was trying to create material that could be used for indoctrinating young Mormons. Organized chronologically and, within the framework of faith, giving much detail about the life of Joseph Smith, Cannon's work is the ancestor of many subsequent Mormon biographies of Joseph that have certain features in common. They get the basic external facts straight, uncritically include the material we earlier described as "folk tradition," and essentially bear testimony to Joseph Smith's divine calling.

General histories—by Herbert H. Bancroft, Orson F. Whitney, and William A. Linn—contained partial biographies. Then in 1902 appeared *The Founder of Mormonism: A Psychological Study of Joseph Smith, Jr.* by Isaac Woodbridge Riley, his published doctoral dissertation, done at Yale.[7] The discipline of psychology was still new, which didn't stop Professor George Trumbull Ladd from making the following introductory statement: "At the time when the subject of the study [Joseph Smith] lived, there was little or no disposition or fitness for considering such manifestations of abnormal psychological development from the scientific point of view." If anything, this was to be a thoroughly modern, enlightened study.

Riley was the first to advance many themes or ideas developed by later scholars:

1. The Smith Family. The narrative of Solomon Mack is presented as proof that in the family "dreams are warnings, visions are messages from on high." Add the history of Lucy Mack Smith—in which he sees "an unthinking credulity," "a positive hankering after the supernatural"—and we are able to conclude that "Joseph's mental outfit is seen to be largely a matter of inheritance." The mother is diagnosed as having melancholia, "a positive intolerance of the sects," and "a marked aloofness from denominationalism." A study of Joseph's genealogy discloses to Riley "serious hereditary weakness" and indeed, through his mother, "a liability to neural instability" (63–64).

2. Dreams. Dreams are seen as basic to the Smith family's religious understanding. Lucy had hers, of course, and she recounted seven dreams of her husband, Joseph Smith Sr. Riley gives a quick and facile dream analysis. Having read his *Encyclopedia Britannica* (9th ed.), Riley pronounces the Smiths as not entirely primitive, for they did not confuse their dreams with daytime experiences, but as "intermediate," for they were not sufficiently advanced to explain the dreams from the material and physical point of view. "Theirs was the mystic view: dreams are warnings from on high, visions are symbolic messages sent to guide the soul" (31). Riley is able to give the "scientific" explanation, which is that the Smith dreams were either hallucinations or illusion. Sensory perceptions were involved in both, especially the visual, which led all dreams to be considered "visions."

3. Influence on the Environment on Joseph Smith. Influences include a ridiculed, rudimentary education. Likely reading material available to Joseph is discussed, but "there is no positive evidence as to his youthful literary pabulum" (43). Especially important was the confusion and wrangling among religious sects, whose shared "somber theology brought an intense melancholy" (50). Such were the preconditions of Joseph Smith's "peculiar psychic experience"—the First Vision followed by the appearances of the Angel Moroni. The religious environment also provides Riley with his preliminary explanation of the early visions: "They may be put in terms of psychic functioning, and may be largely explained by the influences of suggestion and hypnotism" (61). They are not even unusual: Joseph's conversion occurred a year before the average; "the accompanying dreams and visions put him in the rarer third of youth who have dreams and hallucinations." Josiah Royce's analysis of John Bunyan is seen as at least partly valid for Joseph Smith.

4. Pathological Explanations. Putting all of this together, I. Woodbridge Riley does not accuse Joseph Smith of prevarication. Joseph had experiences, all right. But "the apparent objective manifestations were actually subjective symptoms" (68). If we were to ask about the divine aspects or the religious content, our scholar sees no problem: "The theophanic portions of his visions are precisely what occur in a certain form of visual disturbance akin to vertigo." In addition to vertigo, other diagnostic terms advanced as explanations are ophthalmic migraine, melancholic depression, and epileptic convulsions (or convulsive paroxysms) and seizures.

To Riley's credit, he advances epilepsy only as a "working hypothesis" (73). The "infrequency of the youthful attacks" meant that Joseph was afflicted with the ailment only in an "attenuated form." Furthermore, at about age twenty-one, he had a "spontaneous cure." Yet, all things considered, Riley is convinced that "the psychiatric definition of the epileptic fits the prophet to a dot" (74).

Riley is willing to acknowledge that Joseph Smith considered his translations to be inspired. "For all that, his mystic writings may be resolved into their elements of Bible knowledge, petty information, and every-day experience" (193). The Book of Mormon, in short, was "an imaginative elaboration of presentative material." Always up to date, Riley finds that the use of the Urim and Thummim comports comfortably with "a recent experimental study of visions." If Joseph saw Greek or Hebrew letters, or was able to reproduce them, this may have been due to a youthful glance at a Bible in the original tongues, for he was "a good visualizer" (194). The production of the Book of Mormon text was "a veritable piece of automatic writing" (195). The "usual clairvoyant and telepathic embellishments were added" (198).

Generally, even though providing what were then modern psychological explanations, Riley was willing to concede that Joseph Smith had genuine experiences and thought he was inspired. Where was the dividing line between self-deception and conscious duplicity? (208). Without acquitting Joseph of the latter, Riley's interpretation is primarily one of physical-psychological experiences combined with the milieus of a simple-minded family.

5. Hypnotism. But what about the others who believed Joseph? What about the witnesses of the Book of Mormon? In a chapter on "Joseph the Occultist," Riley explains the witnesses by "hypnotic hallucination." For their own vision to occur, there had to be "preparatory manipulation." More broadly, all of the early Latter-day Saints, one gathers, were similarly disposed. Once they accepted Joseph as prophet, he would have "untold influence" (226). "Given, then, such an influence and sensitive subjects, . . . mental suggestion could produce anything [sic] in the way of illusion" (226). As for the testimony of the Eight Witnesses, there are only two possible explanations: pure fabrication or collective hypnosis. Favoring the latter explanation, Riley does not accuse his subject of fraud. Joseph didn't know what he was doing. "To his overwrought imagination, these [achievements] appeared true apostolic gifts" (232).

Not a full biography, Riley's *The Founder of Mormonism* was a provocative, bold attempt to explain the enigmatic Mormon prophet. Drawing upon *fin de siècle* psychological literature, he provided an explanation that was not exactly complimentary but which did allow a certain honesty in Joseph. Its major thesis, that the Prophet had epilepsy, did not fare well as the twentieth century advanced. Riley's book tells more about the state of medical and psychological understanding at the turn of the century and about his own mind-set than it does about Joseph Smith.

At exactly the same time Riley was writing his book, William James was preparing and delivering in Edinburgh the lectures published as *The*

Varieties of Religious Experience (1902). A classic in the scholarly study of religions, *Varieties* has a broader approach and comes from a more important thinker. Yet interesting similarities exist between James and Riley. In a famous first chapter, or lecture, James makes it clear that the origin of a religion in psychological illness in no way precludes its validity. He has nothing but disdain for what he calls "medical materialism," the reductionist view that a religion is explained by pathology. His brief reference to Joseph Smith is scarcely worth mentioning;[8] but clearly James's general attitude, consistent with his own philosophical pragmatism, would be primarily interested, not in the origins of the religion, but in its results—its consequences in the lives of the believers. This may not be far from Riley's willingness to concede that Joseph Smith's revelations were genuine for him.

In 1933 John Henry Evans, a Mormon, published his *Joseph Smith, an American Prophet.*[9] Not a biography in the usual sense, the book offered many vignettes from Joseph's life in rough chronological sequence. Evans could be counted on to be positive, although he did call attention to weaknesses in his subject. Many quotations from contemporary documents were included. The author, an English teacher, had a lively style, approximately on the *Reader's Digest* level, and knew how to retain the reader's interest. After going over Joseph's life in 200 pages, Evans devotes about 100 pages to "the Prophet's religious philosophy" and then, in a final section, grapples with the challenge of explanation. Addressing the possibility of self-deception and hypnotism of others, Evans wrote:

> But the plates did not exist? Very well. Then the man who said they did was an egregious liar, and could not have been a prophet. For see what we must believe if we suppose that he only fancied the plates to be real. We must believe that he imagined he took them out of the hill; that he imagined he carried their fifty pounds home from the hill; that he imagined he was attacked three times on the way home; that he imagined he had to hide them here and there, to keep them from being stolen; that he imagined he had them before him for months, while he worked on them every day; that he not only imagined he showed them to eight men, but that these eight men also imagined they saw and felt the plates. If that does not tax one's credulity, it would be extremely hard to find anything that would.[10]

This work does not pretend to be coolly indifferent. Published by an eastern publisher and distributed nationally, it looked as if it might well serve the purpose of a basic introduction for the indefinite future.

To satisfy Mormon readers who wanted a more consistently chronological narrative, Preston Nibley, an assistant LDS Church historian, published *Joseph Smith the Prophet* in 1944.[11] Clear, straightforward, and unimaginative, this biography marches through Joseph Smith's life, giving the sequence of events as they had come to be accepted by Mormons. There is no bibliography or footnotes, although parenthetical references indicate the source of most quotations. Polygamy is unmentioned. A book for the already convinced, Preston Nibley's biography was ready to reign unchallenged in the Mormon market.

Then came a bombshell. With considerable fanfare in the national media, publisher Alfred A. Knopf of New York City brought out Fawn M. Brodie's *No Man Knows My History: The Life of Joseph Smith the Mormon Prophet.*[12] Church Historian Leonard J. Arrington and I have evaluated this work elsewhere in the context of Mormon historiography.[13] We do not agree with its conclusions and basic interpretation but think it silly to deny that it possesses positive qualities. In 1945 the most thoroughly researched biography of Joseph Smith yet to appear, it decisively repudiates the theory that he had plagiarized the Book of Mormon from a romance by Solomon Spaulding. It conveys the energy of the Prophet and some of his unpredictability. Beautifully written, *No Man* captures the reader's interest and holds it fast through chapter after chapter. National reviewers were profuse in their plaudits.

The Joseph Smith portrayed by Brodie was an impostor, to be sure, but he was an engaging one. He was not even totally dishonest, for he managed to convince himself that he was telling the truth. This idea was not original with Brodie; remember the "self-deception" possibility acknowledged by Riley. For the nonbeliever, such an interpretation might even appear unduly generous. For Brodie herself, who had jettisoned her Mormon beliefs in favor of an atheistic naturalism, there was no way of putting him on the stage as a genuine prophet of God; but she could show him as a charismatic leader, as an audacious claimant of divine religious authority. For most readers, this was good enough, and to this day her book is widely read and recommended.

Mormons, who, of course, could not calmly accept such an interpretation, were quick to respond. The biographies of Preston Nibley and John Henry Evans were reprinted. A direct refutation of Brodie appeared in an issue of the weekly *Church News.*[14] In 1946 the learned Hugh Nibley employed his rapier-like wit against Brodie in his *No Ma'am, That's Not History.*[15] Possibly weakened by its sarcasm and overkill, this lengthy review had important substantive points to make. Nibley chided Brodie for her selective use of evidence; for her hasty, uncritical, and unconvincing use of parallels; for simple factual errors; and for her insistence on a gradual evolution in Joseph Smith's development that, Nibley demonstrates, often clashes directly with the evidence. Above all, he scolds her for pretending to know what was in people's minds. "So Brodie knows that Emma knew that Joseph knew what Emma thought! Is this history?"[16] Later, when Brodie's psychobiographies of Thomas Jefferson and Richard Nixon were torn to shreds by critics, it was easy to point out that her work on Joseph Smith had used the same dubious approach.[17]

Another defender standing in the breach, sword in hand, to defend his prophet was John A. Widtsoe, learned educator and Mormon apostle, whose several articles appeared in the *Improvement Era*. Then, in fulfillment of an assignment from the President of the Church, he published *Joseph Smith: Seeker after Truth, Prophet of God* in fifty-seven chapters.[18] Consistently respectful of his subject, Widtsoe lays out his evidence on topic after topic, occasionally locking horns directly with Brodie. While useful on many specific points and definitely worth reading, Widtsoe is now out of date on several issues.

Since the mid-twentieth century, writing on Joseph Smith has not ceased. If anything, the flow has increased. To say that he continues to attract interest is an understatement. Some of these publications add details about his family or the houses he lived in. Others, I must say, make no real contribution beyond pulling together and restating in the author's words what we know about Joseph Smith's activities in a certain situation. Those works that are interpretive, it seems to me, can be grouped roughly into the following categories.

1. Attacks. What is an "attack" depends, of course, on your point of view. Anti-Mormons have continued to pursue their interest in lectures, pamphlets, radio, and film. For them Joseph Smith was not just a pretender, not sincerely deluded; he was a monster. Other critiques emanating from the anti-Mormon camp have been more substantive, such as the Reverend Wesley P. Walters's effort to demonstrate that there was no religious revival in Palmyra, New York, in 1820, the year of Smith's First Vision.[19] One scholar made an effort to rehabilitate the affidavits from Joseph's neighbors collected by apostate Philastus Hurlbut and published as early as 1834.[20] Polygamy has continued to provide a handle for critics who repeat the old charges that Smith was immoral, with the added suggestion that he exploited the women of his circle. The discovery of the papyri from which, according to the critics, the book of Abraham (in the canonized Pearl of Great Price) was in some sense translated led to a flurry of publication. Finally, the Book of Mormon has rightly been recognized as a vulnerable point, for if it could be overturned, Mormons would be deprived of a basic foundation. Here centering my attention on biography, I have not attempted to enter the complex bibliography on the modern scriptures, although admittedly this is an artificial and prudential demarcation.[21] Suffice it to say that critics of the Book of Mormon and the other modern scriptures are challenging the veracity of the Prophet.

2. Defenses and Appreciations. Examples of scholars who have consistently emphasized the positive aspects of Joseph Smith's life and have responded to critics are Richard Lloyd Anderson, Milton V. Backman Jr., and Hugh Nibley. Thoroughly versed in the canons of modern scholarship and familiar with the primary sources, these and other Mormon writers have not been content to leave the field to enemies of the Prophet. When the historicity of Smith's First Vision was called into question on the grounds that no evidence was found of a revival in Palmyra in 1820, Backman wasted no time in scouring the source material; he found quite sufficient indication of revivalistic activity in the "region."[22] Critics continued to exploit affidavits collected by Philastus Hurlbut in 1833 and 1834. Richard Lloyd Anderson challenged the extent to which these "neighbors" were really acquainted with Joseph Smith and suggested a frame-up.[23] Nibley, in particular, has wittily pointed out the inconsistencies in the anti-Smith writings.[24] As long as attacks continue, one supposes, there will be defenders.

Not in the fray in quite the same way, perhaps, are those who continue to produce biographies. Some of these are close to what in another context would be called "campaign biographies"—that is, fairly superficial narrative treatments of the life, consistently emphasizing the positive. Others, totally uncritically, repeat the standardized, pasteurized version of Joseph Smith's life and season it with later reminiscences and folk traditions beloved by the faithful. I see no need to be supercilious here, for the fact is that all history is drawn on by people according to their interest and sense of relevance. What I have called the ritualization of Mormon history[25] is not limited to the simplified understanding of the Prophet, and the process is by no means unique to Mormons.

Deserving of greater credit as biographies, although still in the appreciative camp, are works by Donna Hill and Richard Lyman Bushman. Hill's *Joseph Smith, the First Mormon*, published by Doubleday in 1977, is perhaps the most satisfactory full biography yet to appear.[26] Although lacking Fawn Brodie's stylistic flair, Hill has done her homework more thoroughly, confronts the major problem areas, and retains our interest as she narrates Joseph's life. Not profound, the book is nevertheless thorough and reflects the expanding body of source material and scholarly studies that had accumulated.

More satisfying for some readers is Richard Bushman's *Joseph Smith and the Beginnings of Mormonism* (1984).[27] A recognized historian, winner of the Bancroft Prize, Bushman is also a devout Mormon. He presents Joseph's life in the traditional mode—that is, as it was experienced and explained by Joseph and those closest to him—but throughout we get Bushman's sensitive, intelligent exposition. Bushman's subject, though, is the young Joseph Smith, for he concludes with the year 1830. We might hope for a second and even a third volume to carry the story to 1844; but in the meantime some of the Prophet's most critical, formative years have been elucidated.[28]

3. New Models of Explanation. Even in the nineteenth century, as we have seen, at least one biographer advanced the suggestion that Joseph Smith was a special kind of spirit medium, thus using a category that was somewhat fashionable in some circles for a few decades. More recently, scholars who do not fit obviously into either the unfriendly or defensive camp have utilized other interpretive models:

4. Political Leader. To the extent that he held public office, as, for example, mayor of Nauvoo, Joseph Smith was a political leader. What I am referring to here is treatment of him that places this activity at the center, not only in the actual decisions of government he was involved but also in his projection of his destiny. Just as he was not merely an ordinary clergy-men but was a prophet, so he was not merely an ordinary politician but was head of the kingdom of God on earth. Some biographies have given little attention to this angle of perception; others ignore it entirely.

In 1967 Klaus J. Hansen published *Quest for Empire: The Political Kingdom of God and the Council of Fifty in Mormon History.*[29] After the efforts of successive gatherings and of trying to achieve separate economic institutions and political autonomy, the Mormons finally were building their own city in Nauvoo, Illinois. There, in early 1844, Joseph Smith proclaimed, "I calculate to be one of the instruments of setting up the kingdom of Daniel by the word of the Lord, and I intend to lay a foundation that will revolutionize the whole world."[30] With mounting opposition both from outsiders and from disaffected insiders, Joseph then proceeded to organize a secret new governing council, the Council of Fifty. Among other things, while anticipating a later take-over in which the Mormon system would dominate, the Fifty participated in the presidential campaign of 1844, promoting—although no one knows how seriously—the candidacy of Joseph Smith. At the same time, some of the Fifty were assigned to plan a migration, which of course required a decision about where the Mormons would go to found their kingdom. Texas, Vancouver

Island, Oregon, and the Great Basin—all were considered. At one point, according to one witness, Joseph Smith even had himself crowned king.[31]

Brilliantly reinterpreting the history in the light of these political aspirations and using minutes of the Fifty that had been previously unknown to scholars, Hansen saw Mormonism as anti-pluralistic—as a bone that was simply indigestible by a pluralistic, democratic America. Joseph Smith in this view became not merely the head of a church, nor even just a prophet, but the self-proclaimed monarch of a new empire. One did not have to adopt the old charges of despotism or dictatorship to recognize that his ambitions, however clothed in religious language, were economic and political.

Such was Hansen's thesis. Mormon historian Marvin Hill has given support to the political emphasis by downplaying the religious, scriptural aspect of the Prophet's role and emphasizing his incompatibility with American society.[32] Retracing Mormon history from its beginning through the Ohio, Missouri, and Illinois periods, Hill demonstrates how the movement appeared to outsiders: as making extravagant claims, increasing in swarming converts, threatening to overwhelm others economically, almost certain to dominate politically, claiming special privileges and divine approbation. The Mormons must have seemed insufferable, and Joseph Smith symbolized and represented the whole system, if, indeed, he was not directly responsible for it. Hill's treatment is a valuable one and, although showing little interest in hearing what the Saints had to say in their own defense, is probably perfectly convincing to many.[33]

Going over approximately the same time span is Kenneth H. Winn, whose doctoral dissertation was published in 1989.[34] He examines, not only the most provocative statements of the Mormons or the hot-tempered reactions of their enemies, but also the explanations and extenuating circumstances. Like Marvin Hill, he recognizes the millenarian anticipations and the political activities that most of their neighbors found offensive. Interestingly, this non-Mormon historian shows greater sympathy for Joseph Smith. Although not biographies, the books of both Hill and Winn present Joseph Smith as primarily a political leader.

5. Destroyer of Skepticism. In 1980 the Reverend Robert Hullinger published *Mormonism's Answer to Skepticism: Why Joseph Smith Wrote the Book of Mormon.*[35] Not at all the usual denigration of Joseph Smith, this book makes considerable effort to understand the context of doubt and infidelity that pervaded America in the early nineteenth century. Growing out of the Enlightenment, criticism of traditional Christianity, which sometimes extended to all religion, was widely disseminated in Joseph

Smith's America. Thomas Paine's *The Age of Reason,* unoriginal though it may have been, popularized the rejection of miracles and traditional religion. Enter Joseph Smith.

What he did was to give his own testimony of modern visions and miracles and, most impressively, to produce the Book of Mormon, which, when read within this context, was a long argument against the modern skeptics.

Hullinger sees Joseph Smith as sincerely motivated, as someone who singlehandedly took on the modern anti-religionists, hitting them with arguments and evidence that could be rejected but which could not be decisively refuted. To be sure, Hullinger does not accept the historicity of the Book of Mormon, but his careful reading allowed him to see one of its major themes. A believing Mormon, agreeing that the Book of Mormon overcomes the doubts and challenges of modernist critics, would insist that it was God through the ancient prophets who had provided this answer for our generation.[36]

6. *Magician.* Prompted by some of Mark Hofmann's forgeries, some people in the 1980s began to see Joseph Smith as a practitioner of rural folk magic. The charge that he had been involved in digging for buried treasure was not new, of course, but now he was portrayed as part of a group who for several years had engaged in this nocturnal activity and practiced strange rites of divination. For a few years, based on a Hofmann forgery of a letter attributed to Martin Harris, Joseph was thought to ascribe extraordinary powers or meaning to the salamander. Brought into this eerie half-light of prescientific behavior were talismans to which he allegedly ascribed spiritual significance and astrological signs by which he allegedly governed his life at crucial points, even including the conceptions and births of his children. At least this was the argument, which was expressed in its most scholarly form by historian D. Michael Quinn.[37]

Quinn did not see magic as inconsistent with the divine calling of prophet. The explanation that any tinkering with magic was either compatible with or superseded by genuine prophetic achievement was expressed by defenders such as Ronald W. Walker and Richard Lloyd Anderson.[38] Yes, they granted, the Smith family was not highly educated and no doubt did accept some of the popular lore of the early nineteenth century. If Joseph was a magician, he was a magician-prophet, or, more accurately, a magician-turned-prophet, for he outgrew his earlier conception of himself as simply leader of a group of rustic treasure hunters. As Richard Bushman wrote:

> The power of Enlightenment skepticism had far less influence on
> Joseph Smith, perhaps at first because rationalism had not penetrated

Smith family culture very deeply. The Prophet showed no sign of wavering when exposed to the scorn of Palmyra's rationalist editors and to the criticism of [Alexander] Campbell himself. Joseph told of the visits of angels, of direct inspiration, of a voice in the chamber of Father Whitmer, without embarrassment.... His world was not created by Enlightenment rationalism with its deathly aversion to superstition. The Prophet brought into modern America elements of a more ancient culture in which the sacred and the profane intermingled and the Saints enjoyed supernatural gifts and powers as the frequent blessing of an interested God.[39]

For Bushman, in some sense, Joseph Smith's openness to realities and experiences beyond the limits of respectable rationalism was a strength, not a weakness.

Two questions must be confronted here. First, how convincing is the evidence that Joseph Smith was involved in the magical activities? The answer varies according to the time—1820, 1825, 1830—and the particular subject of supposed magic. One reviewer, Stephen Robinson, took Quinn to task for logical fallacies and for failing to establish, for example, even the ownership, much less any specific use, of talismans and magic parchments.[40]

Second, just how much of such practices continued to be a part of Joseph's adult life as he brought forth the Book of Mormon, organized a church, received revelations, and led his people for the fourteen years from 1830 to his death in 1844? Most would say that magic entered into the full-blown religion only slightly, if at all. Everything depends on definitions, of course. Some of my university colleagues would dismiss prayer itself as ridiculous mumbo jumbo, some kind of infantile incantation by which naive people think they can influence events.

At any rate, here was a new label. It could even be applied with some respect by those who were using for their comparison such thinkers as Paracelsus. And at a time when "new age" religion even among the educated included mind-altering drugs, astrology, and crystals, it could be high praise to say of Joseph Smith that he was a magus. It could also, of course, be a dismissive form of guilt by association.[41]

7. Mystic. I don't know who first suggested that Joseph Smith might be a kind of mystic. I. Woodbridge Riley used the term rather loosely, as previously noted. Paul M. Edwards, a direct descendant of the Prophet and a leader in the Reorganized Church of Jesus Christ of Latter Day Saints, has suggested that the term describes the tendency in the Smith family, and of course especially in the Prophet, to seek and make contact with the divine.[42] They were not ordinary, practical people, so to speak, but were in some sense mystics.

For those already familiar with others of the nineteenth century of whom the same might be said, this usage has the advantage of making the Smith experiences intelligible. In a valuable corrective to the perception that Americans were all hard-nosed, down-to earth types, Hal Bridges has surveyed several examples of what he called "American mysticism."[43] What we need is a frame of reference in which to place Joseph Smith. This term therefore offers certain advantages. All too often modern people, approaching the subject without any awareness of the larger picture, are quick to see uniqueness, or craziness, in attitudes that had many parallels. If mysticism serves the purpose of breaking down barriers to an understanding of Smith, I suggest, let it be used.

For myself, I find it unhelpful. Bridges's working definition of mysticism is that it "is selfless, direct, transcendent, unitive experience of God or ultimate reality, and the experiment's interpretation of that experience."[44] It seems to exclude the revelations of Joseph Smith, which were not selfless and not unitive. He never lost his own identity, never merged or melted into the divine. I agree with Max Nolan that Joseph Smith's revelations simply do not fit the definitions of classical mysticism as expounded by Plotinus or, closer to the present, St. John of the Cross.[45] There is no real union with the divine in Joseph's experiences, no "flight of the alone to the alone," as Plotinus put it. Nor were his experiences ineffable except in the sense that they could not be fully communicated, for many of them in fact did convey precise messages, even elaborate teachings and instructions.

For strict secularists, of course, both St. Theresa of Avila and Joseph Smith were not to be taken seriously. For them, any genuine connection with God, however we describe it, is quite out of the question. But for those who have become familiar with the literature on mysticism, both Christian and non-Christian, and have some respect for the validity of that experience, perhaps the willingness to accept the possibility of continued interaction between God and humans leaves the door open for the kind of revelations Joseph Smith described.[46]

8. Psychopath. In a general sense, people in Joseph Smith's lifetime could describe him as "crazy," but it was not until the rise of psychology as a learned discipline that the exact nature of his supposed mental derangement could be discussed with any real specificity. The first serious psychological interpretation was that of I. Woodbridge Riley. A little later, Bernard DeVoto, who had his own problems with Mormonism and who had apparently come across some popularized Freudianism, advanced the theory that Joseph Smith was afflicted with paranoia.[47] Neither epilepsy nor paranoia has credibility. After examining the literature, T. L. Brink has no hesitation in rejecting these claims. "No category [of] disease, neurological or psychiatric," he writes, "can account for the complexity of Smith's behavior, or its social dimension."[48]

A thoughtful effort to understand the psychology of Joseph Smith has come from historian Lawrence Foster.[49] Drawing from anthropologist Anthony F. C. Wallace, Foster says that "far from being unique, Joseph Smith's first vision and related experiences were almost a classic model of such phenomena in all times and cultures." Although Foster does not accept the historicity of the First Vision in the literal sense, he is remarkably willing to concede its sincerity and even a kind of validity:

> Even if Joseph's visions reflected his own personal psychology rather than contact with beings from another dimension of reality, the perceived source of a vision by no means determines whether the message itself is not also true in some deeper sense.
>
> Joseph Smith was one of the most complex individuals who ever lived; if he interpreted the deeply felt inner truth of his prophetic mission as an objective experience, that interpretation in no way invalidates the truth of the mission itself. Surely if God works through fallible human agency, then it may well be that he has to operate at times through psychological experiences perceived as literally true. This may be necessary in order to communicate a complex divine message to the limited human agents through whom that message must be transmitted.[50]

More recently, in 1992, Foster advanced a more specific psychological interpretation—that Joseph Smith was a manic-depressive.[51] Not a psychiatrist or psychologist, Foster bases his interpretation on a survey of the literature. Several of the characteristics now associated with manic depression were found in the Mormon prophet's life, especially at the end: he was expansive and grandiose, manically enthusiastic, sexually hyperactive, and of course intermittently depressed. To his credit, Foster was both tentative and careful in his conclusions.

If Joseph Smith was manic-depressive to any degree, even though this may explain some of his characteristic reactions, it did not prevent him from being enormously productive in both ideas and institutional innovations. Foster, who is not Mormon, may not agree with the religious views, but he knows that validity is independent of the subject's mental or physical condition. He quotes William James: "If there were such a thing as inspiration from a higher realm, it might well be that the neurotic temperament would furnish the chief condition of the requisite receptivity."[52]

A variation is the interpretation of LDS Jungian psychiatrist C. Jess Groesbeck, who sees family dynamics as crucial.[53] Reading through the details of the family history as recalled by Joseph's mother, Lucy Mack Smith, Groesbeck discerns serious tension between the father and the mother. Obsessed with a search for the true church, she sought answers in organized religion. Joseph Sr., on the other hand, was clinically depressed as a result of losing the family's resources in speculation. He had a series of dreams, which Groesbeck interprets, sometimes on multiple levels, as a reflection of the frustration, the differences between husband and wife, and the longing for a solution. For a time, Alvin, the oldest son, played the role of healer and breadwinner. After Alvin's tragic death, Hyrum and Joseph had to take over. Joseph's visions and founding of the Church, therefore, served the purpose not only of restoring the true church but also of solving a family problem—bringing father and mother back together.

Groesbeck is careful not to deny the reality of the First Vision, "a remarkable, compensatory collective response from the archetypal level of the psyche in which multiple, significant problems were resolved for Joseph himself, his father, for his mother and other members of his family, for his forefathers, and"—note the jump from the individual and familial to the universal—"finally for many others in his generation."[54]

In the early 1990s, William D. Morain, an orthopedic surgeon, and Robert D. Anderson, a Freudian psychiatrist, separately interpreted Joseph Smith largely in terms of his childhood operation.[55] My original reaction is to be unconvinced. As William James wrote of the early Roman Catholic effort to explain Luther's Reformation as the result of his desire to marry a nun: "The effects are infinitely wider than the alleged causes, and for the most part opposite in nature."[56] Anderson's detailed correlation of the members of the Smith family with those of Lehi's family in the Book of Mormon is similarly deficient.[57]

9. Genius. A term quite readily used by many now to describe Joseph Smith is genius. We find in Fawn Brodie a kind of reluctant concession to his creativity, the extraordinary quality of his imagination. Historian Jan Shipps has used this term as well, although she has also suggested that Joseph can be fruitfully considered to be a kind of prodigy.[58] Lawrence Foster, while seeing manic depression as the underlying condition, is also not reluctant to concede genius to Smith. The term had been used by William James in describing many religious innovators.

In 1992 Yale literary scholar Harold Bloom devoted a surprising number of pages to Joseph Smith.[59] Using a term made fashionable by Max Weber, Bloom praises Smith's charisma: "Whatever account of charisma is accepted, the Mormon prophet possessed that quality to a degree unsurpassed in American history." But it is not Joseph Smith's charismatic leadership that is Bloom's main interest but rather his "imaginative vitality." As a "Jewish Gnostic," Bloom is not expressing belief in Joseph Smith, but his admiration is unsparing: "My observation certainly does find enormous validity in Smith's imaginative recapture of crucial elements in the archaic Jewish religion, elements evaded by normative Judaism, and by the Church after it. The God of Joseph Smith is a daring revival of the God of some of the Kabbalists and Gnostics, prophetic sages who, like Smith himself, asserted that they had returned to the true religion of Yahweh or Jehovah."[60] However we might agree or disagree with Bloom's analysis, or his emphasis, he is clearly quite willing to see Joseph Smith as "an authentic religious genius."[61]

What all of these explanatory models have in common is a professed desire to understand Joseph Smith by putting him into a recognized category but one that avoids the uncomfortable alternatives of true prophet or fraud. Those who have advanced the newer interpretations intend to be complimentary or at least to separate themselves from those who are simply shouting denunciations. Some of these authors even cling to a belief in Joseph Smith's prophetic calling, simply arguing that God, as in biblical times, used someone shaped by secondary influences. Others among the modern writers by no means accept Joseph as a prophet but obviously admire him and do not wish to be among his old-fashioned denouncers. In that sense, they see themselves as occupying a middle ground.

Most believing Mormons are unfamiliar with these scholarly reappraisals. To the extent that they might find such analyses convincing, however, they would simply insist on combining models. If Joseph Smith was a political leader, for example, he was for them a prophet, part of whose role, as circumstances developed, was also to provide political leadership. If Joseph challenged the skeptics of his time, he was simply doing what a prophet does, under divine inspiration, in speaking to the needs of his generation. If he was a magician or magus, his followers would say, he was one selected by God and who then moved into the larger, vastly more significant role of prophet. If he was a mystic (a term most Latter-day Saints would not find descriptive of their founder), he was one who, far from focusing his primary concern on his own union with the divine, transformed his vocation into that of prophetically mediating between God and human beings. They would not relish a term like psychopath but, with William James, might well accept the idea that God takes a person with a given set of strengths and weaknesses—personal and familial, psychological and physical—and uses that person as an instrument. The same would be true of Joseph as genius. Of the many who have a high intelligence quotient, a few achieve greatness in different areas of life. The significant thing for believing Latter-day Saints would be that God selected this particular genius, if you will, and used him. Cutting through to the heart of the matter, they are usually content to see Joseph Smith as a prophet.

Notes

1. Charles Mackay, *History of the Mormons: or, Latter-day Saints, with Memoirs of the Life and Death of Joseph Smith, the "American Mahomet"* (Auburn, N.Y.: Derby and Miller, 1852). On Mackay as a historian, see Leonard J. Arrington, "Charles Mackay and His 'True and Impartial History' of the Mormons," *Utah Historical Quarterly* 36 (Winter 1968): 24–40.

2. Lucy Mack Smith, *Biographical Sketches of Joseph Smith the Prophet, and His Progenitors for Many Generations* (Liverpool: Latter-day Saints' Book Depot, 1853). A "corrected" edition was published in Salt Lake City in 1902. RLDS editions were published in 1880, 1908, and 1912.

3. Jan Shipps, "The Prophet, His Mother, and Early Mormonism: Mother Smith's History as a Passageway to Understanding," mimeograph, LDS Church History Library.

4. Edward W. Tullidge, *Life of Joseph, the Prophet* (New York: Tullidge & Crandall, 1878; rpt. Plano, Ill.: Board of Publication of the Reorganized Church of Jesus Christ of Latter Day Saints, 1880). On Tullidge as a historian, see Davis Bitton and Leonard J. Arrington, *Mormons and Their Historians* (Salt Lake City: University of Utah Press, 1988).

5. See my "Mormonism's Encounter with Spiritualism," in my compilation of essays, *The Ritualization of Mormon History and Other Essays* (Urbana: University of Illinois Press, 1994).

6. George Q. Cannon, *The Life of Joseph Smith, the Prophet* (Salt Lake City: Juvenile Instructor Office, 1888). A second edition appeared in 1907 followed by a Tahitian translation in 1925.

7. I. Woodbridge Riley, *The Founder of Mormonism: A Psychological Study of Joseph Smith, Jr.* (New York: Dodd Mead & Co., 1902). Additional quotations from this source are cited parenthetically in the text.

8. William James, *The Varieties of Religious Experience: A Study in Human Nature* (New York: Longmans, Green, and Co., 1902). He had been discussing the revelations of Mohammed, which are pronounced "from the unconscious sphere." Then: "In the case of Joseph Smith (who had prophetic revelations innumerable in addition to the revealed translation of the old plates which resulted in the Book of Mormon), although there may have been a motor element, the inspiration seems to have been predominantly sensorial." The "peep-stones" were "apparently a case

of crystal-gazing." James gives no real analysis of the revelations in the Doctrine and Covenants, which one might think would attract the scholar's interest. He does reproduce an interesting letter from "an eminent Mormon" (I am guessing it was Joseph F. Smith), including this statement: "This Church has at its head a prophet, seer, and revelator, who gives to man God's holy will. Revelation is the means through which the will of God is declared directly and in fullness to man. These revelations are got through dreams of sleep or in waking visions of the mind, by voices without visional appearance, or by actual manifestations of the Holy Presence before the eye. We believe that God has come in person and spoken to our prophet and revelator."

9. John Henry Evans, *Joseph Smith: An American Prophet* (New York: Macmillan, 1933).

10. Ibid., 427–28.

11. Preston Nibley, *Joseph Smith, the Prophet* (Salt Lake City: Deseret News Press, 1944).

12. Fawn M. Brodie, *No Man Knows My History: The Life of Joseph Smith, the Mormon Prophet,* 2d ed. rev. (1945; New York: Alfred A. Knopf, 1971). The second edition is substantially unchanged but also has an afterword.

13. Bitton and Arrington, *Mormons and Their Historians*, 111–15.

14. "An Appraisal of the So-Called Brodie Book," *LDS Church News*, May 11, 1946.

15. Hugh Nibley, *No Ma'am, That's Not History: A Brief Review of Mrs. Brodie's Reluctant Vindication of a Prophet She Seeks to Expose* (Salt Lake City: Bookcraft, 1946). Incorporating the changes of subsequent editions, is his *Tinkling Cymbals and Sounding Brass,* edited by David J. Whittaker (Salt Lake City: Deseret Book/ Provo, Utah: Foundation for Ancient Research and Mormon Studies, 1991).

16. Ibid., 34.

17. Louis Midgley, "The Brodie Connection: Thomas Jefferson and Joseph Smith," *BYU Studies* 20 (Fall 1979): 59–67. On the Nixon biography, see Frank Gannon, "The Good Dog Richard Affair," in *Orthodoxy: The American Spectator Anniversary Anthology,* edited by R. Emmett Tyrell Jr. (New York: Harper & Row, 1987), 442–52. For a general evaluation of Brodie, see F. L. Stewart, *Exploding the Myth about Joseph Smith, the Mormon Prophet* (New York: House of Stewart Publishing, 1967).

18. John A. Widtsoe, *Joseph Smith: Seeker after Truth, Prophet of God* (Salt Lake City: Deseret News, 1951).

19. Wesley P. Walters, "New Light on Mormon Origins from the Palmyra Revival," *Evangelical Theological Society Bulletin* 10 (1967): 227–41; and *Dialogue: A Journal of Mormon Thought* 4 (Spring 1969): 60–81.

20. Rodger I. Anderson, *Joseph Smith's New York Reputation Reexamined* (Salt Lake City: Signature Books, 1990), critically reviewed by Richard Lloyd Anderson in *Review of Books on the Book of Mormon* 3 (1991): 52–80.

21. The easiest way to keep up with the ongoing research on the Book of Mormon on both sides is to follow FARMS publications.

22. Milton V. Backman, *Joseph Smith's First Vision* (Salt Lake City: Bookcraft, 1971). See also Milton V. Backman, *Eyewitness Accounts of the Restoration* (Salt Lake City: Deseret Book, 1983).

23. See Richard Lloyd Anderson, Review of Rodger I. Anderson, *Joseph Smith's New York Reputation Reexamined*, cited above. See also Richard L. Anderson, *Joseph Smith's New England Heritage* (Salt Lake City: Deseret Book, 1971).

24. In addition to Nibley, *No Ma'am, That's Not History*, see also Hugh Nibley, *Censoring the Joseph Smith Story* (Salt Lake City: Deseret Book, 1961); and his *The Myth Makers* (Salt Lake City: Deseret Book, 1961).

25. Bitton, *The Ritualization of Mormon History*.

26. Donna Hill, *Joseph Smith, the First Mormon* (Garden City, N.Y.: Doubleday, 1977).

27. Richard Lyman Bushman, *Joseph Smith and the Beginnings of Mormonism* (Urbana: University of Illinois Press, 1984).

28. In time for the bicentennial of Joseph Smith's birth, Bushman's full biography appeared: Richard Lyman Bushman, *Joseph Smith: Rough Stone Rolling* (New York: Alfred A. Knopf, 2005). Another biography taking a thoroughly naturalistic approach is Dan Vogel, *Joseph Smith: The Making of a Prophet* (Salt Lake City: Signature Books, 2004).

29. Klaus J. Hansen, *Quest for Empire: The Political Kingdom of God and the Council of Fifty in Mormon History* (East Lansing: Michigan State University Press, 1967).

30. Joseph Smith Jr. et al., *History of the Church of Jesus Christ of Latter-day Saints*, edited by B. H. Roberts, 2d ed. rev. (6 vols., 1902–12, Vol. 7, 1932), 6:364.

31. Insisting that Joseph's kingship was connected with the temple ceremonies and was decidedly not of this world is Gordon C. Thomasson, "Foolsmate," *Dialogue: A Journal of Mormon Thought* 6 (Autumn–Winter 1971): 148–51.

32. Marvin S. Hill, *Quest for Refuge: The Mormon Flight from American Pluralism* (Salt Lake City: Signature Books, 1989).

33. The most penetrating review, by Gordon D. Pollock, criticizes Hill for a feeble, naive definition of class and an unclear understanding of pluralism. *Journal for the Scientific Study of Religion* 29 (1990): 418–19.

34. Kenneth H. Winn, *Exiles in a Land of Liberty: Mormons in America, 1830–1846* (Chapel Hill: University of North Carolina Press, 1989).

35. Robert Hullinger, *Mormonism's Answer to Skepticism: Why Joseph Smith Wrote the Book of Mormon* (St. Louis: Clayton Publishing, 1980). The work has been republished under the title *Joseph Smith's Response to Skepticism* (Salt Lake City: Signature Books, 1992).

36. Richard L. Bushman emphasizes the extent to which Joseph Smith did not use miracles as proof, but he acknowledges that this was sometimes done. Faith and the witness of the Holy Ghost are the important things: "This is our evidence." Bushman, "How Did the Prophet Joseph Smith Respond to Skepticism in His Time?" *Ensign,* February 1990, 61–63.

37. D. Michael Quinn, *Early Mormonism and the Magic World View* (Salt Lake City: Signature Books, 1987).

38. Richard L. Anderson, "The Mature Joseph Smith and Treasure Seeking," *BYU Studies* 24 (Fall 1984): 489–560; Ronald W. Walker, "Joseph Smith: The Palmyra Seer," *BYU Studies* 24 (Fall 1984): 461–72.

39. Bushman, *Joseph Smith and the Beginnings of Mormonism*, 184.

40. Stephen Robinson, Review of D. Michael Quinn, *Early Mormonism and the Magic World View* in *BYU Studies* 27 (Fall 1987): 88–95. See also reviews in the same issue by William A. Wilson and Benson Whittle.

41. Appearing after I had originally written this chapter was John L. Brooke, *The Refiner's Fire: The Making of Mormon Cosmology, 1644–1844* (Cambridge, England: Cambridge University Press, 1994), which sees Joseph Smith as one who tapped into the tradition of backwoods magic but also borrowed from something called the "hermetic" tradition, a cover term that includes a great many ingredients, to put it mildly. For my negative review of Brooke's misguided polemic, which predictably was lauded by secular professional historians and current anti-Mormons, see *BYU Studies* 34 (1994–95): 182–92.

42. Paul M. Edwards, "The Secular Smiths," *Journal of Mormon History* 4 (1977): 3–17.

43. Hal Bridges, *American Mysticism: From William James to Zen* (New York: Harper & Row, 1970).

44. Ibid., 4.

45. Max Nolan, "Joseph Smith and Mysticism," *Journal of Mormon History* 10 (1983): 105–16.

46. I am aware that the great mystics had little regard for visions and voices, although some of them experienced such manifestations. Bridges, *American Mysticism*, 7. It is instructive to review the many manifestations, often quite sensory if not sensual, of St. Theresa of Avila and St. Ignatius Loyola—both of whom lived in the sixteenth century—by comparison with the far more linear, verbal, communicative revelations of Joseph Smith.

47. Bernard DeVoto, "The Centennial of Mormonism," *American Mercury* 19 (January 1930): 1–13; see also "Joseph Smith" in *Dictionary of American Biography* (1935); Leland A. Fetzer, "Bernard DeVoto and the Mormon Tradition," *Dialogue: A Journal of Mormon Thought* 3–4 (Autumn–Winter 1971): 23–38.

48. T. L. Brink, "Joseph Smith: A Study in Analytical Psychology" (Ph.D. diss., University of Chicago, 1978), 272–73.

49 Lawrence Foster, "First Visions: Personal Observations on Joseph Smith's Religious Experience," *Sunstone* 8 (September–October 1983): 39–43.

50. Ibid., 42.

51. Lawrence Foster, "The Psychology of Religious Genius: Joseph Smith and the Origins of New Religious Movements," Paper presented at the annual meeting of the Mormon History Association, St. George, Utah, May 16, 1992.

52. Ibid.

53. C. Jess Groesbeck, "The Smiths and Their Dreams and Visions," *Sunstone*

12 (March 1988): 22–29.

54. The existence of different versions of the vision "in no way indicates that all of the aspects of the vision were not experienced in the actual event. In no way would it invalidate the vision in its complexity and intricacy as a psychic datum, answering the needs of Joseph Smith in a personal way." Ibid., 29.

55. William D. Morain, "The Sword of Laban: Joseph Smith, Jr., and the Unconscious," Paper presented at the annual meeting of the Mormon History Association, Ogden, Utah, May 1993, and his subsequent book, *The Sword of Laban: Joseph Smith, Jr., and the Dissociated Mind* (Washington, D.C.: American Psychiatric Press, 1998); Robert D. Anderson, "The Sword of Laban: The Book of Mormon as Autobiography," Paper presented at Sunstone Symposium, Salt Lake City, August 1993, and his *Inside the Mind of Joseph Smith: Psychobiography and the Book of Mormon* (Salt Lake City: Signature Books, 1999).

56. James, *The Varieties of Religious Experience*, 21 note.

57. Groesbeck, "The Smiths and Their Dreams and Visions," 73, made the following perceptive comments on Robert Anderson's paper: "There are too many things in Joseph's life that are not accounted for in the Book of Mormon and, vice versa, the Book of Mormon has too many things in it that do not just relate to Joseph's life."

58. "Joseph Smith [like Benjamin Franklin] was also a 'human multitude,' an extraordinarily talented individual—a genius beyond question." Jan Shipps, "The Prophet Puzzle: Suggestions Leading towards a More Comprehensive Interpretation of Joseph Smith," *Journal of Mormon History* 1 (1974): 19.

59. Harold Bloom, "The Religion-Making Imagination of Joseph Smith," *Yale Review* 80 (1992): 26–43; repeated and expanded in Harold Bloom, *The American Religion: The Emergence of the Post-Christian Nation* (New York: Simon & Schuster, 1992). My references here are to the article.

60. Bloom, "The Religion-Making Imagination of Joseph Smith," 29.

61. See "Four LDS Views on Harold Bloom: A Roundtable," *BYU Studies* 35, no. 1 (1995): 173–204. Introduced by M. Gerald Bradford, the essays are by Eugene England, Truman G. Madsen, Charles Randall Paul, and Richard F. Haglund Jr. Haglund's comments are especially important in recognizing the fundamental inaccuracy and political motivation of Bloom's interpretation.

Epilogue

I feel like shouting hallelujah, all the time, when I think that I ever knew Joseph Smith, the Prophet whom the Lord raised up and ordained, and to whom He gave keys to powers to build up the kingdom of God on earth and sustain it. —Brigham Young[1]

The blood of Joe Smith, spilled by murderous hands, will be like the fabled dragon's teeth sown broadcast, that every where sprang up armed men. —Horace Greeley[2]

This work has examined different images of the man Joseph Smith, friendly and unfriendly. I make no claim to having exhausted the possibilities of this kind of analysis. My *The Martyrdom Remembered: A One-Hundred-Fifty-Year Perspective on the Assassination of Joseph Smith* (Salt Lake City: Aspen Books, 1994) studies the image of that single momentous event; but other aspects of Joseph Smith's life and influence could bear an equally detailed scrutiny. My focus here, however, has not been on the facts of historical episodes but rather on the images they created in the minds of others affected by Joseph Smith.

Presuppositions and assumptions do indeed serve as lenses that select, ignore, emphasize, and frame, resulting in different perspectives and conclusions. It is a truism that people act, not according to the way things are, but the way they think they are. During his lifetime, different people perceived Joseph Smith differently and behaved accordingly. The same is true of the present. If our paradigm of reality—the map of possibilities by which we govern our lives—allows room for God, angels, miracles, prophets, and the like, we are in the population that at least potentially might follow Joseph Smith or someone like him. If our paradigm rules out such possibilities, we, of course, look for alternative explanations.[3]

Joseph Smith should not have been surprised that many in the materialistic America of the 1830s saw him as a con man; certainly, peddlers of snake oil, or their equivalent, were on every side. Many people were suspicious of all religious claims, even those of Jesus of Nazareth. The miracle, perhaps, is that Smith found some people still living within a framework more like ancient Israel's—or who could move into that framework—than Alexis de Tocqueville's America.

Who then *was* Joseph Smith? Was he a prophet of God? Let's try something easier. Was Andrew Jackson a great president? Or was Christopher Columbus a hero or a villain? Such questions do not lend themselves to answers on which everyone will agree. Clearly the presuppositions and values of the observer strongly influence the answer one finds satisfying.

Like all human beings, Joseph Smith played several roles.[4] He was a son, a brother, a husband, a father, a friend. How well he fulfilled these roles may be subject to discussion, but those related to him in these ways were staunchly loyal, holding him in the highest regard. He was also a businessman, for he dealt with money and building projects and retail stores. Some have suggested that he was sometimes naive, granting credit too readily or getting caught up in speculation.

As an administrator he can be evaluated by those trained in organizational behavior, a discipline that did not exist in his lifetime. On occasion he may have erred in his choice of advisors—one thinks especially of John C. Bennett—but he used very effectively the highly loyal Hyrum and had the vision and acuity to give increasing prominence to the Twelve Apostles.

As a leader how did Joseph Smith measure up? Because of the complexity of the concept "leadership," on which an extensive literature now exists, the question is not simple. There are different leadership styles. But of certain things there is little room for doubt. For example, Joseph had charisma; he could capture the attention of a crowd and could effectively communicate his own sincerity. Even through the terrible trials of Ohio, Missouri, and Illinois, he retained a surprisingly large portion of his following. And new disciples continued to flock in. Even those who disliked him and disdained his religion would, I think, concede that in terms of practical results he was indeed a leader.

Consideration of different roles could go on and on. As singer, for all I know, Joseph Smith may have been a disaster. As a foot racer he probably would not have led at the finish line, for his childhood surgery left him with a slight limp. As a wrestler, we happen to know that he was a tough competitor, which may say something about both his physical strength and the determination of his character.

But role theory is concerned primarily with social roles.[5] What, then, about Joseph Smith's basic claim to being a prophet of God? In a University of Chicago doctoral dissertation, T. L. Brink, after considering the old charge that Joseph Smith was an impostor, concludes: "Psychoanalysis has identified generalized patterns of imposture, and the life and behavior of Joseph Smith clearly do not conform to those patterns."[6]

But does this mean that Joseph Smith was exactly what he claimed to be? Brink's words of summary are carefully chosen: Was Joseph Smith a self-deluded enthusiast? To the extent that he was totally committed to his religious vocation, he was an enthusiast. To the extent that he confused psychic reality with physical reality, he was deluded. But to the extent that he formulated a new system of myths, symbols, rituals, and social organization, which his followers found relevant to their needs, he was a true prophet.[7] Within Brink's frame of reference, this is a highly positive evaluation. What is being said here, if I understand it correctly, is that, to those who accepted Joseph Smith as a prophet, he *was* a prophet. He functioned as a prophet; he gave them direction, communicated the will of God (or what they accepted as such), and acted as a "forthteller" in taking stock of the state of the world and calling people to a standard. He also told about the future, thus fulfilling the prophetic role of "foreteller."

The obverse of the medal is not so complimentary. To those who did not accept Joseph Smith, he was no prophet at all. To them he was indeed some kind of raving fanatic, a pretender, a megalomaniac. We are left with the different perceptions, different images. Insofar as the object of this book has been to set forth some of these images, we might well stop here. For secularists who find claims to divine calling unthinkable, for the perfectly adequate reason that, for them, God does not exist, the question *does* end here. For them it was never a serious question to begin with.

But those who believe in a God capable of revealing himself might still entertain the question. Is it possible that this man of the nineteenth century was in fact an instrument of God, someone who channeled a divine message to the human race?

Most theists, including most Christians, rule out any such possibility without feeling any obligation to examine what Joseph Smith said and did. Others have looked over the facts of his life, however cursorily, and found what they deem to be incompatibilities with his claim. For example, a true prophet would not practice polygamy, or a true prophet would not fire a revolver at his assassins. The list goes on and on.

In such statements, there is always an undisclosed syllogism by which one defines in advance the means by which God must reveal himself. Major premise: a true prophet would not do X. Minor premise: Joseph Smith did X. Conclusion: Joseph Smith was not a true prophet. The same reasoning sufficed for all who rejected the biblical prophets and indeed the messianic mission of Jesus Christ. Such logic is indeed airtight, but the conclusion is embedded in the rigid definition of the major premise.

Believers in God would agree, I think, that the one who knows who is and who is not a prophet of God—indeed, the decisive and only final authority on the subject—is God. Not claiming access to the divine mind, I, as a historian, must humbly confess my inability to proceed further *as a historian.* The tools of the historian do have limitations.

When Joseph Smith said, "No man knows my history," he was admitting that he had no way of providing such irresistible evidence in his favor that all must accept it. "Just wait and see," he was saying. "You will know later who I am." In this sense, he could easily have applied to himself the words of the Book of Mormon prophet Nephi as he takes leave of his readers: "And if they are not the words of Christ, judge ye—for Christ will show unto you, with power and great glory, that they are his words, at the last day; and you and I shall stand face to face before his bar; and ye shall know that I have been commanded of him to write these things, notwithstanding my weakness" (2 Ne. 33:11).

"God knows I am his prophet," Joseph Smith says in essence, "and some day you too will know. In the meantime, if you will sincerely pray to God, if you will put the teachings into your heart and life, confirmation is available. You will have a personal knowledge fully satisfying to yourself." At least this process seems to have what made people like Brigham Young Joseph's undeviating followers who felt like "shouting hallelujah."

Back in the days before the corruption of our language, before the flattening of our reality into a stark, naturalistic, horizontal plane, there used to be a name for the leap, the signing on to something magnificently demanding and all-encompassing, the living out of something as if it were true, the growing conviction of the reality of things hoped for, things unseen. It used to be called faith.

Notes

1. Brigham Young, October 6, 1855, *Journal of Discourses*, 26 vols. (Liverpool and London: Latter-day Saints' Book Depot, 1854–86), 3:51.

2 Horace Greeley, quoted in *Nauvoo Neighbor*, July 24, 1844.

3. This basic point is spelled out most profoundly by Kant. As it affects our

scientific understanding, the most influential work of this generation has been Thomas Kuhn, *The Structure of Scientific Revolutions* (Chicago: University Press, 1970). On a more accessible level, I like E. F. Schumacher's *A Guide for the Perplexed* (New York: Harper & Row, 1977).

4. I do not regard human beings as only the sum of the social roles they play, an oversimplification unfairly attributed to G. H. Mead.

5. J. A. Jackson, ed., *Role* (1972; rpt., New York: Cambridge University Press, 2010); Erving Goffman, *The Presentation of the Self in Everyday Life* (1956; rpt., New York: Doubleday Anchor, 1959).

6. T. L. Brink, "Joseph Smith: A Study in Analytical Psychology" (Ph.D. diss., University of Chicago, 1978), 281. Notice that Brink is writing twenty years after Phyllis Greenacre, "The Impostor," *Psychoanalytic Quarterly* 27 (1958): 359–82, quoted with approval by Fawn Brodie, *No Man Knows My History: The Life of Joseph Smith, the Mormon Prophet* (1945; 2d ed., New York: Alfred A. Knopf, 1971), 418–19.

7. Brink, "Joseph Smith: A Study in Analytical Psychology," 282.

Select Bibliography

Note: This bibliography represents its status as of November 2005 when Davis Bitton was updating the chapters in this book. If he had been alive to see the first volumes in the massive Joseph Smith Papers project appear from the newly established Church Historian's Press in 2008 and 2009, he would have been among its heartiest supporters.

A "complete" bibliography of Joseph Smith is not so easy to create as some might imagine. Setting aside for the moment the unpublished material in the LDS Church History Library and other archives, we discover that almost everything published about the Church in its first fourteen years (and to some extent afterwards) mentions Joseph Smith or relates to him by implication. Every biography of early Mormons, for example, will likely contain references to the Prophet. Anything written on any of the scriptures he produced—Book of Mormon, Doctrine and Covenants, Pearl of Great Price—relates to him at least indirectly. I do not attempt to list studies relating specifically to the scriptures here. Since 1989, *Review of Books on the Book of Mormon* has been useful in staying abreast of many such writings, but for works published earlier the task is much more challenging.

When *BYU Studies* published its index volume in 1992, covering volumes 1 to 31, the subject index under the heading "Smith, Joseph" included more than six columns of entries in small print. From 1943 to 1985, an annual Joseph Smith memorial sermon was delivered at the Institute of Religion, Utah State University. Each year several papers are presented at conventions, to say nothing of sermons or less scholarly commentary in magazines for a popular audience or the depressing wasteland of anti-Mormon pamphlets. Although some might smile at the comparison, Joseph Smith, like Shakespeare and Montaigne, Petrarch and Luther, Emerson and Marx, shows every indication of inspiring a continued interest and thus an uninterrupted flow of scholarship year after year after year.

The following works are not necessarily "recommended" titles and are certainly not all equal in value. While I have deliberately omitted some of the sermons on the one side and some of the irresponsible diatribes on the other, the list still includes works that those on either extreme would dismiss as worthless. Of the many sermons, editorials, and newspaper articles mentioning Joseph Smith I have here listed only a few.

An alternative bibliography covering much of the same ground but differing in emphasis is David J. Whittaker, "Joseph Smith in Recent Research: A Selected Bibliography," in David J. Whittaker, ed., *Mormon Americana: A Guide to Sources and Collections in the United States* (Provo, Utah: BYU Studies, 1995).

Published Primary Sources

Arrington, Leonard J., ed. "James Gordon Bennett's 1831 Report on 'The Mormonites.'" *BYU Studies* 10 (Spring 1970): 353–64.

Burton, Alma P., comp. *Discourses of the Prophet Joseph Smith.* Salt Lake City: Deseret Book, 1977.

Cannon, Brian Q. "John C. Calhoun, Jr., Meets the Prophet Joseph Smith Shortly before the Departure for Carthage." *BYU Studies* 33 (1993): 772–80.

Cannon, Donald Q. "Reverend George Moore Comments on Nauvoo, the Mormons, and Joseph Smith." *Western Illinois Regional Studies* 5 (1982): 5–16.

———. *The Wisdom of Joseph Smith.* Orem, Utah: Grandin Books, 1983.

Cannon, Donald Q., and Larry E. Dahl. *The Prophet Joseph Smith's King Follett Discourse.* Provo, Utah: BYU Religious Studies Center, 1983.

Cook, Lyndon W., ed. "'A More Virtuous Man Never Existed on the Footstool of the Great Jehovah': George Miller on Joseph Smith." *BYU Studies* 19 (Spring 1979): 402–7.

Cook, Lyndon W. *The Revelations of the Prophet Joseph Smith: A Historical and Biographical Commentary of the Doctrine and Covenants.* Provo, Utah: Seventy's Mission Bookstore, 1981.

Ehat, Andrew F., and Lyndon W. Cook, eds. *The Words of Joseph Smith: The Contemporary Accounts of the Nauvoo Discourses of the Prophet Joseph.* Provo, Utah: Brigham Young University Press, 1980.

Faulring, Scott H., ed. *An American Prophet's Record: The Diaries and Journals of Joseph Smith.* Salt Lake City: Signature Books, 1987.

Heidt, Stephen C., comp. *Un-Canonized Revelations of the Prophet Joseph Smith.* N.p: Oquirrh Mountain Publishing, 1994.

Huntress, Keith. *Murder of an American Prophet: Events and Prejudice Surrounding the Killings of Joseph and Hyrum Smith; Carthage, Illinois, June 27, 1844.* San Francisco: Chandler Publishing, 1960.

Jessee, Dean C., ed. "Howard Coray's Recollections of Joseph Smith." *BYU Studies* 17 (Spring 1977): 341–47.

———. *The Papers of Joseph Smith.* 2 vols. *Vol. 1: Autobiographical and Historical Writings.* Salt Lake City: Deseret Book, 1989; *Vol. 2: Journals, 1832–1842.* Salt Lake City: Deseret Books, 1992.

———. *The Personal Writings of Joseph Smith.* Salt Lake City: Deseret Book, 1984.

Jones, Dan. "The Martyrdom of Joseph Smith and His Brother Hyrum." *BYU Studies* 24 (Winter 1984): 78–109.

Kirkham, Francis W. *A New Witness for Christ in America.* 2 vols. Independence, Mo.: Zion's Printing and Publishing, 1942–51.

Marquardt, H. Michael, ed. *Joseph Smith's 1832–34 Diary; Also, Joseph Smith's 1832 Account of His Early Life.* Salt Lake City: Modern Microfilm, 1979.

———. *Joseph Smith's 1835–36 Diary.* Salt Lake City: Modern Microfilm, 1979.

Millet, Robert L., ed. *Joseph Smith: Selected Sermons and Writings.* In Sources of American Spirituality Series. New York/Mahwah, NJ: Paulist Press, 1989.

Nelson, Leland R., comp. *The Journal of Joseph: The Personal Diary of a Modern Prophet.* Provo, Utah: Council Press, 1979.

Partridge, G. F., ed. "The Death of a Mormon Dictator." *New England Quarterly* 9 (1936): 583–617.

Smith, Joseph, Jr., et al. *History of the Church of Jesus Christ of Latter-day Saints.* Edited by B. H. Roberts, 2d ed. rev. 6 vols. Salt Lake City: Deseret News, 1902–12. Vol. 7. Salt Lake City: Deseret News, 1932. Salt Lake City: Deseret Book, 1970 printing.

———. "General Smith's Views of the Powers and Policy of the Government of the United States." *Dialogue: A Journal of Mormon Thought* 3, no. 3 (Autumn 1968): 28–34.

Smith, Joseph Fielding, comp. *Teachings of the Prophet Joseph Smith.* Salt Lake City: Deseret Book, 1976 printing.

Van Wagoner, Richard S., and Steven C. Walker, eds. "The Joseph/Hyrum Smith Funeral Sermon." *BYU Studies* 23 (Winter 1983): 3–18.

Books

Anderson, Mary Audentia. *Ancestry and Posterity of Joseph Smith and Emma Hale*. Independence, Mo.: Herald House, 1929.

Anderson, Richard Lloyd. *Joseph Smith's New England Heritage*. Salt Lake City: Deseret Book, 1971.

———. *"His Mother's Manuscript": An Intimate View of Joseph Smith*. Provo, Utah: Brigham Young University, 1976.

Anderson, Rodger I. *Joseph Smith's New York Reputation Reexamined*. Salt Lake City: Signature Books, 1990.

Andrus, Hyrum. *Joseph Smith: The Man and the Seer*. Salt Lake City: Deseret Book, 1960.

———. *Joseph Smith and World Government*. Salt Lake City: Deseret Book, 1958.

Andrus, Hyrum L., and Helen Mae Andrus, comps. *They Knew the Prophet*. Salt Lake City: Bookcraft, 1974.

Backman, Milton V. *Eyewitness Accounts of the Restoration*. Salt Lake City: Deseret Book, 1983.

———. *Joseph Smith and the Doctrine and Covenants*. Salt Lake City: Deseret Book, 1992.

———. *Joseph Smith's First Vision: The First Vision in Its Historical Context*. Salt Lake City: Bookcraft, 1971.

———. *Joseph Smith's First Vision: Confirming Evidences and Contemporary Accounts*. 2d ed., rev. and enl. Salt Lake City: Bookcraft, 1980.

Barrett, Ivan J. *Great Moments in the Life of Joseph Smith*. Provo, Utah: Brigham Young University Press, 1963.

———. *Joseph Smith, the Extraordinary*. Provo, Utah: Brigham Young University Press, 1964.

———. *The Last Seven Days of the Life of Joseph Smith*. Provo, Utah: Brigham Young University, 1962.

Beardsley, Harry M. *Joseph Smith and His Mormon Empire*. Boston: Houghton Mifflin, 1931.

Bennett, John C. *The History of the Saints: An Exposé of Joe Smith and Mormonism*. Boston: Leland & Whiting, 1842.

Berrett, William E., Lowell L. Bennion, and T. Edgar Lyon. *Contributions of Joseph Smith*. Salt Lake City: Deseret Book, 1940.

Bitton, Davis. *The Martyrdom Remembered: A One-Hundred-Fifty-Year Perspective on the Assassination of Joseph Smith*. Salt Lake City: Aspen Books, 1994.

Black, Susan Easton, and Charles D. Tate Jr., eds. *Joseph Smith: The Prophet, the Man*. Provo, Utah: BYU Religious Studies Center, 1993.

Blake, Reed. *24 Hours to Martyrdom*. Salt Lake City: Bookcraft, 1973.

Bloom, Harold. *The American Religion: The Emergence of the Post-Christian Nation*. New York: Simon & Schuster, 1992.

Brewster, Hoyt W., Jr. *Martyrs of the Kingdom*. Salt Lake City: Bookcraft, 1990.

Briggs, Kay W. *Brother Joseph: Stories and Lessons from the Life of the Prophet*. Salt Lake City: Bookcraft, 1994.

Brodie, Fawn M. *No Man Knows My History: The Life of Joseph Smith the Mormon Prophet*. New York: Alfred A. Knopf, 1945.

Bushman, Richard L. *Joseph Smith and the Beginnings of Mormonism*. Urbana: University of Illinois Press, 1984.

______. *Joseph Smith and Skepticism*. Provo, Utah: Brigham Young University Press, 1974.

Cannon, George Q. *The Latter-day Prophet: History of Joseph Smith Written for Young People*. Salt Lake City: Juvenile Instructor, 1900.

______. *The Life of Joseph Smith, the Prophet*. Salt Lake City: Juvenile Instructor Office, 1888. Rpt., Salt Lake City: Deseret Book, 1986.

Carmer, Carl. *The Farm Boy and the Angel*. Garden City, N.Y.: Doubleday, 1970.

Caswall, Henry. *The Prophet of the Nineteenth Century*. London: Rivingtons, 1843.

Chase, Daryl. *Joseph the Prophet: As He Lives in the Hearts of His People*. Salt Lake City: Deseret Book, 1944.

Cheville, Roy A. *Joseph and Emma Smith: Companions for Seventeen and a Half Years, 1827–1844*. Independence, Mo.: Herald Publishing House, 1977.

Clark, George Edward. *I Cry Joseph: Fifty-four Evidences of the Divine Calling of Joseph Smith*. N.p., privately published, 1952.

Conkling, J. Christopher. *A Joseph Smith Chronology*. Salt Lake City: Deseret Book, 1979.

Cook, Lyndon W. *Joseph Smith and the Law of Consecration*. Provo, Utah: Grandin Book Company, 1985.

Crowther, Duane S. *The Life of Joseph Smith, 1805–1844*. Bountiful, Utah: Horizon Publishers, 1989.

______. *The Prophecies of Joseph Smith*. Salt Lake City: Bookcraft, 1963.

Curtis, Lindsay R. *The Making of a Prophet*. Salt Lake City: Deseret Book, 1967.

Doxey, Stephen B. *Joseph Smith and the Constitution: A Subjective Analysis*. N.p., 1985.

Draper, Maurice L. *The Founding Prophet: An Administrative Biography of Joseph Smith Jr.* Independence, Mo.: Herald Publishing House, 1991.

Durham, G. Homer. *Joseph Smith: Prophet-Statesman.* Salt Lake City: Bookcraft, 1944.

Evans, John Henry. *Joseph Smith: An American Prophet.* New York: Macmillan, 1933. Reprinted, 1943, 1946, 1961, 1966, 1985, 1989.

Fischer, Norma J. *Portrait of a Prophet.* Salt Lake City: Bookcraft, 1960.

Gibbons, Francis M. *Joseph Smith: Martyr, Prophet of God.* Salt Lake City: Deseret Book, 1977.

Gibbons, Ted. *Like a Lamb to the Slaughter.* Orem, Utah: Keepsake Paperbacks, 1990.

Gillmor, B. F. *Joseph Smith, The Mormon Prophet: A Study of a Religious Psychopath.* Kansas City: Medical Herald, 1914.

Grant, Carter E. *Important Events during the 38½ Years of the Prophet's Life.* Sandy, Utah: Privately published, 1960.

Gregg, Thomas. *The Prophet of Palmyra: Mormonism Reviewed and Examined in the Life, Character, and Career of Its Founder.* New York: John B. Alden, 1890.

Hartshorn, Leon R. *Joseph Smith, Prophet of the Restoration.* Salt Lake City: Deseret Book, 1970.

Heinerman, John. *Joseph Smith and Natural Foods.* Manti, Utah: Mountain Valley Productions, 1976.

________. *Joseph Smith and Herbal Medicine.* Monrovia, Calif.: Majority of One Press, 1980.

Hill, Donna. *Joseph Smith: The First Mormon.* Garden City, N.Y.: Doubleday, 1977.

Hogan, Mervin B. *Joseph Smith and Free Masonry.* Salt Lake City: Author, 1983.

________. *Joseph Smith, Man and Mason.* Salt Lake City: Author, 1983.

________. *Joseph Smith, The Frontier Prophet.* Salt Lake City: Author, 1987.

________. *Joseph Smith's Embracement of Freemasonry.* Salt Lake City: Author, 1988.

________. *The Two Joseph Smith Masonic Experiences.* Salt Lake City: Author, 1987.

Howard, Marcia. *Joseph Hears God's Call.* Independence, Mo.: Herald House, 1982.

Howard, Richard P. *Restoration Scriptures: A Study of Their Textual Development.* Independence, Mo.: Reorganized Church of Jesus Christ of Latter Day Saints, Department of Religious Education, 1969.

Hullinger, Robert N. *The Mormon Answer to Skepticism: Why Joseph Smith Wrote the Book of Mormon.* St. Louis: Clayton Publishing House, 1980. Reprinted as *Joseph Smith's Response to Skepticism.* Salt Lake City: Signature Books, 1992.

Jackson, Ronald Vern. *The Seer, Joseph Smith: His Education from the Most High.* Salt Lake City: Hawkes Publications, 1977.

Johnson, J. Edward. *Joseph Smith.* Berkeley, Calif.: Gillick Press, 1944.

Jones, Gracia N. *The Priceless Gifts: Celebrating the Holidays with Joseph and Emma Smith.* Murray, Utah: Roylance Publishing, 1989.

Lundwall, N. B., ed. *The Fate of the Persecutors of the Prophet Joseph Smith.* Salt Lake City: Bookcraft, 1952.

McCloud, Susan Evans. *Joseph Smith: A Photobiography.* Salt Lake City: Aspen Books, 1992.

McConkie, Mark L. *The Father of the Prophet: Stories and Insights from the Life of Joseph Smith Sr.* Salt Lake City: Bookcraft, 1993.

McConkie, Joseph Fielding. *His Name Shall Be Joseph: Ancient Prophecies of the Latter-day Seer.* Salt Lake City: Hawkes Publishing, 1980.

McConkie, Joseph Fielding, and Robert L. Millet. *Joseph Smith: The Choice Seer.* Salt Lake City: Bookcraft, 1996.

Madsen, Truman. *Joseph Smith among the Prophets.* Salt Lake City: Deseret Book, 1965. Pamphlet.

______. *Joseph Smith the Prophet.* Salt Lake City: Bookcraft, 1989.

Matthews, Robert J. *"A Plainer Translation": Joseph Smith's Translation of the Bible: A History and Commentary.* Provo, Utah: Brigham Young University Press, 1975.

Millet, Robert L., ed. *"To Be Learned Is Good If. . ."*. Salt Lake City: Bookcraft, 1987. Separate chapters listed below under articles.

Morris, Nephi L. *Prophecies of Joseph Smith and Their Fulfillment.* Salt Lake City: Deseret Book, 1920.

Nibley, Hugh. *Eduard Meyer's Comparison of Mohammed and Joseph Smith.* Provo, Utah: FARMS, 1987.

______. *Tinkling Cymbals and Sounding Brass: The Art of Telling Tales about Joseph Smith and Brigham Young.* Salt Lake City: Deseret Book and Provo, Utah: FARMS, 1991. Includes *No, Ma'am, That's Not History: A Brief Review of Mrs. Brodie's Reluctant Vindication of a Prophet She Seeks to Expose* (1946); *Censoring the Joseph Smith Story* (1961); and *The Myth Makers* (1961).

Nibley, Preston. *Joseph Smith, the Prophet.* Salt Lake City: Deseret News Press, 1946.

Parry, Edwin F., comp. *Stories about Joseph Smith the Prophet*. Salt Lake City: Deseret News, 1934.

Parry, Jay A., and Steven Songer. *Joseph Smith: The Boy . . . The Prophet*. Salt Lake City: Bookcraft, 1981.

Persuitte, David. *Joseph Smith and the Origins of the Book of Mormon*. Jefferson, N.C.: McFarland, 1985. Reviewed in *Review of Books on the Book of Mormon* 1 (1990).

Petersen, Mark E. *The Forerunners*. Salt Lake City: Bookcraft, 1979.

Peterson, LaMar. *Hearts Made Glad: The Charges of Intemperance against Joseph Smith, the Mormon Prophet*. Salt Lake City: Dumac Press, 1975.

Porter, Larry C., and Susan Easton Black, eds. *The Prophet Joseph: Essays on the Life and Mission of Joseph Smith*. Salt Lake City: Deseret Book, 1988. Separate chapters listed below under articles.

Pratt, David N. *Joseph Smith: America's Son of Perdition*. Unity, Maine: Privately printed, 1988.

Proctor, Scot Facer, and Maurine Jensen Proctor. *Witness of the Light: A Photographic Journey in the Footsteps of the American Prophet Joseph Smith*. Salt Lake City: Deseret Book, 1991.

Quinn, D. Michael. *Early Mormonism and the Magic World View*. Salt Lake City: Signature Books, 1987.

Riley, I. Woodbridge. *The Founder of Mormonism: A Psychological Study of Joseph Smith Jr*. London: William Heinemann, 1903.

Roberts, B. H. *Joseph Smith, the Prophet-Teacher*. 1908; rpt., Princeton, N.J.: Deseret Club of Princeton University, 1967.

Sampson, Joe. *Written by the Finger of God: A Testimony of Joseph Smith's Translations: Decoding Ancient Languages*. N.p.: Wellspring Publishing, 1994.

Smith, Henry A. *The Day They Martyred the Prophet*. Salt Lake City: Bookcraft, 1963.

Stewart, F. L. *Exploding the Myth about Joseph Smith, the Mormon Prophet*. New York: House of Stewart Publications, 1967.

Stewart, John J. *Joseph Smith, Democracy's Unknown Prophet*. Salt Lake City: Mercury Publishing, 1960.

———. *Joseph Smith: The Mormon Prophet*. Salt Lake City: Mercury Publishing, 1966.

Stokes, William Lee. *Joseph Smith and the Creation*. Salt Lake City: Starstone, 1991.

Tanner, Jerald, and Sandra Tanner. *Joseph Smith and Polygamy*. Salt Lake City: Modern Microfilm, 1966.

______. *Joseph Smith and Money Digging*. Salt Lake City: Modern Microfilm, 1970.

Taves, Ernest H. *Trouble Enough: Joseph Smith and the Book of Mormon*. Buffalo, N.Y.: Prometheus Books, 1984.

Tinney, Thomas Milton. *The Royal Family of the Prophet Joseph Smith Jr.* Salt Lake City: Green Family Organization, 1973.

Tracy, Shannon M. *In Search of Joseph*. Orem, Utah: Kenning House, 1995.

Tullidge, Edward. *Life of Joseph Smith, the Prophet*. New York: Privately printed, 1878.

Underwood, Grant. *The Millenarian World of Early Mormonism*. Urbana: University of Illinois Press, 1993.

Widtsoe, John A. *Joseph Smith as a Scientist*. Salt Lake City: General Board of the Young Men's Mutual Improvement Association, 1908.

______. *Joseph Smith: Seeker after Truth, Prophet of God*. Salt Lake City: Deseret News, 1951.

Articles

Alexander, Thomas G. "'A New and Everlasting Covenant': An Approach to the Theology of Joseph Smith." In *New Views of Mormon History: Essays in Honor of Leonard J. Arrington*, edited by Davis Bitton and Maureen Ursenbach Beecher. Salt Lake City: University of Utah Press, 1987, 43–62.

______. "The Place of Joseph Smith in the Development of American Religion: A Historiographical Inquiry." *Journal of Mormon History* 5 (1978): 3–17.

Allaman, John Lee. "Joseph Smith's Visits to Henderson County." *Western Illinois Regional Studies* 8 (Spring 1985): 46–55.

Allen, James B. "Emergence of a Fundamental: The Expanding Role of Joseph Smith's First Vision in Mormon Religious Thought." *Journal of Mormon History* 7 (1980): 43–61.

______. "The Significance of Joseph Smith's First Vision in Mormon Thought," *Dialogue: A Journal of Mormon Thought* 1 (Autumn 1966): 29–45.

Anderson, A. Gary. "The Mack Family and Marlow, New Hampshire." In *Regional Studies in Latter-day Saint Church History: New England*. Edited by Donald Q. Cannon (Provo, Utah: BYU Department of Church History and Doctrine, 1988), 43–52.

Anderson, Richard Lloyd. "Circumstantial Confirmation of the First Vision through Reminiscences." *BYU Studies* 9, no. 3 (1969): 373–404.

Anderson, Richard Lloyd. "Christian Ethics in Joseph Smith Biography." In *Expressions of Faith: Testimonies of Latter-day Saint Scholars*. Salt Lake City: Deseret Book/Provo, Utah: FARMS, 1996.

———. "The Credibility of the Book of Mormon Translators." In *Book of Mormon Authorship: New Light on Ancient Origins*. Edited by Noel B. Reynolds. Provo, Utah: BYU Religious Studies Center, 1982, 213–37.

———. "Joseph Smith and the Millenarian Time Table." *BYU Studies* 3, no. 3 (1961): 55–66.

———. "Joseph Smith's Final Self-Appraisal." In *The Prophet Joseph: Essays on the Life and Mission of Joseph Smith*. Edited by Larry C. Porter and Susan Easton Black. Salt Lake City: Deseret Book, 1988, 320–32.

———. "Joseph Smith's New York Reputation Reappraised." *BYU Studies* 10, no. 3 (1970): 283–314.

———. "Joseph Smith's Prophecies of Martyrdom." In *Eighth Annual Sidney B. Sperry Symposium*. Provo, Utah: Church Educational System Religious Instruction, 1980, 1–14.

———. "The Mature Joseph Smith and Treasure Searching." *BYU Studies* 24, no. 4 (1984): 489–560.

———. "The Reliability of the Early History of Lucy and Joseph Smith." *Dialogue: A Journal of Mormon Thought* 4, no. 2 (Summer 1969): 12–28.

———. "The Religious Dimension of Emma's Letters to Joseph." In *Joseph Smith: The Prophet, the Man*. Edited by Susan Easton Black and Charles D. Tate Jr. Provo, Utah: BYU Religious Studies Center, 1993, 117–25.

———. Review of Rodger I. Anderson, *Joseph Smith's New York Reputation Re-examined*. In *Review of Books on the Book of Mormon* 3 (1991): 52–80.

Anderson, Robert D. "Toward an Introduction to a Psychobiography of Joseph Smith." *Dialogue: A Journal of Mormon Thought* 27, no. 3 (Fall 1994): 249–72.

Andrus, Hyrum L. "Joseph Smith and the Law of Consecration." *Seminar on the Prophet Joseph Smith*. Provo, Utah: Adult Education and Extension Services, 1962.

———. "Joseph Smith and the West." *BYU Studies* 2, no. 2 (1960): 129–47.

Arrington, Leonard J. "Joseph Smith." In *The Presidents of the Church*. Edited by Leonard J. Arrington. Salt Lake City: Deseret Book, 1986) 3–42.

______. "The Looseness of Zion: Joseph Smith and the Lighter View." *Task Papers in LDS History, No. 7*. Salt Lake City: LDS Historical Department, 1976.

______. "Joseph Smith, Builder of Ideal Communities." In *The Prophet Joseph: Essays on the Life and Mission of Joseph Smith*. Edited by Larry C. Porter and Susan Easton Black. Salt Lake City: Deseret Book, 1988, 115–37.

Bachman, Danel W. "Joseph Smith, a True Martyr." In *Joseph Smith: The Prophet, the Man*. Edited by Susan Easton Black and Charles D. Tate Jr. Provo, Utah: BYU Religious Studies Center, 1993, 317–32.

Backman, Milton V., Jr. "Awakenings in the Burned-Over District: New Light on the Historical Setting of the First Vision." *BYU Studies* 9 (Spring 1969): 301–20.

______. "Defender of the First Vision." In *Regional Studies in Latter-day Saint Church History: New York*. Edited by Larry C. Porter, Milton V. Backman Jr., and Susan Easton Black. Provo, Utah: BYU Department of Church History and Doctrine, 1992, 33–48.

______. "Establish a House of Prayer, a House of God: The Kirtland Temple." In *The Prophet Joseph: Essays on the Life and Mission of Joseph Smith*. Edited by Larry C. Porter and Susan Easton Black. Salt Lake City: Deseret Book, 1988, 208–25.

______. "Joseph Smith and the Restitution of All Things." In *Joseph Smith: The Prophet, the Man*. Edited by Susan Easton Black and Charles D. Tate Jr. Provo, Utah: BYU Religious Studies Center, 1993, 89–99.

______. "Joseph Smith's First Vision: Cornerstone of a Latter-day Faith." In *"To Be Learned Is Good If . . ."*. Edited by Robert L. Millet. Salt Lake City: Bookcraft, 1987, 21–41.

______. "Lo, Here! Lo, There! Early in the Spring of 1820." In *The Prophet Joseph: Essays on the Life and Mission of Joseph Smith*. Edited by Larry C. Porter and Susan Easton Black. Salt Lake City: Deseret Book, 1988, 19–35.

Barlow, Philip L. "Before Mormonism: Joseph Smith's Use of the Bible, 1820–1829." *Journal of the American Academy of Religion* 57 (Winter 1989): 739–71.

______. "Joseph Smith's Revision of the Bible: Fraudulent, Pathologic, or Prophetic?" *Harvard Theological Review* 83 (1990): 1–30.

Barrett, Ivan S. "Joseph Smith's Personality." *Seminar on the Prophet Joseph Smith*. Provo, Utah: Adult Education and Extension Services, 1962.

Baugh, Alexander L. "Joseph Smith's Athletic Nature." In *Joseph Smith: The Prophet, the Man*. Edited by Susan Easton Black and Charles D. Tate Jr. Provo, Utah: BYU Religious Studies Center, 1993, 137–50.

______. "Parting the Veil: The Visions of Joseph Smith." *BYU Studies* 38, no. 1 (1999): 22–69.

Benson, Alvin K. "Joseph Smith on Modern Science." In *Joseph Smith: The Prophet, the Man*. Edited by Susan Easton Black and Charles D. Tate Jr. Provo, Utah: BYU Religious Studies Center, 1993, 151–67.

Bentley, Joseph I. "Legal Trials of Joseph Smith." *Encyclopedia of Mormonism*. 4 vols. New York: Macmillan, 1992, 3:1346–48.

Bergera, Gary James. "Joseph Smith and the Hazards of Charismatic Leadership." *John Whitmer Historical Association Journal* 6 (1986): 33–42.

Bernauer, Barbara Hands. "Still 'Side by Side': The Final Burial of Joseph and Hyrum Smith." *John Whitmer Historical Association Journal* 11 (1991): 17–33.

Berrett, LaMar C. "An Impressive Letter from the Pen of Joseph Smith." *BYU Studies* 11 (Summer 1971): 517–23.

______. "Joseph, a Family Man." In *The Prophet Joseph: Essays on the Life and Mission of Joseph Smith*. Edited by Larry C. Porter and Susan Easton Black. Salt Lake City: Deseret Book, 1988, 36–48.

Bitton, Davis. "Joseph Smith in the Mormon Folk Memory." *Restoration Studies* 1 (1980): 75–94.

______. "The Martyrdom of Joseph Smith in Early Mormon Writings." *John Whitmer Historical Association Journal* 1 (1981): 29–39.

Black, Susan Easton. "Hiram, Ohio: Tribulation." In *The Prophet Joseph: Essays on the Life and Mission of Joseph Smith*. Edited by Larry C. Porter and Susan Easton Black. Salt Lake City: Deseret Book, 1988), 161–74.

______. "Isaac Hale: Antagonist of Joseph Smith." *In Regional Studies in Latter-day Saint Church History: New York*. Edited by Larry C. Porter, Milton V. Backman Jr., and Susan Easton Black. Provo, Utah: BYU Department of Church History and Doctrine, 1990, 93–111.

______. "Joseph's Experience in Hiram, Ohio: A Time of Contrasts." *In Regional Studies in Latter-day Saint History: Ohio*. Edited by

Milton V. Backman Jr. Provo, Utah: BYU Department of Church History and Doctrine, 1990, 27–44.

Bloom, Harold. "The Religion-Making Imagination of Joseph Smith," *Yale Review* 80 (April 1992): 26–43.

Booth, Howard J. "An Image of Joseph Smith Jr.: A Personality Study." *Courage: A Journal of History, Thought and Action* 1 (September 1970): 4–14.

Bringhurst, Newell G. "Joseph Smith, the Mormons, and Antebellum Reform—A Closer Look." *John Whitmer Historical Association Journal* 14 (1994): 73–91.

Brink, T. L. "Joseph Smith: The Verdict of Depth Psychology." *Journal of Mormon History* 3 (1976): 73–83.

Buerger, David John. "Salvation in the Theology of Joseph Smith." In *Line upon Line: Essays in Mormon Doctrine*. Edited by Gary James Bergera. Salt Lake City: Signature Books, 1989, 159–69.

Bushman, Richard L. "The First Vision Story Revisited." *Dialogue: A Journal of Mormon Thought* 4 (Spring 1969): 82–93.

______. "Joseph Smith's Family Background." In *The Prophet Joseph: Essays on the Life and Mission of Joseph Smith*. Edited by Larry C. Porter and Susan Easton Black. Salt Lake City: Deseret Book, 1988, 1–18.

______. "Joseph Smith in the Current Age." In *Joseph Smith: The Prophet, the Man*. Edited by Susan Easton Black and Charles D. Tate Jr. Provo, Utah: BYU Religious Studies Center, 1993, 33–48.

______. "Treasure-seeking Then and Now." *Sunstone* 11 (September 1987): 5–6.

______. "The Theology of Councils." In *Revelation, Reason, and Faith: Essays in Honor of Truman G. Madsen*. Edited by Donald W. Parry, Daniel C. Peterson, and Stephen D. Ricks. Provo, Utah: FARMS, 2002, 433–46.

Bushman, Richard L., and Dean C. Jessee. "The Prophet." *Encyclopedia of Mormonism*. 4 vols. New York: Macmillan, 1992, 3:1331–39.

Cannon, Donald Q. "The Founding of Nauvoo." In *The Prophet Joseph: Essays on the Life and Mission of Joseph Smith*. Edited by Larry C. Porter and Susan Easton Black. Salt Lake City: Deseret Book, 1988, 246–60.

______. "Joseph Smith and the University of Nauvoo." In *Joseph Smith: The Prophet, the Man*. Edited by Susan Easton Black and Charles D. Tate Jr. Provo, Utah: BYU Religious Studies Center, 1993, 285–300.

———. "The King Follett Discourse: Joseph Smith's Greatest Sermon in Historical Perspective." *BYU Studies* 18 (Winter 1978): 179–92.

Cannon, M. Hamlin, ed. "Bankruptcy Proceedings against Joseph Smith in Illinois." *Pacific Historical Review* 14 (December 1945): 425–33.

Clark, James. "Joseph Smith and the Lebolo Egyptian Papyri." *BYU Studies* 8 (Winter 1968): 195–203.

Collins, William P. "Thoughts on the Mormon Scriptures: An Outsider's View of the Inspiration of Joseph Smith." *Dialogue: A Journal of Mormon Thought* 15, no. 3 (Autumn 1982): 49–59.

Crawley, Peter. "A Comment on Joseph Smith's Account of His First Vision and the 1820 Revival." *Dialogue: A Journal of Mormon Thought* 6, no. 1 (Spring 1971): 106–9.

Dahl, Larry E. "The Theological Significance of the First Vision." In *Studies in Scripture, Vol. 2: The Pearl of Great Price.* Edited by Robert L. Millet and Kent P. Jackson. Salt Lake City: Randall Book, 1985.

Dillenberger, John. "Grace and Works in Martin Luther and Joseph Smith." In *Reflections on Mormonism: Judaeo-Christian Parallels.* Edited by Truman G. Madsen. Provo, Utah: BYU Religious Studies Center, 1978, 175–86. Also in *Sunstone* 3 (May–June 1978): 18–21.

Durham, Reed C., Jr. "Joseph Smith's Own Story of a Serious Childhood Illness." *BYU Studies* 10, no. 4 (1970): 480–82.

Edwards, Paul M. "The Secular Smiths." *Journal of Mormon History* 4 (1977): 3–17.

Ehat, Andrew F. "It Seems like Heaven Began on Earth: Joseph Smith and the Constitution of the Kingdom of God." *BYU Studies* 20, no. 3 (1980): 253–80.

Ellsworth, Paul D. "Mobocracy and the Rule of Law: American Press Reaction to the Murder of Joseph Smith." *BYU Studies* 20, no. 1 (1979): 71–82.

Enders, Donald L. "The Joseph Smith Sr. Family: Farmers of the Genesee." In *Joseph Smith: The Prophet, the Man.* Edited by Susan Easton Black and Charles D. Tate Jr. Provo, Utah: BYU Religious Studies Center, Brigham Young University, 1993, 213–25.

Esplin Ronald K. "Discipleship: Brigham Young and Joseph Smith." In *Joseph Smith: The Prophet, the Man.* Edited by Susan Easton Black and Charles D. Tate Jr. Provo, Utah: BYU Religious Studies Center, 1993, 241–69.

———. "Joseph, Brigham, and the Twelve: A Succession of Continuity." *BYU Studies* 21 (Summer 1981): 301–41.

______. "Joseph Smith's Mission and Timetable: 'God Will Protect Me until My Work Is Done.'" In *The Prophet Joseph: Essays on the Life and Mission of Joseph Smith*. Edited by Larry C. Porter and Susan Easton Black. Salt Lake City: Deseret Book, 1988, 280–319.

______. "A Place Prepared: Joseph, Brigham and the Quest for Promised Refuge in the West." *Journal of Mormon History* 9 (1982): 85–111.

Foster, Lawrence. "First Visions: Personal Observations on Joseph Smith's Religious Experience." *Sunstone* 8, no. 5 (September–October 1983): 39–43.

Garr, Arnold K. "Joseph Smith: Man of Forgiveness." In *Joseph Smith: The Prophet, the Man*. Edited by Susan Easton Black and Charles D. Tate Jr. Provo, Utah: BYU Religious Studies Center, Brigham Young University, 1993, 127–36.

Garrard, LaMar A. "Traditions of Honesty and Integrity in the Smith Family." In *"To Be Learned Is Good If . . ."* Edited by Robert L. Millet. Salt Lake City: Bookcraft, 1987.

Garvey, Keven. "The Prophet from Palmyra: Joseph Smith and the Rise of Mormonism." In *Psychoanalytical Perspectives on Religion, Sect, and Cult*. Edited by David A. Halperin. Boston: John Wright, 1983.

Gayler, George R. "Attempts by the State of Missouri to Extradite Joseph Smith, 1841–1843." *Missouri Historical Review* 58 (October 1963): 21–36.

______. "Governor Ford and the Death of Joseph and Hyrum Smith." *Journal of the Illinois State Historical Society* 50 (1957): 391–411.

Godfrey, Kenneth W. "Joseph Smith and the Masons." *Journal of the Illinois State Historical Society* 64 (Spring 1971): 79–90.

______. "A New Look at the Alleged Little Known Discourse of Joseph Smith." *BYU Studies* 9 (Autumn 1968): 49–53.

______. "Non-Mormon Views of the Martyrdom: A Look at Some Early Published Accounts." *John Whitmer Historical Association Journal* 17 (1987): 12–20.

______. "Remembering the Deaths of Joseph and Hyrum Smith." In *Joseph Smith: The Prophet, the Man*. Edited by Susan Easton Black and Charles D. Tate Jr. Provo, Utah: BYU Religious Studies Center, Brigham Young University, 1993, 301–15.

______. "The Road to Carthage Led West." *BYU Studies* 8 (Winter 1968): 204–5.

Goodyear, Imogene. "Joseph Smith and Polygamy: An Alternative View." *John Whitmer Historical Association Journal* 4 (1984): 16–21.

Green, Arnold H. "The Muhammed-Joseph Smith Comparison: Subjective Metaphor or a Sociology of Prophethood." In *Mormons and Muslims*. Edited by Spencer J. Palmer. Provo, Utah: BYU Religious Studies Center, 1983.

Green, Arnold H., and Lawrence P. Goldrup. "Joseph Smith, an American Muhammed? An Essay on the Perils of Historical Analogy." *Dialogue: A Journal of Mormon Thought* 6, no. 1 (Spring 1971): 46–58.

Groesbeck, C. Jess. "The Smiths and Their Dreams and Visions," *Sunstone* 12, no. 2 (March 1988): 22–29.

Hale, Van. "The Doctrinal Impact of the King Follett Discourse." *BYU Studies* 18 (Winter 1978): 209–25.

———. "The King Follett Discourse: Textual History and Criticism." *Sunstone* 8, no. 5 (September–October 1983): 5–12.

Hansen, Klaus. "Joseph Smith and the Political Kingdom of God." *American West* 5 (1968): 20–24, 63.

Hartley, William G. "Close Friends as Witnesses: Joseph Smith and the Joseph Knight Families." In *Joseph Smith: The Prophet, the Man*. Edited by Susan Easton Black and Charles D. Tate Jr. Provo, Utah: BYU Religious Studies Center, 1993, 271–83.

———. "'Upon You My Fellow Servants': Restoration of the Priesthood." In *The Prophet Joseph: Essays on the Life and Mission of Joseph Smith*. Edited by Larry C. Porter and Susan Easton Black. Salt Lake City: Deseret Book, 1988, 49–72.

Hess, John W. "Recollections of the Prophet Joseph Smith." *Juvenile Instructor* 27 (May 15, 1892): 302–4; 27 (August 1, 1892): 470–72.

Hickman, Martin B. "The Political Legacy of Joseph Smith." *Dialogue: A Journal of Mormon Thought* 3 (Autumn 1968): 22–27.

Hicks, Michael. "Joseph Smith, W. W. Phelps, and the Poetic Paraphrase of 'The Vision.'" *Journal of Mormon History* 20, 2 (Fall 1994): 63–84.

Hill, Marvin S. "Brodie Revisited: A Reappraisal." *Dialogue: A Journal of Mormon Thought* 7 (Winter 1972): 72–85.

———. "The First Vision Controversy: A Critique and Reconciliation." *Dialogue: A Journal of Mormon Thought* 15, no. 2 (Summer 1982): 31–46.

———. "Joseph Smith and the 1826 Trial: New Evidence and New Difficulties." *BYU Studies* 12 (Winter 1972): 223–33.

———. "Joseph Smith the Man: Some Reflections on a Subject of Controversy." *BYU Studies* 21, no. 1 (1981): 175–86.

———. "Money-Digging Folklore and the Beginnings of Mormonism: An Interpretive Suggestion." *BYU Studies* 24, no. 4 (1984): 473–88.

________. "The 'New Mormon History' Reassessed in Light of Recent Books on Joseph Smith and Mormon Origins." *Dialogue: A Journal of Mormon Thought* 21, no. 3 (Fall 1988): 115–27.

________. "On the First Vision and Its Import in the Shaping of Early Mormonism." *Dialogue: A Journal of Mormon Thought* 12, no. 1 (Spring 1979): 90–99.

________. "The 'Prophet Puzzle' Assembled; or, How to Treat Our Historical Diplopia Toward Joseph Smith." *Journal of Mormon History* 3 (1976): 101–5.

________. "Secular or Sectarian History? A Critique of *No Man Knows My History*." *Church History* 43 (March 1974): 78–96.

Hogan, Mervin B. "Henry Clay, Joseph Smith, and the Presidency." *The Royal Arch Mason* (Winter 1986): 229–34.

________. "Joseph Smith: A Modern Enigma." *The Royal Arch Mason* (Spring 1967): 3–11, 30.

Howard, Richard P. "An Analysis of Six Contemporary Accounts Touching Joseph Smith's First Vision." *Restoration Studies* 1 (1980): 95–117.

________. "Joseph Smith's First Vision: The RLDS Tradition." *Journal of Mormon History* 7 (1980): 23–29.

Hullinger, Robert N. "Joseph Smith, Defender of Faith." *Concordia Theological Monthly* 42 (February 1971): 72–87.

Huntress, Keith. "Governor Thomas Ford and the Murderers of Joseph Smith." *Dialogue: A Journal of Mormon Thought* 4 (Summer 1969): 41–52.

Jessee, Dean C. "The Early Accounts of Joseph Smith's First Vision." *BYU Studies* 9, no. 3 (1969): 275–94.

________. "Joseph Smith and the Beginnings of Mormon Record Keeping." In *The Prophet Joseph: Essays on the Life and Mission of Joseph Smith*. Edited by Larry C. Porter and Susan Easton Black. Salt Lake City: Deseret Book, 1988, 138–60.

________. "Joseph Smith's 19 July 1840 Discourse." *BYU Studies* 19, no. 3 (1979): 390–94.

________. "Priceless Words and Fallible Memories: Joseph Smith as Seen in the Effort to Preserve His Discourses." *BYU Studies* 31 (Spring 1991): 19–40.

________. "The Reliability of Joseph Smith's History." *Journal of Mormon History* 3 (1976): 23–46.

________. "Sources for the Study of Joseph Smith." In *Mormon Americana: A Guide to Sources and Collections in the United States*. Provo, Utah: BYU Studies, 1995.

________. "Return to Carthage: Writing the History of Joseph Smith's Martyrdom." *Journal of Mormon History* 8 (1981): 3–19.

________. "The Writing of Joseph Smith's History." *BYU Studies* 11 (Summer 1971): 439–73.

________. "Writings of Joseph Smith." *Encyclopedia of Mormonism*. New York: Macmillan, 1992, 3:1343–46.

Johnson Clark V. "Let Far West Be Holy and Consecrated." In *The Prophet Joseph: Essays on the Life and Mission of Joseph Smith*. Edited by Larry C. Porter and Susan Easton Black. Salt Lake City: Deseret Book, 1988, 226–45.

Jolley, Clifton Holt. "The Martyrdom of Joseph Smith: An Archetypal Study." *Utah Historical Quarterly* 44 (Fall 1976): 329–50.

King, Arthur Henry. "Joseph Smith As a Writer." In his *The Abundance of the Heart*. Salt Lake City: Bookcraft, 1986, 197–205.

Lambert, Neal E., and Richard H. Cracroft. "Literary Form and Historical Understanding: Joseph Smith's First Vision." *Journal of Mormon History* 7 (1980): 33–42.

Larsen, David R. "The Case against the Alleged Psychotic Joe Smith; or One Hallucinating Jose, Imaginary or Real?" *Journal of the Association of Mormon Counselors and Psychotherapists* 10 (January 1984): 10–11, 23.

Larson, Stan. "The King Follett Discourse: A Newly Amalgamated Text." *BYU Studies* 18 (Winter 1978): 193–208.

Launius, Roger D. "Joseph Smith's Encounter with Spiritualism." *Restoration Trails Forum* 9 (November 1983): 3, 8.

________. "The Murders in Carthage: Non-Mormon Reports of the Assassination of the Smith Brothers." *John Whitmer Historical Association Journal* 15 (1995): 17–34.

Ludlow, Daniel H. "A Tribute to Joseph Smith Jr." In *The Prophet Joseph: Essays on the Life and Mission of Joseph Smith*. Edited by Larry C. Porter and Susan Easton Black. Salt Lake City: Deseret Book, 1988, 333–48.

Lyon, T. Edgar. "Joseph Smith: The Wentworth Letter and Religious America of 1842." *Joseph Smith Memorial Sermons*. Logan, Utah: LDS Institute of Religion, 1966, Vol. 2:116–27.

McCollum, Adele Brannon. "The First Vision: Re-Visioning Historical Experience." In *Literature of Belief: Sacred Scripture and Religious Experience*. Edited by Neal A. Lambert. Provo, Utah: BYU Religious Studies Center, 1981, 177–96.

McConkie, Bruce R. "Joseph Smith: A Revealor of Christ." *Speeches of the Year*. Provo, Utah: Brigham Young University, 1978.

______. "This Generation Shall Have My Word Through You." Paper delivered at the Sperry Symposium. Provo, Utah: Brigham Young University, 1979. Published in *Hearken, O Ye People: Discourses on the Doctrine and Covenants*. No editor identified. Sandy, Utah: Randall Book 1984, 79–92. Edited version in *Ensign*, June 1980, 54–59.

McKinlay, Daniel B. "The Martyrdom: Joseph and Hyrum Smith as Testators." *Revelation, Reason, and Faith: Essays in Honor of Truman G. Madsen*. Edited by Donald W. Parry, Daniel C. Peterson, and Stephen D. Ricks. Provo, Utah: FARMS, 2002, 477–98.

Madsen, Ann N., and Susan Easton Black. "Joseph and Joseph: He Shall Be Like Unto Me (2 Nephi 3:15)." In *The Old Testament and the Latter-day Saints*. No editor identified. Salt Lake City: Randall Books, 1986, 125–40.

Madsen, Gordon A. "Joseph Smith's 1826 Trial: The Legal Setting." *BYU Studies* 30, no. 2 (1990): 91–108.

Madsen, Truman G. "Joseph Smith and the Problem of Ethics." In *Perspectives in Mormon Ethics: Personal, Social, Legal, and Medical*. Edited by Donna G. Hill. Salt Lake City: Publishers Press, 1983, 29–48. Reprinted from *Seminar on the Prophet Joseph Smith*. Provo, Utah: Adult Education and Extension Services, 1962, 43–62.

______. "Joseph Smith and the Sources of Love." *Dialogue: A Journal of Mormon Thought* 1, no. 1 (Spring 1966): 122–34.

______. "Teachings of Joseph Smith." *Encyclopedia of Mormonism*. 4 vols. New York: Macmillan, 1992, 3:1339–43.

Matthews, Robert J. "Joseph Smith—Translator." In *Joseph Smith: The Prophet, the Man*. Edited by Susan Easton Black and Charles D. Tate Jr. Provo, Utah: BYU Religious Studies Center, 1993, 77–87.

______. "The Prophet Translates the Bible by the Spirit of Revelation." In *The Prophet Joseph: Essays on the Life and Mission of Joseph Smith*. Edited by Larry C. Porter and Susan Easton Black. Salt Lake City: Deseret Book, 1988, 175–191.

Melville, J. Keith. "Joseph Smith, the Constitution, and Individual Liberties." *BYU Studies* 28, no. 2 (1988): 65–74.

Merrill, Byron R. "Joseph Smith and the Lamanites." In *Joseph Smith: The Prophet, the Man*. Edited by Susan Easton Black and Charles D. Tate Jr. Provo, Utah: BYU Religious Studies Center, 1993, 187–202.

Midgley, Louis. "The Brodie Connection: Thomas Jefferson and Joseph Smith." *BYU Studies* 20, no. 1 (Fall 1979): 59–67.

Millet, Robert L. "Joseph Smith and Modern Mormonism: Orthodoxy, Neoorthodoxy, Tension, and Tradition." *BYU Studies* 29, no. 3 (1989): 49–68.

———. "Joseph Smith among the Prophets." In *Joseph Smith: The Prophet, the Man*. Edited by Susan Easton Black and Charles D. Tate Jr. Provo, Utah: BYU Religious Studies Center, 1993, 15–31.

———. "Joseph Smith, the Book of Mormon, and the Nature of God." In *"To Be Learned Is Good If . . ."*. Edited by Robert L. Millet. Salt Lake City: Bookcraft, 1987.

———. "Joseph Smith's Translation of the Bible: Impact on Mormon Theology." *Religious Studies and Theology* 7 (January 1987): 43–53.

———. "Joseph Smith's Translation of the Bible and the Synoptic Problem." *John Whitmer Historical Association Journal* 5 (1985): 41–46.

Moench, Melodie. "Joseph Smith: Prophet, Priest, and King." *Task Papers in LDS History*, No. 25. Salt Lake City: LDS Historical Department, 1978.

Murdoch, Norman H. "Joseph Smith, the Book of Mormon, and Mormonism: A Review Essay." *New York History* 67 (1986): 224–30.

Nibley, Hugh. "Their Portrait of a Prophet." In *Nibley on the Timely and the Timeless*. Provo, Utah: BYU Religious Studies Center, 1978.

Nibley, Preston. "Joseph Smith and the Three Witnesses." In *1961 Seminar on the Prophet Joseph Smith*. Compiled by Truman G. Madsen. Provo, Utah: Brigham Young University, 1961, 16–24.

Nolan, Max. "Joseph Smith and Mysticism." *Journal of Mormon History* 10 (1983): 105–116.

Oaks, Dallin H., and Joseph I. Bentley. "Joseph Smith and Legal Process: In the Wake of the Steamboat *Nauvoo*." *BYU Studies* 19, no. 2 (1979): 167–98.

Olsen, Steven L. "Joseph Smith and the Structure of Mormon Identity." *Dialogue: A Journal of Mormon Thought* 14 (Autumn 1981): 89–100.

———. "Joseph Smith's Concept of the City of Zion." In *Joseph Smith: The Prophet, the Man*. Edited by Susan Easton Black and Charles D. Tate Jr. Provo, Utah: BYU Religious Studies Center, 1993, 203–11.

Owens, Lance S. "Joseph Smith and the Kabbalah: The Occult Connection." *Dialogue: A Journal of Mormon Thought* 27, no. 3 (Fall 1994): 117–94.

Parry, Keith. "Joseph Smith and the Clash of Sacred Cultures." *Dialogue: A Journal of Mormon Thought* 18 (Winter 1985): 65–80.

Partridge, Elinore H. "Characteristics of Joseph Smith's Style and Notes on the Authorship of the *Lectures on Faith*." *Task Papers in LDS History*, No. 14. Salt Lake City: LDS Historical Department, 1976.

Paul, Robert. "Joseph Smith and the Manchester (New York) Library." *BYU Studies* 22, no. 3 (1982): 333–56.

______. "Joseph Smith and the Plurality of Worlds Idea." *Dialogue: A Journal of Mormon Thought* 19, no. 2 (Summer 1986): 12–36.

Paulsen, David L., and Blake Thomas Ostler. "Sin, Suffering, and Soul-Making: Joseph Smith on the Problem of Evil." In *Revelation, Reason, and Faith: Essays in Honor of Truman G. Madsen*. Edited by Donald W. Parry, Daniel C. Peterson, and Stephen D. Ricks. Provo, Utah: FARMS, BYU, 2002, 237–84.

Perkins, Keith W. "The Prophet Joseph Smith in 'the Ohio': The Schoolmaster." In *The Prophet Joseph: Essays on the Life and Mission of Joseph Smith*. Edited by Larry C. Porter and Susan Easton Black. Salt Lake City: Deseret Book, 1988, 90–114.

Petersen, Roger K. "Joseph Smith: Prophet-Poet." In *Eighth Sidney B. Sperry Symposium*. Provo, Utah: BYU College of Religious Instruction, 1980, 265–79.

Peterson, Paul H. "Understanding Joseph: A Review of Published Documentary Sources." In *Joseph Smith: The Prophet, the Man*. Edited by Susan Easton Black and Charles D. Tate Jr. Provo, Utah: BYU Religious Studies Center, 1993, 101–16.

Poll, Richard D. "Joseph Smith and the Presidency." *Dialogue: A Journal of Mormon Thought* 3, no. 3 (Autumn 1968): 17–21.

Porter, Larry C. "'The Field Is White Already to Harvest': Earliest Missionary Labors and the Book of Mormon." In *The Prophet Joseph: Essays on the Life and Mission of Joseph Smith*. Edited by Larry C. Porter and Susan Easton Black. Salt Lake City: Deseret Book, 1988, 73–89.

Poulson, Richard C. "Fate and the Persecutors of Joseph Smith: Transmutations of an American Myth." *Dialogue: A Journal of Mormon Thought* 11, no. 4 (Winter 1978): 63–70.

Proper, David R. "Joseph Smith and Salem." *Essex Institute Historical Collections* 100 (April 1964): 88–97.

Quinn, D. Michael. "The Mormon Succession Crisis of 1844." *BYU Studies* 16 (Winter 1976): 187–233.

Raisanen, Heikki. "Joseph Smith und die Bibel: Die Leistung des Mormonischen Propheten in neuer Beleuchtung." *Theologische Literaturzeitung* 109 (February 1984): 81–92.

Ricks, Stephen D., and Daniel C. Peterson. "Joseph Smith and 'Magic': Methodological Reflections on the Use of a Term." In *"To Be Learned Is Good If . . ."* Edited by Robert L. Millet. Salt Lake City: Bookcraft, 1987, 129–47.

Riddle, Chauncey C. "As a Prophet Thinketh in His Heart, So Is He: The Mind of Joseph Smith." In *The Prophet Joseph: Essays on the Life and Mission of Joseph Smith.* Edited by Larry C. Porter and Susan Easton Black. Salt Lake City: Deseret Book, 1988, 262–79.

Romig, Ronald E., and Lachlan Mackay. "What Did Joseph [Smith] Look Like?" *Saints Herald*, December 1994, 8–10, 12.

Rust, Richard Dilworth. "'I Love All Men Who Dive': Herman Melville and Joseph Smith." *BYU Studies* 38, no. 1 (1999): 151–69.

Searle, Howard C. "Authorship of the History of Joseph Smith: A Review Essay." *BYU Studies* 21 (Winter 1981): 101–22.

Shipps, Jan. "The Prophet Puzzle: Suggestions Leading toward a More Comprehensive Interpretation of Joseph Smith." *Journal of Mormon History* 1 (1974): 3–20.

Skinner, Andrew C. "Joseph Smith Vindicated Again: Enoch, Moses 7:48, and Apocryphal Sources." In *Revelation, Reason, and Faith: Essays in Honor of Truman G. Madsen.* Edited by Donald W. Parry, Daniel C. Peterson, and Stephen D. Ricks. Provo, Utah: FARMS, 2002, 365–82.

Smith, Brian L. "Joseph Smith: Gifted Learner, Master Teacher, Prophetic Seer." In *Joseph Smith: The Prophet, the Man.* Edited by Susan Easton Black and Charles D. Tate Jr. Provo, Utah: BYU Religious Studies Center, 1993, 169–86.

Snow, Edgar C., Jr. "One Face of the Hero: In Search of the Mythological Joseph Smith." *Dialogue: A Journal of Mormon Thought* 27, no. 3 (Fall 1994): 233–47.

Sondrup, Steven P. "The Articles of Faith: Language of Confession in Mormon Belief." In *Literature of Belief: Sacred Scripture and Religious Experience.* Edited by Neal A. Lambert. Provo, Utah: BYU Religious Studies Center, 1981, 197–215.

Stott, Graham St. John. "Just War, Holy War, and Joseph Smith Jr." In *Restoration Studies* 4 (1988): 134–41.

Taylor, Alan. "Rediscovering the Context of Joseph Smith's Treasure Seeking." *Dialogue: A Journal of Mormon Thought* 19 (1986): 18–28.

Tickemyer, Garland E. "Joseph Smith and Process Theology." *Dialogue: A Journal of Mormon Thought* 17 (Autumn 1984): 75–85.

Turner, Rodney. "Joseph Smith and the Apocalypse of John." *The New Testament and the Latter-day Saints*. No editor identified. Orem, Utah: Randall Book, 1987, 319–45.

Van Orden, Bruce A. "The Compassion of Joseph Smith." In *"To Be Learned Is Good If . . ."*. Edited by Robert L. Millet. Salt Lake City: Bookcraft, 1987, 43–57.

______. "Zion's Camp: A Refiner's Fire." In *The Prophet Joseph: Essays on the Life and Mission of Joseph Smith*. Edited by Larry C. Porter and Susan Easton Black. Salt Lake City: Deseret Book, 1988, 192–207.

Van Wagoner, Richard, and Steven C. Walker. "Joseph Smith: The Gift of Seeing." *Dialogue: A Journal of Mormon Thought* 15, no. 2 (Summer 1982): 48–68.

Vernon, Glenn N. "Joseph Smith and the Challenge of Change." *Seminar on the Prophet Joseph Smith*. Provo, Utah: Adult Education and Extension Services, 1962.

Vlahos, Clare D. "Joseph Smith Jr.'s Conception of Revelation." In *Restoration Studies* 2 (1983): 63–74.

Vogel, Dan. "The Locations of Joseph Smith's Early Treasure Quests." *Dialogue: A Journal of Mormon Thought* 27, no. 3 (Fall 1994): 197–231.

Vogel, Dan, and Brent Lee Metcalfe. "Joseph Smith's Scriptural Cosmology." In *The Word of God: Essays on Mormon Scripture*. Edited by Dan Vogel. Salt Lake City: Signature Books, 1990, 187–219.

Voros, J. Frederic, Jr. "Was the Book of Mormon Buried with King Follett? The Essential Unity of Joseph's Message" *Sunstone* 11, no. 1 (March 1987): 15–18.

Walker, Ronald W. "Joseph Smith: The Palmyra Seer." *BYU Studies* 24, no. 4 (1984): 461–72.

______. "The Persisting Idea of American Treasure Hunting." *BYU Studies* 24, no. 4 (1984): 429–59.

Walters, Wesley P. "From Occult to Cult with Joseph Smith." *Journal of Pastoral Theology* 1 (Summer 1977): 121–31.

______. "Joseph Smith's Bainbridge, N.Y., Court Trials." *Westminster Theological Journal* 36 (Winter 1974): 123–44.

______. "Joseph Smith's First Vision Story Revisited." *Journal of Pastoral Practice* 4 (Summer 1980): 92–109.

______. "New Light on Mormon Origins from the Palmyra Revival." *Evangelical Theological Society Bulletin* 10 (1967): 227–41. Also published in *Dialogue: A Journal of Mormon Thought* 4 (Spring 1969): 60–81.

Williams, Peter W. "New World Revelation: Joseph Smith and the Rise of Mormonism." In *America's Religions: Traditions and Cultures*. New York: Macmillan, 1990, 219–25.

Winder, Lorie. "In Search of the Real Joseph Smith." *Sunstone* 5 (November/December 1980): 30–34.

Wirthlin, Leroy S. "Joseph Smith's Boyhood Operation: An 1813 Surgical Success." *BYU Studies* 21, no. 2 (1981): 131–54.

———. "Nathan Smith (1762–1828), Surgical Consultant to Joseph Smith." *BYU Studies* 17, no. 3 (1977): 319–37.

Zucker, Louis C. "Joseph Smith as a Student of Hebrew." *Dialogue: A Journal of Mormon Thought* 3, no. 2 (Summer 1968): 41–55.

Sermons and Church Magazines

Allen, James B. "Eight Contemporary Accounts of Joseph Smith's First Vision—What Do We Learn from Them?" *Improvement Era* 73 (April 1970): 4–13.

———. "Was Joseph Smith a Serious Candidate for President of the United States?" *Ensign*, September 1973, 21–22.

Anderson, Lavina Fielding. "139-Year-Old Portraits of Joseph and Emma Smith." *Ensign*, March 1981, 62–64.

Anderson, Richard Lloyd. "The Alvin Smith Story: Fact and Fiction." *Ensign*, August 1987, 58–72.

———. "By the Gift and Power of God." *Ensign*, September 1977, 79–85.

———. "Confirming Records of Moroni's Coming." *Improvement Era* 73 (September 1970): 4–8.

———. "Heritage of a Prophet." *Ensign*, February 1971, 15–19.

———. "Joseph Smith's Brothers: Nauvoo and After." *Ensign*, September 1979, 30–33.

———. "Joseph Smith's Home Environment." *Ensign*, July 1971, 57–59.

———. "Joseph Smith's Testimony of the First Vision." *Ensign*, April 1996, 10–21.

———. "Parallel Prophets: Paul and Joseph Smith." *Ensign*, April 1985, 12–17.

———. "The Personality of the Prophet." *New Era*, December 1987, 14–19.

———. "The Trustworthiness of Young Joseph Smith." *Improvement Era* 73 (October 1970): 82–89.

Arrington, Leonard J. "The Human Qualities of Joseph Smith, the Prophet." *Ensign*, January 1971, 35–38.

______. "Joseph Smith and the Lighter View." *New Era*, August 1976, 8–13.

Backman, Milton V., Jr. "Confirming Witnesses of the First Vision." *Ensign*, January 1986, 32–37.

______. "Did Brigham Young Confirm or Expound on Joseph Smith's First Vision?" *Ensign*, April 1992, 59–60.

______. "Joseph Smith, Popularizer or Restorer?" *Improvement Era* 70 (March–April 1967): 58–61, 76–83.

______. "Joseph Smith's Recitals of the First Vision." *Ensign*, January 1985, 8–17.

Baker, LeGrand L. "On to Carthage to Die." *Improvement Era* 72 (June 1969): 10–15.

Ball, Isaac B. "The Poetic Qualities in the Writings of Joseph Smith." *Improvement Era* 38 (December 1935): 734–35.

Ballard, M. Russell. "The Family of Joseph Smith." *Ensign*, November 1991, 5–7.

Berrett, William E. "Joseph Smith: Five Qualities of Leadership." *New Era*, June 1977, 40–43.

Black, Susan Easton. "I Am Not Any Longer to Be Alone." *Ensign*, January 1989, 50–56.

Bushman, Richard L. "The Character of Joseph Smith: Insights from His Holographs." *Ensign*, April 1977, 11–13.

______. "How Did the Prophet Joseph Smith Respond to Skepticism in His Time?" *Ensign*, February 1990, 61–63.

Cannon, Donald Q., Larry E. Dahl, and John W. Welch. "The Restoration of Major Doctrines Through Joseph Smith." *Ensign*, January 1989, 26–33; February 1989, 6–13.

Cummings, B. F. "The Prophet's Last Letters." *Improvement Era* 18 (March 1915): 388–93.

Done, Willard. "Joseph Smith as a Man." *Improvement Era* 9 (December 1905): 114–22.

Durham, G. Homer. "Joseph Smith and the Political World." *Improvement Era* 55 (October 1952): 712–13, 746–51.

______. "Joseph Smith's Statecraft." *Improvement Era* 45 (December 1942): 782–83, 823–26.

Esplin, Ronald K. "God Will Protect Me until My Work Is Done." *Ensign*, August 1989, 16–21.

Evans, John Henry. "Genius or Seer?" *Improvement Era* 9 (December 1905): 170–78.

Gates, Susa Young. "What Joseph Smith Did for the Womanhood of the Church." *Improvement Era* 9 (December 1905): 179–83. Reprinted in *Improvement Era* 73 (November 1970): 43–46.

Gibbons, Francis M. "The Savior and Joseph Smith—Alike Yet Unlike." *Ensign*, May 1991, 32–33.

Grant, Carter E. "The Joseph Smith Home." *Improvement Era* 62 (December 1959): 898–99, 976–80.

Green, Doyle L. "Are These Portraits of the Prophet Joseph Smith?" *Improvement Era*, December 1966.

Hart, Charles H. "Joseph the Prophet." *Improvement Era* 23 (April 1920): 491–95.

Hartley, William G. "Joseph Smith and Nauvoo's Youth." *Ensign*, September 1979, 26–29.

Hatch, Ephraim. "What Did Joseph Smith Look Like?" *Ensign*, March 1981, 65–73.

Hinckley, Gordon B. "Praise to the Man." *Ensign*, August 1983, 2–6.

Horton, George A., Jr. "Ancient Gifts for a New Dispensation: The Prophet Joseph Smith Restored Major Documents Recorded by Earlier Prophets." *Ensign*, January 1993, 11–13.

————. "Prophecies in the Bible about Joseph Smith." *Ensign*, January 1989, 20–25.

Howard, Richard P. "Christmas Day, 1832: Joseph Smith Responds to the Nullification Crisis." *Saints' Herald* 116 (May 1969): 54.

————. "'Try the Spirits' Wrote Joseph Jr., in 1842." *Saints' Herald* 131 (September 1984): 24.

Jackson, Kent P. "Moroni's Message to Joseph Smith." *Ensign*, August 1990, 13–16.

Jessee, Dean C. "Joseph Smith Jr.—In His Own Words." *Ensign*, December 1984, 22–31; January 1985, 18–24.

————. "Joseph Smith's Reputation among Historians." *Ensign*, September 1979, 56–61.

————. "The Spirituality of Joseph Smith." *Ensign*, September 1978, 14–20.

————. and William G. Hartley. "Joseph Smith's Missionary Journal." *New Era*, February 1974, 34–36.

"Joseph Smith, The Prophet." *Young Woman's Journal* 17 (December 1906): 537–48.

Josephson, Marba C. "What Did the Prophet Joseph Smith Look Like?" *Improvement Era* 56 (May 1953): 311–15, 371–75.

Kimball, Spencer W. "The Pattern of Martyrdom." *Improvement Era*, May 1946, 286, 316–18.

King, Arthur Henry. "A Man Who Speaks to Our Time from Eternity." *Ensign*, March 1989, 12–16.

Knight, Hal. "Joseph Smith as a City Planner." *Improvement Era* 72 (December 1969): 11, 14.

Knowles, Duane C. "Foes Became His Friends." *Ensign*, January 1993, 27–30.

Lund, Gerald N. "A Prophet for the Fulness of Times." *Ensign*, January 1997, 50–54.

McConkie, Bruce R. "This Generation Shall Have My Word through You." *Ensign*, June 1980, 54–59.

Madsen, Truman G. "Joseph Smith and the Depth of Discipleship." *Ninth Annual Religious Education Symposium, Church Education System*, 43–47.

______. "Joseph Smith's Reputation among Theologians." *Ensign*, September 1979, 61–63.

Matthews, Robert J. "Joseph Smith's Inspired Translation of the Bible." *Ensign*, December 1972, 61–63.

______. Joseph Smith's Efforts to Publish His Bible Translation." *Ensign*, January 1983, 57–64.

______. "Plain and Precious Things Restored." *Ensign*, July 1982, 14–20.

Maxwell, Neal A. "A Choice Seer." *Ensign*, August 1986, 6–15.

______. "Joseph, the Seer." *Ensign*, November 1983, 54–56.

______. "My Servant Joseph." *Ensign*, May 1992, 37–39.

Millet, Robert L. "Joseph Smith and the New Testament." *Ensign*, December 1986, 28–34.

Osmond, Alfred. "Joseph Smith as Educator." *Improvement Era* 17 (January-February 1914): 259–62, 360–65.

Parry, Edwin F. "Joseph Smith's Last Prophecy." *Improvement Era* 24 (July 1921): 797–99.

Perkins, Keith. "Thou Art Still Chosen." *Ensign*, January 1993, 14–19.

Porter, Larry C. "Christmas with the Prophet Joseph." *Ensign*, December 1978, 9–11.

______. "How Did the U.S. Press React When Joseph and Hyrum Were Murdered?" *Ensign*, April 1984, 22–23.

Reeder, William H., Jr. "Proclamation of the Twelve Apostles on the Death of Joseph Smith." *Improvement Era* 52 (March 1949): 149, 176–77.

Roberts, B. H. "Joseph Smith the Modern American Prophet." *Improvement Era* 23 (April 1920): 526–32.

———. "The Probability of Joseph Smith's Story." *Improvement Era* 7 (March–April 1904): 321–31, 417–32.

Skidmore, Rex A. "Joseph Smith: A Leader and Lover of Recreation." *Improvement Era* 43 (December 1940): 716–17, 762–63.

Smith, Calvin N. "Joseph Smith as a Public Speaker." *Improvement Era* 69 (April 1966): 277–79, 308–12.

Stewart, D. Michael. "What Do We Know about the Purported Statement of Joseph Smith that the Constitution Would Hang by a Thread and that the Elders Would Save It?" *Ensign*, June 1976, 64–65.

Taylor, J. Lewis. "Joseph Smith the Prophet: A Self-Portrait." *Ensign*, June 1973, 40–44.

Top, Brent L. "'I Was With My Family': Joseph Smith—Devoted Husband, Father, Son, and Brother." *Ensign*, August 1991, 22–27.

Wadsworth, Richard. "Does the Book of Mormon Prophesy of Joseph Smith?" *Ensign*, April 1989, 52–53.

Widtsoe, John A. "Did Joseph Smith Introduce Plural Marriage?" *Improvement Era* 49 (November 1946): 721, 766–77.

———. "How Can Joseph Smith Be Explained?" *Improvement Era* 49 (October 1946): 641, 670–71.

———. "Was Joseph Smith Honest in Business?" *Improvement Era* 49 (September 1946): 577, 604–07.

———. "What Manner of Boy and Youth Was Joseph Smith?" *Improvement Era* 49 (August 1946): 513, 542–43.

———. "What Was the Vocabulary of Joseph Smith?" *Improvement Era* 54 (June 1951): 399, 476–77.

———. "What Were the Sources of Joseph Smith's Greatness?" *Ensign*, December 1987, 26–27.

———. "Why Did Joseph Smith Become a Mason?" *Improvement Era* 53 (September 1950): 694–95.

Wirthlin, LeRoy S. "Joseph Smith's Surgeon." *Ensign*, March 1978, 58–60.

Woodford, Robert J. "How the Revelations in the Doctrine and Covenants Were Received and Compiled." *Ensign*, January 1985, 26–33.

Young, S. Dilworth. "What Joseph Smith Teaches Us of Jesus Christ." *Ensign*, December 1973, 41–44.

Theses and Dissertations

Andrus, Helen Mae H. "A Study of Joseph Smith's Teachings and Practices as They Influence Welfare in the LDS Church." M.A. thesis, Brigham Young University, 1952.

Andrus, Hyrum L. "Joseph Smith: Social Philosopher, Theorist, Prophet." Doctor of Social Science diss., Syracuse University, 1955.

Brink, T. L. "Joseph Smith: A Study in Analytical Psychology." Ph.D. diss., University of Chicago, 1978.

Cheesman, Paul R. "An Analysis of the Accounts Relating to Joseph Smith's Early Visions." M.A. thesis, Brigham Young University, 1965.

Ehat, Andrew F. "Joseph Smith's Introduction of Temple Ordinances and the 1844 Mormon Succession Question." M.A. thesis, Brigham Young University, 1983.

Goshay, Thomas Gerard. "An Examination of the Biblical Scholarship of Joseph Smith, the Mormon Prophet." B.D. thesis, Talbot Theological Seminary, 1962.

Gottfredson, Montchesney Riddle. "The Relationship of the Extant Eschatalogically Oriented Work of Joseph Smith to That of Selected Twentieth-Century New Testament Scholars." Ph.D. diss., Brigham Young University, 1967.

Graham, Bruce L. "The Presidential Campaign of Joseph Smith Jr., 1844." M.A. thesis, Lamar University, 1976.

Guthrie, Gary Dean. "Joseph Smith as an Administrator." M.A. thesis, Brigham Young University, 1969.

Hansen, Warren David. "Re-Establishing Community: An Analysis of Joseph Smith's Social Thought in the Context of Philosophical Tradition." Ph.D. diss., Rutgers University, 1980.

Harris, James Roy. "A Comparison of the Educational Thought of Joseph Smith with That of Certain Contemporary Educators." Ed.D. diss., Brigham Young University, 1965.

Jones, Edward T. "The Theology of Thomas Dick and Its Possible Relationship to That of Joseph Smith." M.A. thesis, Brigham Young University, 1969.

Launius, Roger D. "Zion's Camp and the Redemption of Jackson County, Missouri." M.A. thesis, Louisiana State University, 1978.

McBrien, Dean D. "The Influence of the Frontier on Joseph Smith." Ph.D. diss., George Washington University, 1929.

McCarl, William B. "The Visual Image of Joseph Smith." M.A. thesis, Brigham Young University, 1962.

McConkie, Joseph Fielding. "A Historical Explanation of the Views of the Church of Jesus Christ of Latter-day Saints and the Reorganized Church of Jesus Christ of Latter Day Saints on Four Distinctive Aspects of the Doctrine of Deity Taught by the Prophet Joseph Smith." M.A. thesis, Brigham Young University, 1968.

McLaws, Monte B. "Joseph Smith, 1838–1839." M.A. thesis, Arizona State University, 1963.

Norton, Walter A. "Joseph Smith as a Jacksonian Man of Letters: His Literary Development As Evidenced in His Newspaper Writings." M.A. thesis, Brigham Young University, 1976.

Olive, Cherel Jane Ellsworth. "Mazeway Reformation and Revitalization Movements: The Wallace Model as Applied to the Development of Mormonism." M.A. thesis, University of Nevada, Las Vegas, 1977.

Petersen, Roger Kent. "Joseph Smith, Prophet-Poet: A Literary Analysis of Writings Commonly Associated with His Name." Ph.D. diss., Brigham Young University, 1981.

Peterson, Elmer. "The Character of Joseph Smith: A Study Based on His Own Literary Production." M.A. thesis, Brigham Young University, 1938.

Porter, Larry C. "A Study of the Origins of the Church of Jesus Christ of Latter-day Saints in the States of New York and Pennsylvania." Ph.D. diss., Brigham Young University, 1971.

Robertson, Raymond Dale. "Joseph Smith in Historical Perspective." M.A. thesis, Ball State University, 1972.

Searle, Howard C. "Early Mormon Historiography: Writing the History of the Mormons, 1830–1858." Ph.D. diss., University of California, Los Angeles, 1979.

Smith, Calvin N. "A Critical Analysis of the Public Speaking of Joseph Smith." Ph.D. diss., Purdue University, 1965.

Takayama, Machiko. "Poetic Language in Nineteenth Century Mormonism: A Study of Semiotic Phenomenology in Communication and Culture." Ph.D. diss., Southern Illinois University, 1990.

Thompson, Edward George. "A Study of the Political Involvements in the Career of Joseph Smith." M.A. thesis, Brigham Young University, 1966.

Tickemyer, Garland E. "The Philosophy of Joseph Smith and Its Educational Implications." Ph.D. diss., University of Texas, 1963.

Ward, Lane Dennis. "The Teaching Methods of Joseph Smith." Ed.D. diss., Brigham Young University, 1979.

_______. "The World and Joseph Smith." M.A. thesis, Brigham Young University, 1980.

Whipple, Walter L. "An Analysis of Textual Changes in 'The Book of Abraham' and in the 'Writings of Joseph Smith, the Prophet,' in the Pearl of Great Price." M.A. thesis, Brigham Young University, 1959.

Whitney, Clarissa I. "A Critical Analysis of the Forensic and Religious Speaking of Joseph Smith." M.A. thesis, California State College, Fullerton, 1967.

Unpublished Papers

Anderson, Robert D. "The Autobiography of Joseph Smith in Third Nephi." Sunstone Symposium, 1994.

_______. "The Sword of Laban: The Book of Mormon as Autobiography." Sunstone Symposium, August 1993. Audiocassette tape in my possession including comment by C. Jess Groesbeck.

Ashurst-McGee, Mark R. "Joseph Smith, the Kinderhook Plates, and the Question of Revelation." Mormon History Association, May 1996.

Bolton, Andrew. "Was Joseph Smith a Socialist?" Mormon History Association, July 1987.

Bradley, Donald P. "To Prove You All as I Did Abraham: The Abrahamic Trials of Joseph and Emma Smith." Mormon History Association, May 1996.

Bushman, Richard L. "Lucy Smith's and Oliver Cowdery's Prophet: Two Constructions of Joseph Smith." Mormon History Association, May 1997.

_______. "The Visionary World of Joseph Smith." Mormon History Association, June 1995.

Chisholm, Scott. "Joseph Smith on the Frontier: The Book of Mormon as American Dream Machine." Sunstone Symposium, August 1997.

Compton, Todd. "Polygamy, Polygyny, Polyandry: An Overview of Joseph Smith's Plural Wives." Sunstone Symposium, August 1995.

Crabb, A. Richard. "Why Did Joseph Smith Let Nauvoo Die?" Mormon History Association, May 1989.

Ehat, Andrew. "The Last Charge of Joseph Smith to the Twelve." Mormon History Association, May 1996.

_______. "Melchizedek Priesthood Restoration." Mormon History Association, May 1996

England, Eugene. "Joseph Smith and the Dilemmas of American Romanticism." Mormon History Association, May 1980.

Foster, Lawrence. "The Psychology of Religious Genius: Joseph Smith and the Origins of New Religious Movements." Mormon History Association, St. George, Utah, May 16, 1992.

Geary, Edward A. "Joseph Smith Jr., Henry James Sr., and the Emerson Generation." Mormon History Association, May 1980.

Godfrey, Kenneth. "Joseph Smith, Son, Husband, Father: The Roots for a Family-Centered Society." Mormon History Association, May 1980.

———. "Joseph Smith, The Hill Cumorah, and Book of Mormon Geography: A Historical Study, 1823–1844." Mormon History Association, May 1989.

———. "Return to Carthage: The Martyrdom of Joseph and Hyrum Smith Revisited." Mormon History Association, May 1989.

Griggs, C. Wilfred. "Joseph Smith and Apocalypticism in History." Mormon History Association, May 1980.

Groesbeck, C. Jess. "Joseph Smith and His Nauvoo Dreams: A Step in His Individuation." Mormon History Association, June 1990.

———. "Joseph Smith and His Path of Individuation." Sunstone Symposium, 1991.

———. "Joseph Smith and the Archetype of Eternal Marriage." Sunstone Symposium, August 1995.

———. "Joseph Smith and the Book of Mormon—The Archetypal Connection (A Basis for Faith in a New World)." Sunstone Symposium, 1994.

Groesbeck, C. Jess, M.D., Sharon Groesbeck and David Groesbeck. "Joseph Smith and the Shaman's Vision: A Psychoanalytic Exploration in Mormonism." Photocopy of typescript in my possession.

Hamilton, Marshall. "People vs. the Prophet: Joseph Smith and the Criminal Process in Nauvoo." Mormon History Association, June 1990.

Jessee, Dean C. "The Writings of Joseph Smith." Mormon History Association, June 1995.

Jorgensen, Lynne Watkins. "The 'Mantle of the Prophet': A Collective Spiritual Experience." Mormon History Association, June 1995.

———. "The Mantle of the Prophet Joseph Passes to Brother Brigham and the Twelve Apostles: A Collective Spiritual Witness." Sunstone Symposium, August 1995.

Madsen, Gordon. "Joseph Smith as Guardian: The Lawrence Estate." Mormon History Association, May 1996.

Madsen, Gordon A. "The Lawrence Estate Revisited: Joseph Smith and Illinois Law Regarding Guardianships." Nauvoo Symposium, 1989.

Marsh, W. Jeffrey. "Chosen Vessels unto Me: The Apostle Paul and the Prophet Joseph Smith." Sidney B. Sperry Symposium, October 1994.

Melland, Ian. "Was Joseph Smith a True Believer? The Functionalist Argument Reconsidered." Mormon History Association, May 1997.

Morain, William D. "The Sword of Laban: Joseph Smith Jr. and the Unconscious." Mormon History Association, May 1993.

Nolan, Max. "Joseph Smith and Joseph Priestley: A Study in Contrasts." Mormon History Association, July 1987.

Olsen, Steven L. "The Joseph Smith Story: Structure and Ideology." Mormon History Association, May 1980.

Owens, Lance. "The Gnostic Joseph: Early Mormonism as a Classical Heresy." Sunstone Symposium, August 1992.

______. "The Prophet's Bride: Joseph Smith, Sacred Sexuality, and the Occult Tradition." Mormon History Association, May 1994.

______. "A Similarity of Priesthood: Joseph Smith and the Hermetic Tradition." Sunstone Symposium, 1994.

Parkin, Warren S. "Redefining Martyrdom: The One Hundred-Fiftieth Anniversary of the Murder of Joseph Smith." Sunstone Symposium, 1994.

Paul, Robert. "Joseph Smith and Isaac Newton: In Quest of the Philosopher's Stone." Mormon History Association, July 1987.

Pollock, Gordon D. "The Prophet before the Bar: The Richmond Court Transcript." Mormon History Association, May 1988.

Porter, Larry C. "Joseph Smith: Prophet, Teacher, Theologian." Nauvoo Symposium, 1989.

Shipps, Jan. "The Prophet, His Mother, and Early Mormonism: Mother Smith's History as a Passageway to Understanding." Mormon History Association, May 1978.

Simmons, Larry. "Tibet's Diamond Vehicle, John the Revelator's Clear Precious Stone, and Joseph Smith's Secret Treasure." Sunstone Symposium, August 1984.

Smith, George D. "The Summer of 1842: A Chronological View of Joseph Smith's Day-to-day Relationships with the 12 Wives He Had

Married after His First Wife, Emma." Sunstone Symposium, July 1998.

Snow, Edgar C., Jr. "'King Warrior Magician Lover': Joseph Smith as Mormon Masculine Archetype." Sunstone Symposium, August 1997.

Vogel, Dan. "Joseph Smith's Family Dynamics." Sunstone Symposium, July 1998. C. Jess Groesbeck, commentator.

Vogel, Dan. "Joseph Smith's Treasure Seeking Revisited: An Appraisal of Some Recent Interpretations." Mormon History Association, May 1993.

______. "The 'Prophet Puzzle' Revisited." Mormon History Association, May 1996.

Walker, Ronald W. "Beyond Magic: Telling the Unknown Story of Joseph Smith." Mormon History Association, May 1986.

Walton, Michael. "Joseph Smith and Science: The Methodist Connection." Sunstone Symposium, Friday, August 1984.

Index

Also available from
GREG KOFFORD BOOKS

Perspectives on Mormon Theology Series

Brian D. Birch and Loyd Ericson, series editors

(forthcoming)

This series will feature multiple volumes published on particular theological topics of interest in Latter-day Saint thought. Volumes will be co-edited by leading scholars and graduate students whose interests and knowledge will ensure that the essays in each volume represent quality scholarship and acknowledge the diversity of thought found and expressed in Mormon theological studies. Topics for the first few volumes include: revelation, apostasy, atonement, scripture, and grace.

The *Perspectives on Mormon Theology* series will bring together the best of new and previously published essays on various theological subjects. Each volume will be both a valued resource for academics in Mormon Studies and an illuminating introduction to the broad and sophisticated approaches to Mormon theology.

Excavating Mormon Pasts:
The New Historiography of the Last Half Century

Newell G. Bringhurst and
Lavina Fielding Anderson

Paperback, ISBN: 978-1-58958-115-9

Special Book Award - John Whitmer Historical Association

Mormonism was born less than 200 years ago, but in that short time it has developed into a dynamic world religious movement. With that growth has come the inevitable restructuring and reevaluation of its history and doctrine. Mormon and non-Mormon scholars alike have viewed Joseph Smith's religion as fertile soil for religious, historical and sociological studies. Many early attempts to either defend or defame the Church were at best sloppy and often dishonest. It has taken decades for Mormon scholarship to mature to its present state. The editors of this book have assembled 16 essays addressing the substantial number of published works in the field of Mormon studies from 1950 to the present. The contributors come from various segments of the Mormon tradition and fairly represent the broad intellectual spectrum of that tradition. Each essay focuses on a particular aspect of Mormonism (history, women's issues, polygamy, etc.), and each is careful to evenhandedly evaluate the strengths and weaknesses of the books under discussion. More importantly, each volume is placed in context with other, related works, giving the reader a panoramic view of contemporary research. Students of Mormonism will find this collection of historiographical essays an invaluable addition to their libraries.

On the Road with Joseph Smith: An Author's Diary

Richard L. Bushman

Paperback, ISBN 978-1-58958-102-9

After living with Joseph Smith for seven years and delivering the final proofs of his landmark study, *Joseph Smith: Rough Stone Rolling* to Knopf in July 2005, biographer Richard Lyman Bushman went "on the road" for a year, crisscrossing the country from coast to coast, delivering addresses on Joseph Smith and attending book-signings for the new biography.

Bushman confesses to hope and humility as he awaits reviews. He frets at the polarization that dismissed the book as either too hard on Joseph Smith or too easy. He yields to a very human compulsion to check sales figures on Amazon.com, but partway through the process stepped back with the recognition, "The book seems to be cutting its own path now, just as [I] hoped."

For readers coming to grips with the ongoing puzzle of the Prophet and the troublesome dimensions of their own faith, Richard Bushman, openly but not insistently presents himself as a believer. "I believe enough to take Joseph Smith seriously," he says. He draws comfort both from what he calls his "mantra" ("Today I will be a follower of Jesus Christ") and also from ongoing engagement with the intellectual challenges of explaining Joseph Smith.

Praise for *On the Road With Joseph Smith*:

"The diary is possibly unparalleled—an author of a recent book candidly dissecting his experiences with both Mormon and non-Mormon audiences . . . certainly deserves wider distribution—in part because it shows a talented historian laying open his vulnerabilities, and also because it shows how much any historian lays on the line when he writes about Joseph Smith."
-Dennis Lythgoe, *Deseret News*

"By turns humorous and poignant, this behind-the-scenes look at Richard Bushman's public and private ruminations about Joseph Smith reveals a great deal—not only about the inner life of one of our greatest scholars, but about Mormonism at the dawn of the 21st century."
-Jana Riess, co-author of *Mormonism for Dummies*

The Brigham Young University Book of Mormon Symposium Series

Various Authors

Nine-volume paperback box set, ISBN: 978-1-58958-087-9

A series of lectures delivered at BYU by a wide and exciting array of the finest gospel scholars in the Church. Get valuable insights from foremost authorities including General authorities, BYU Professors and Church Educational System instructors. No gospel library will be complete without this valuable resource. Anyone interested in knowing what the top gospel scholars in the Church are saying about such important subjects as historiography, geography, and faith in Christ will be sure to enjoy this handsome box set. This is the perfect gift for any student of the Book of Mormon.

Contributors include: Neal A. Maxwell, Boyd K. Packer, Jeffrey R. Holland, Russell M. Nelson, Dallin H. Oaks, Gerald N. Lund, Dean L. Larsen, Joseph Fielding McConkie, Richard Neitzel Holzapfel, Truman G. Madsen, John W. Welch, Robert J. Matthews, Daniel H. Ludlow, Stephen D. Ricks, Grant Underwood, Robert L. Millet, Susan Easton Black, H. Donl Peterson, John L. Sorenson, Monte S. Nyman, Daniel C. Peterson, Stephen E. Robinson, Carolyn J. Rasmus, Dennis L. Largey, C. Max Caldwell, Andrew C. Skinner, S. Michael Wilcox, Paul R. Cheesman, K. Douglas Bassett, Douglas E. Brinley, Richard O. Cowan, Donald W. Parry, Bruce A. Van Orden, Kenneth W. Anderson, Leland Gentry, S. Kent Brown, H. Dean Garrett, Lee L. Donaldson, Robert E. Parsons, S. Brent Farley, Rodney Turner, Larry E. Dahl, Mae Blanch, Rex C. Reeve Jr., E. Dale LeBaron, Clyde J. Williams, Chauncey C. Riddle, Kent P. Jackson, Daniel K. Judd, Neal E. Lambert, Michael W. Middleton, R. Wayne Shute, John M. Butler, and many more!

The History of Mormons in Argentina

Néstor Curbelo

English, ISBN: 978-1-58958-052-7

Originally published in Spanish, Curbelo's The History of the Mormons in Argentina is a groundbreaking book detailing the growth of the Church in this Latin American country.

Through numerous interviews and access to other primary resources, Curbelo has constructed a timeline, and then documents the story of the Church's growth. Starting with a brief discussion of Parley P. Pratt's assignment to preside over the Pacific and South American regions, continuing on with the translation of the scriptures into Spanish, the opening of the first missions in South America, and the building of temples, the book provides a survey history of the Church in Argentina. This book will be of interest not only to history buffs but also to thousands of past, present, and future missionaries.

Translated by Erin Jennings

Mormon Polygamous Families:
Life in the Principle

Jessie L. Embry

Paperback, ISBN: 978-1-58958-098-5
Hardcover, ISBN: 978-1-58958-114-2

Mormons and non-Mormons all have their views about how polygamy was practiced in the Church of Jesus Christ of Latter-day Saints during the late nineteenth and early twentieth centuries. Embry has examined the participants themselves in order to understand how men and women living a nineteenth-century Victorian lifestyle adapted to polygamy. Based on records and oral histories with husbands, wives, and children who lived in Mormon polygamous households, this study explores the diverse experiences of individual families and stereotypes about polygamy. The interviews are in some cases the only sources of primary information on how plural families were organized. In addition, children from monogamous families who grew up during the same period were interviewed to form a comparison group. When carefully examined, most of the stereotypes about polygamous marriages do not hold true. In this work it becomes clear that Mormon polygamous families were not much different from Mormon monogamous families and non-Mormon families of the same era. Embry offers a new perspective on the Mormon practice of polygamy that enables readers to gain better understanding of Mormonism historically.

Mormonism and Evolution:
The Authoritative LDS Statements

Edited by William E. Evenson and Duane E. Jeffrey

Paperback, ISBN: 978-1-58958-093-0

The Church of Jesus Christ of Latter-day Saints (the Mormon Church) has generally been viewed by the public as anti-evolutionary in its doctrine and teachings. But official statements on the subject by the Church's highest governing quorum and/or president have been considerably more open and diverse than is popularly believed.

This book compiles in full all known authoritative statements (either authored or formally approved for publication) by the Church's highest leaders on the topics of evolution and the origin of human beings. The editors provide historical context for these statements that allows the reader to see what stimulated the issuing of each particular document and how they stand in relation to one another.

A Different God?
Mitt Romney the Religious Right and the Mormon Question

Craig L. Foster

Paperback, ISBN: 978-1-58958-117-3

In the contested terrain of American politics, nowhere is the conflict more intense, even brutal, than in the territory of public life also claimed by religion. Mitt Romney's 2007–08 presidential campaign is a textbook example.

Religious historian (and ardent Republican) Craig L. Foster revisits that campaign with an astute focus on the never-quite-contained hostility that Romney triggered among America's religious right. Although few political campaign are known for their kindness, the back-stabbing, mean-spirited attacks, eruptions of irrationalism, and downright lies exploded into one of the meanest chapters of recent American political history.

Foster readjusts rosy views of America as the tolerant, pluralistic society against the context of its lengthy, colorful, and bruising history of religious discrimination and oppression against many religious groups, among them Mormonism. Mormons are now respected and admired--although the image hasn't tilted enough to work for Romney instead of against him. Their turbulent past of suspicion, marginalization, physical violence, and being deprived of voting rights has sometimes made them, in turn, suspicious, hostile, and politically naive. How much of this pattern of mutual name-calling stems from theology and how much from theocratic ideals?

Foster appraises Romney's success and strengths—and also places where he stumbled, analyzing an intriguing pattern of "what-ifs?" of policy, personality, and positioning. But perhaps even more intriguing is the anti-Romney campaign launched by a divided and fragmenting religious right who pulled together in a rare show of unity to chill a Mormon's presidential aspirations. What does Romney's campaign and the resistance of the religious right mean for America in the twenty-first century?

In this meticulously researched, comprehensively documented, and passionately argued analysis of a still-ongoing campaign, Craig Foster poses questions that go beyond both Romney and the religious right to engage the soul of American politics.

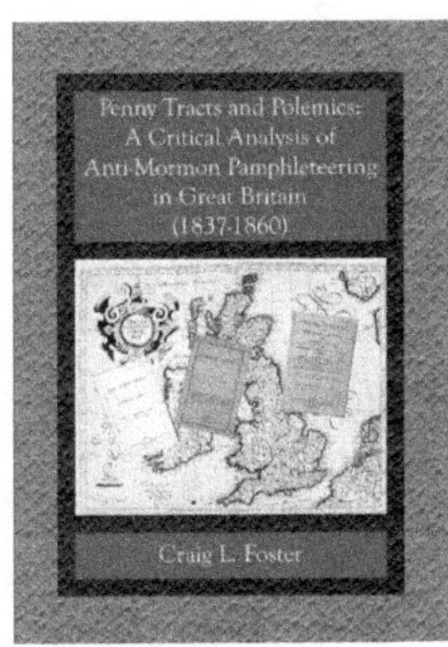

Penny Tracts and Polemics: A Critical Analysis of Anti-Mormon Pamphleteering in Great Britain, 1837–1860

Craig L. Foster

Hardcover, ISBN: 978-1-58958-005-3

By 1860, Mormonism had enjoyed a presence in Great Britain for over twenty years. Mormon missionaries experienced unprecedented success in conversions and many new converts had left Britain's shores for a new life and a new religion in the far western mountains of the American continent.

With the success of the Mormons came tales of duplicity, priestcraft, sexual seduction, and uninhibited depravity among the new religious adherents. Thousands of pamphlets were sold or given to the British populace as a way of discouraging people from joining the Mormon Church. Foster places the creation of these English anti-Mormon pamphlets in their historical context. He discusses the authors, the impact of the publications and the Mormon response. With illustrations and detailed bibliography.

The Gift and Power:
Translating the Book of Mormon

Brant A. Gardner

Hardcover, ISBN: 978-1-58958-131-9

From Brant A. Gardner, the author of the highly praised *Second Witness* commentaries on the Book of Mormon, comes *The Gift and Power: Translating the Book of Mormon*. In this first book-length treatment of the translation process, Gardner closely examines the accounts surrounding Joseph Smith's translation of the Book of Mormon to answer a wide spectrum of questions about the process, including: Did the Prophet use seerstones common to folk magicians of his time? How did he use them? And, what is the relationship to the golden plates and the printed text?

Approaching the topic in three sections, part 1 examines the stories told about Joseph, folk magic, and the translation. Part 2 examines the available evidence to determine how closely the English text replicates the original plate text. And part 3 seeks to explain how seer stones worked, why they no longer work, and how Joseph Smith could have produced a translation with them.

Second Witness:
Analytical and Contextual Commentatry on the Book of Mormon

Brant A. Gardner

Second Witness, a new six-volume series from Greg Kofford Books, takes a detailed, verse-by-verse look at the Book of Mormon. It marshals the best of modern scholarship and new insights into a consistent picture of the Book of Mormon as a historical document. Taking a faithful but scholarly approach to the text and reading it through the insights of linguistics, anthropology, and ethnohistory, the commentary approaches the text from a variety of perspectives: how it was created, how it relates to history and culture, and what religious insights it provides.

The commentary accepts the best modern scholarship, which focuses on a particular region of Mesoamerica as the most plausible location for the Book of Mormon's setting. For the first time, that location—its peoples, cultures, and historical trends—are used as the backdrop for reading the text. The historical background is not presented as proof, but rather as an explanatory context.

The commentary does not forget Mormon's purpose in writing. It discusses the doctrinal and theological aspects of the text and highlights the way in which Mormon created it to meet his goal of "convincing . . . the Jew and Gentile that Jesus is the Christ, the Eternal God."

Praise for the *Second Witness* series:

"Gardner not only provides a unique tool for understanding the Book of Mormon as an ancient document written by real, living prophets, but he sets a standard for Latter-day Saint thinking and writing about scripture, providing a model for all who follow. . . . No other reference source will prove as thorough and valuable for serious readers of the Book of Mormon."

-Neal A. Maxwell Institute, Brigham Young University

1. 1st Nephi: 978-1-58958-041-1	4. Alma: 978-1-58958-044-2
2. 2nd Nephi–Jacob: 978-1-58958-042-8	5. Helaman–3rd Nephi: 978-1-58958-045-9
3. Enos–Mosiah: 978-1-58958-043-5	6. 4th Nephi–Moroni: 978-1-58958-046-6

Complete set: 978-1-58958-047-3

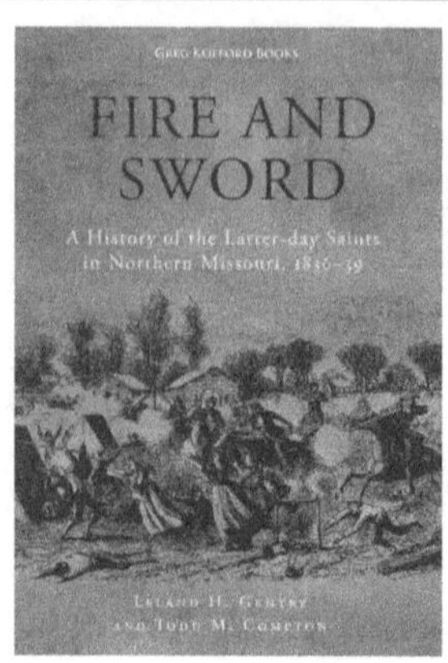

Fire and Sword:
A History of the Latter-day Saints in Northern Missouri, 1836-39

Leland Homer Gentry
and Todd M. Compton

Hardcover, ISBN: 978-1-58958-103-6

Many Mormon dreams flourished in Missouri. So did many Mormon nightmares.

The Missouri period—especially from the summer of 1838 when Joseph took over vigorous, personal direction of this new Zion until the spring of 1839 when he escaped after five months of imprisonment—represents a moment of intense crisis in Mormon history. Representing the greatest extremes of devotion and violence, commitment and intolerance, physical suffering and terror—mobbings, battles, massacres, and political "knockdowns"—it shadowed the Mormon psyche for a century.

Leland Gentry was the first to step beyond this disturbing period as a one-sided symbol of religious persecution and move toward understanding it with careful documentation and evenhanded analysis. In Fire and Sword, Todd Compton collaborates with Gentry to update this foundational work with four decades of new scholarship, more insightful critical theory, and the wealth of resources that have become electronically available in the last few years.

Compton gives full credit to Leland Gentry's extraordinary achievement, particularly in documenting the existence of Danites and in attempting to tell the Missourians' side of the story; but he also goes far beyond it, gracefully drawing into the dialogue signal interpretations written since Gentry and introducing the raw urgency of personal writings, eyewitness journalists, and bemused politicians seesawing between human compassion and partisan harshness. In the lush Missouri landscape of the Mormon imagination where Adam and Eve had walked out of the garden and where Adam would return to preside over his posterity, the towering religious creativity of Joseph Smith and clash of religious stereotypes created a swift and traumatic frontier drama that changed the Church.

"Swell Suffering":

A Biography of Maurine Whipple

Veda Tebbs Hale

Paperback, ISBN: 978-1-58958-124-1
Hardcover, ISBN: 978-1-58958-122-7

Maurine Whipple, author of what some critics consider Mormonism's greatest novel, *The Giant Joshua,* is an enigma. Her prize-winning novel has never been out of print, and its portrayal of the founding of St. George draws on her own family history to produce its unforgettable and candid portrait of plural marriage's challenges. Yet Maurine's life is full of contradictions and unanswered questions. Veda Tebbs Hale, a personal friend of the paradoxical novelist, answers these questions with sympathy and tact, nailing each insight down with thorough research in Whipple's vast but under-utilized collected papers.

Praise for *"Swell Suffering"*:

"Hale achieves an admirable balance of compassion and objectivity toward an author who seemed fated to offend those who offered to love or befriend her. . . . Readers of this biography will be reminded that Whipple was a full peer of such Utah writers as Virginia Sorensen, Fawn Brodie, and Juanita Brooks, all of whom achieved national fame for their literary and historical works during the mid-twentieth century"

—Levi S. Peterson, author of *The Backslider* and *Juanita Brooks: Mormon Historian*

Modern Polygamy and Mormon Fundamentalism:
The Generations after the Manifesto

Brian C. Hales

Paperback, ISBN: 978-1-58958-109-8

**Winner of the John Whitmer Historical Association's
Smith-Pettit Best Book Award**

This fascinating study seeks to trace the historical tapestry that is early Mormon polygamy, details the official discontinuation of the practice by the Church, and, for the first time, describes the many zeal-driven organizations that arose in the wake of that decision. Among the polygamous groups discussed are the LeBaronites, whose "blood atonement" killings sent fear throughout Mormon communities in the late seventies and the eighties; the FLDS Church, which made news recently over its construction of a compound and temple in Texas (Warren Jeffs, the leader of that church, is now standing trial on two felony counts after his being profiled on America's Most Wanted resulted in his capture); and the Allred and Kingston groups, two major factions with substantial membership statistics both in and out of the United States. All these fascinating histories, along with those of the smaller independent groups, are examined and explained in a way that all can appreciate.

Praise for *Modern Polygamy and Mormon Fundamentalism*:

"This book is the most thorough and comprehensive study written on the sugbject to date, providing readers with a clear, candid, and broad sweeping overview of the history, teachings, and practices of modern fundamentalist groups."
—Alexander L. Baugh, Associate Professor of Church History and Doctrine, Brigham Young University

"This is My Doctrine": The Development of Mormon Theology

Charles R. Harrell

Hardcover, ISBN: 978-1-58958-103-6

The principal doctrines defining Mormonism today often bear little resemblance to those it started out with in the early 1830s. This book shows that these doctrines did not originate in a vacuum but were rather prompted and informed by the religious culture from which Mormonism arose. Early Mormons, like their early Christian and even earlier Israelite predecessors, brought with them their own varied culturally conditioned theological presuppositions (a process of convergence) and only later acquired a more distinctive theological outlook (a process of differentiation).

In this first-of-its-kind comprehensive treatment of the development of Mormon theology, Charles Harrell traces the history of Latter-day Saint doctrines from the times of the Old Testament to the present. He describes how Mormonism has carried on the tradition of the biblical authors, early Christians, and later Protestants in reinterpreting scripture to accommodate new theological ideas while attempting to uphold the integrity and authority of the scriptures. In the process, he probes three questions: How did Mormon doctrines develop? What are the scriptural underpinnings of these doctrines? And what do critical scholars make of these same scriptures? In this enlightening study, Harrell systematically peels back the doctrinal accretions of time to provide a fresh new look at Mormon theology.

"*This Is My Doctrine*" will provide those already versed in Mormonism's theological tradition with a new and richer perspective of Mormon theology. Those unacquainted with Mormonism will gain an appreciation for how Mormon theology fits into the larger Jewish and Christian theological traditions.

LDS Biographical Encyclopedia

Andrew Jenson

Hardcover, ISBN: 978-1-58958-031-2

In the Preface to the first volume Jenson writes, "On the rolls of the Church of Jesus Christ of Latter-day Saints are found the names of a host of men and women of worth—heroes and heroines of a higher type—who have been and are willing to sacrifice fortune and life for the sake of their religion. It is for the purpose of perpetuating the memory of these, and to place on record deeds worthy of imitation, that [this set] makes its appearance."

With over 5,000 biographical entries of "heroes and heroines" complete with more than 2,000 photographs, the *LDS Biographical Encyclopedia* is an essential reference for the study of early Church history. Nearly anyone with pioneer heritage will find exciting and interesting history about ancestors in these volumes.

Andrew Jenson was an assistant historian for the Church of Jesus Christ of Latter-day Saints from 1897 to 1941.

A House for the Most High: The Story of the Original Nauvoo Temple

Matthew McBride

Hardcover, ISBN: 978-1-58958-016-9

This awe-inspiring book is a tribute to the perseverance of the human spirit. *A House for the Most High* is a groundbreaking work from beginning to end with its faithful and comprehensive documentation of the Nauvoo Temple's conception. The behind-the-scenes stories of those determined Saints involved in the great struggle to raise the sacred edifice bring a new appreciation to all readers. McBride's painstaking research now gives us access to valuable first-hand accounts that are drawn straight from the newspaper articles, private diaries, journals, and letters of the steadfast participants.

The opening of this volume gives the reader an extraordinary window into the early temple-building labors of the besieged Church of Jesus Christ of Latter-day Saints, the development of what would become temple-related doctrines in the decade prior to the Nauvoo era, and the 1839 advent of the Saints in Illinois. The main body of this fascinating history covers the significant years, starting from 1840, when this temple was first considered, to the temple's early destruction by a devastating natural disaster. A well-thought-out conclusion completes the epic by telling of the repurchase of the temple lot by the Church in 1937, the lot's excavation in 1962, and the grand announcement in 1999 that the temple would indeed be rebuilt. Also included are an astonishing appendix containing rare and fascinating eyewitness descriptions of the temple and a bibliography of all major source materials. Mormons and non-Mormons alike will discover, within the pages of this book, a true sense of wonder and gratitude for a determined people whose sole desire was to build a sacred and holy temple for the worship of their God.

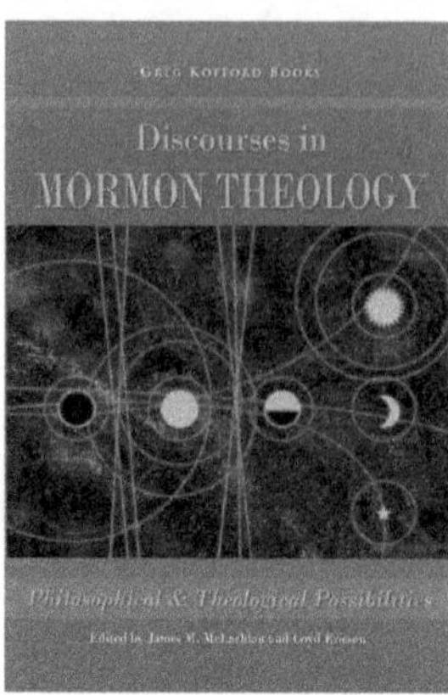

Discourses in Mormon Theology: Philosophical and Theological Possibilities

Edited by
James M. McLachlan and Loyd Ericson

Hardcover, ISBN: 978-1-58958-103-6

A mere two hundred years old, Mormonism is still in its infancy compared to other theological disciplines (Judaism, Catholicism, Buddhism, etc.). This volume will introduce its reader to the rich blend of theological viewpoints that exist within Mormonism. The essays break new ground in Mormon studies by exploring the vast expanse of philosophical territory left largely untouched by traditional approaches to Mormon theology. It presents philosophical and theological essays by many of the finest minds associated with Mormonism in an organized and easy-to-understand manner and provides the reader with a window into the fascinating diversity amongst Mormon philosophers. Open-minded students of pure religion will appreciate this volume's thoughtful inquiries.

These essays were delivered at the first conference of the Society for Mormon Philosophy and Theology. Authors include Grant Underwood, Blake T. Ostler, Dennis Potter, Margaret Merrill Toscano, James E. Faulconer, and Robert L. Millet

Praise for *Discourses in Mormon Theology*:

"In short, *Discourses in Mormon Theology* is an excellent compilation of essays that are sure to feed both the mind and soul. It reminds all of us that beyond the white shirts and ties there exists a universe of theological and moral sensitivity that cries out for study and acclamation."

-Jeff Needle, Association for Mormon Letters

Who Are the Children of Lehi?
DNA and the Book of Mormon

D. Jeffrey Meldrum
and Trent D. Stephens

Hardcover, ISBN: 978-1-58958-048-0
Paperback, ISBN: 978-1-58958-129-6

How does the Book of Mormon, keystone of the LDS faith, stand up to data about DNA sequencing that puts the ancestors of modern Native Americans in northeast Asia instead of Palestine?

In *Who Are the Children of Lehi?* Meldrum and Stephens examine the merits and the fallacies of DNA-based interpretations that challenge the Book of Mormon's historicity. They provide clear guides to the science, summarize the studies, illuminate technical points with easy-to-grasp examples, and spell out the data's implications.

The results? There is no straight-line conclusion between DNA evidence and "Lamanites." The Book of Mormon's validity lies beyond the purview of scientific empiricism—as it always has. And finally, inspiringly, they affirm Lehi's kinship as one of covenant, not genes.

Modern Mormonism: Myths and Realities

Robert L. Millet

Paperback, ISBN: 978-1-58958-127-2

What answer may a Latter-day Saint make to accusations from those of other faiths that "Mormons aren't Christians," or "You think God is a man," and "You worship a different Jesus"? Not only are these charges disconcerting, but the hostility with which they are frequently hurled is equally likely to catch Latter-day Saints off guard.

Now Robert L. Millet, veteran of hundreds of such verbal battles, cogently, helpfully, and scripturally provides important clarifications for Latter-day Saints about eleven of the most frequent myths used to discredit the Church. Along the way, he models how to conduct such a Bible based discussion respectfully, weaving in enlightenment from LDS scriptures and quotations from religious figures in other faiths, ranging from the early church fathers to the archbishop of Canterbury.

Millet enlivens this book with personal experiences as a boy growing up in an area where Mormons were a minuscule and not particularly welcome minority, in one-on-one conversations with men of faith who believed differently, and with his own BYU students who also had lessons to learn about interfaith dialogue. He pleads for greater cooperation in dealing with the genuine moral and social evils afflicting the world, and concludes with his own ardent and reverent testimony of the Savior.

Exploring Mormon Thought Series

Blake T. Ostler

In volume one, *The Attributes of God*, Blake T. Ostler explores Christian and Mormon notions about God. ISBN: 978-1-58958-003-9

In volume two, *The Problems of Theism and the Love of God*, Blake Ostler explores issues related to soteriology, or the theory of salvation. ISBN: 978-1-58958-095-4

In volume three, *Of God and Gods*, Ostler analyzes and responds to the arguments of contemporary international theologians, reconstructs and interprets Joseph Smith's important King Follett Discourse and Sermon in the Grove, and argues persuasively for the Mormon doctrine of "robust deification." ISBN: 978-1-58958-107-4

Praise for the *Exploring Mormon Thought* series:

"These books are the most important works on Mormon theology ever written. There is nothing currently available that is even close to the rigor and sophistication of these volumes. B. H. Roberts and John A. Widtsoe may have had interesting insights in the early part of the twentieth century, but they had neither the temperament nor the training to give a rigorous defense of their views in dialogue with a wider stream of Christian theology. Sterling McMurrin and Truman Madsen had the capacity to engage Mormon theology at this level, but neither one did."

—Neal A. Maxwell Institute, Brigham Young University

Hugh Nibley: A Consecrated Life

Boyd Jay Petersen

Hardcover, ISBN: 978-1-58958-019-0

Winner of the Mormon History Association's Best Biography Award

As one of the LDS Church's most widely recognized scholars, Hugh Nibley is both an icon and an enigma. Through complete access to Nibley's correspondence, journals, notes, and papers, Petersen has painted a portrait that reveals the man behind the legend.

Starting with a foreword written by Zina Nibley Petersen and finishing with appendices that include some of the best of Nibley's personal correspondence, the biography reveals aspects of the tapestry of the life of one who has truly consecrated his life to the service of the Lord.

Praise for *A Consecrated Life*:

"Hugh Nibley is generally touted as one of Mormonism's greatest minds and perhaps its most prolific scholarly apologist. Just as hefty as some of Nibley's largest tomes, this authorized biography is delightfully accessible and full of the scholar's delicious wordplay and wit, not to mention some astonishing war stories and insights into Nibley's phenomenal acquisition of languages. Introduced by a personable foreword from the author's wife (who is Nibley's daughter), the book is written with enthusiasm, respect and insight. . . . On the whole, Petersen is a careful scholar who provides helpful historical context. . . . This project is far from hagiography. It fills an important gap in LDS history and will appeal to a wide Mormon audience."

—Publishers Weekly

"Well written and thoroughly researched, Petersen's biography is a must-have for anyone struggling to reconcile faith and reason."

—Greg Taggart, Association for Mormon Letters

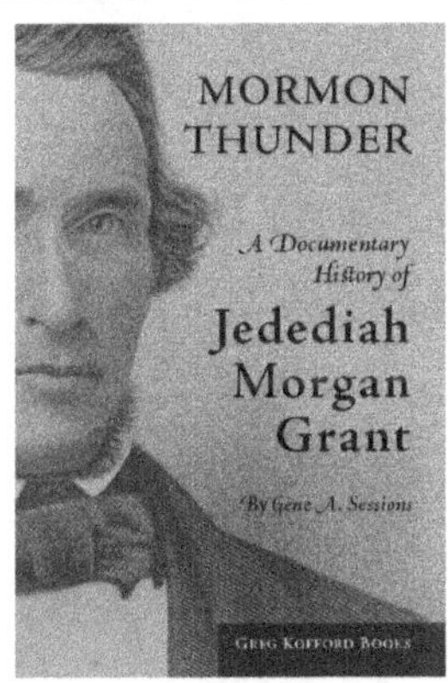

Mormon Thunder:
A Documentary History of Jedediah Morgan Grant

Gene A. Sessions

Paperback, ISBN: 978-1-58958-111-1

Jedediah Morgan Grant was a man who knew no compromise when it came to principles—and his principles were clearly representative, argues Gene A. Sessions, of Mormonism's first generation. His life is a glimpse of a Mormon world whose disappearance coincided with the death of this "pious yet rambunctiously radical preacher, flogging away at his people, demanding otherworldliness and constant sacrifice." It was "an eschatological, premillennial world in which every individual teetered between salvation and damnation and in which unsanitary privies and appropriating a stray cow held the same potential for eternal doom as blasphemy and adultery."

Updated and newly illustrated with more photographs, this second edition of the award-winning documentary history (first published in 1982) chronicles Grant's ubiquitous role in the Mormon history of the 1840s and '50s. In addition to serving as counselor to Brigham Young during two tumultuous and influential years at the end of his life, he also portentously befriended Thomas L. Kane, worked to temper his unruly brother-in-law William Smith, captained a company of emigrants into the Salt Lake Valley in 1847, and journeyed to the East on several missions to bolster the position of the Mormons during the crises surrounding the runaway judges affair and the public revelation of polygamy.

Jedediah Morgan Grant's voice rises powerfully in these pages, startling in its urgency in summoning his people to sacrifice and moving in its tenderness as he communicated to his family. From hastily scribbled letters to extemporaneous sermons exhorting obedience, and the notations of still stunned listeners, the sound of "Mormon Thunder" rolls again in "a boisterous amplification of what Mormonism really was, and would never be again."

Hearken, O Ye People: The Historical Setting of Joseph Smith's Ohio Revelations

Mark Lyman Staker

Hardcover, ISBN: 978-1-58958-113-5

2010 Best Book Award - John Whitmer Historical Association

2011 Best Book Award - Mormon History Association

More of Mormonism's canonized revelations originated in or near Kirtland than any other place. Yet many of the events connected with those revelations and their 1830s historical context have faded over time. Mark Staker reconstructs the cultural experiences by which Kirtland's Latter-day Saints made sense of the revelations Joseph Smith pronounced. This volume rebuilds that exciting decade using clues from numerous archives, privately held records, museum collections, and even the soil where early members planted corn and homes. From this vast array of sources he shapes a detailed narrative of weather, religious backgrounds, dialect differences, race relations, theological discussions, food preparation, frontier violence, astronomical phenomena, and myriad daily customs of nineteenth-century life. The result is a "from the ground up" experience that today's Latter-day Saints can all but walk into and touch.

Praise for *Hearken O Ye People*:

"I am not aware of a more deeply researched and richly contextualized study of any period of Mormon church history than Mark Staker's study of Mormons in Ohio. We learn about everything from the details of Alexander Campbell's views on priesthood authority to the road conditions and weather on the four Lamanite missionaries' journey from New York to Ohio. All the Ohio revelations and even the First Vision are made to pulse with new meaning. This book sets a new standard of in-depth research in Latter-day Saint history."

-Richard Bushman, author of *Joseph Smith: Rough Stone Rolling*

"To be well-informed, any student of Latter-day Saint history and doctrine must now be acquainted with the remarkable research of Mark Staker on the important history of the church in the Kirtland, Ohio, area."

-Neal A. Maxwell Institute, Brigham Young University

"Let the Earth Bring Forth"
Evolution and Scripture

Howard C. Stutz

Paperback, ISBN: 978-1-58958-126-5

A century ago in 1809, Charles Darwin was born. Fifty years later, he published a scientific treatise describing the process of speciation that launched what appeared to be a challenge to the traditional religious interpretation of how life was created on earth. The controversy has erupted anew in the last decade as Creationists and Young Earth adherents challenge school curricula and try to displace "the theory of evolution."

This book is filled with fascinating examples of speciation by the well-known process of mutation but also by the less well-known processes of sexual recombination and polyploidy. In addition to the fossil record, Howard Stutz examines the evidence from the embryo stages of human beings and other creatures to show how selection and differentiation moved development in certain favored directions while leaving behind evidence of earlier, discarded developments. Anatomy, biochemistry, and genetics are all examined in their turn.

With rigorously scientific clarity but in language accessible to a popular audience, the book proceeds to its conclusion, reached after a lifetime of study: the divine map of creation is one supported by both scientific evidence and the scriptures. This is a book to be read, not only for its fascinating scientific insights, but also for a new appreciation of well-known scriptures.

The Wasp

Hardcover, ISBN: 978-1-58958-050-3

A newspaper published in Nauvoo from April 16, 1842, through April 26, 1843, *The Wasp* provides a crucial window into firsthand accounts of the happenings and concerns of the Saints in Nauvoo. It was initially edited by William Smith, younger brother of Joseph Smith. William was succeeded by John Taylor as editor and Taylor and Wilford Woodruff as printers and publishers. Some of the main stories covered in the newspaper are the August 1842 elections where local candidates endorsed by the Mormons easily won against their opponents, the fall from grace of John C. Bennett, the attempt by the state of Missouri to extradite Joseph Smith as an accessory in the attempted murder of Lilburn W. Boggs, and the Illinois legislature's effort to repeal the Nauvoo charter.

With a foreword by Peter Crawley putting the newspaper in historical context, this first-ever reproduction of the entire run of the *The Wasp* is essential to anyone interested in the Nauvoo period of Mormonism.